direct hit

winning
direct marketing campaigns

**MERLIN STONE, DEREK DAVIES and
ALISON BOND**

PITMAN PUBLISHING

PITMAN PUBLISHING
128 Long Acre, London WC2E 9AN

A Division of Pearson Professional Limited

First published in Great Britain 1995

© Pearson Professional Limited 1995

British Library Cataloguing in Publication Data
A CIP catalogue record for this book can be obtained from the British Library.

ISBN 0 273 61689 7

10 9 8 7 6 5 4 3 2 1

Typeset by Northern Phototypesetting Co Ltd., Bolton
Printed and bound in Great Britain by Bell & Bain Ltd, Glasgow

The Publishers' policy is to use paper manufactured from sustainable forests.

contents

1

what is 'the direct hit'?

- The discipline of direct marketing is about making direct (and hopefully profitable) contact with individual customers, and receiving responses directly from them.

- Rapid growth in the use of direct marketing – in virtually every market – has been stimulated by changes in marketing media and information technology.

- Direct marketing's strengths lie in its targetability, measurability and testability, and also in its focus on acquiring, retaining and developing customers and maximizing their lifetime value.

introduction

Knowing how to score a direct hit on your customer through direct marketing is an essential part of marketing. The key principle of direct marketing is that at least part of the communication you have with your customer is direct – to named customers. From this simple principle of the "direct hit" has grown a whole new discipline. However, it has not grown quickly. The seeds of direct marketing as we use it today were sown way back in the nineteenth century at the birth of the US mail order industry, which served so well the needs of remote farmers, ranchers, settlers and new townships.

Today, this geographical justification for direct marketing has been replaced by our needs for much more cost-effective, measurable and reliable ways of managing customers. Technology has made it so much easier for us to communicate directly with our customers, while changes in tastes and media fragmentation have made conventional mass marketing techniques less effective in getting the response you want from your customers – though of course they are still very powerful in developing and sustaining branding.

Direct marketing is now a key discipline within marketing. It is:

- **Direct** because its communications go directly between you and your customer, with no intermediary.
- **Marketing**, because it helps you meet your customers' needs and your profit, sales or other objectives.
- **A discipline**, because by following a set of rules and procedures, you can achieve good results.

Direct marketing is very much part of mainstream marketing, but has three additional characteristics.

1. It is based on direct responses. Direct marketing communications invite your customers to respond – by mail, telephone, redeemable retail vouchers etc. The response may range from enquiry and giving information to ordering. This opportunity for monitoring feedback is critical to direct marketing.

2. Direct marketing is measurable. In any direct marketing campaign responses are measured, evaluated and analyzed. Responses can be through any medium – telephone, mail, fax etc. Measuring responses leads to accountability. All costs can be related to response and return on investment calculated. Traditional advertising relies on market research techniques based on samples to measure effectiveness. Direct marketers use transaction data for this. This is one reason why direct marketing has been called scientific advertising. Direct marketers conduct their tests in controlled environments. Whilst environments do change, direct marketing is as near to a science as marketing will ever achieve.

3. Direct marketing usually requires you to build and maintain a database of customers and prospects. This gives you better understanding of your market and can give you competitive advantage.

technical definition

> **Direct marketing** is the planned implementation, recording, analysis and tracking of customers' direct response behaviour over time in order to derive future marketing strategies for developing long-term customer loyalty and ensuring continued business growth.

Let's consider this definition in more detail:

- **Planning** – all direct marketing activities are part of a controlled marketing strategy. Prior market analysis and achievable objectives are fundamental to effective planning.
- **Recording** – implies the information is stored and capable of manipulation and retrieval from the database.
- **Tracking** – means marketing information is monitored over time, and in the best case over customers' active buying life with your company, enabling their lifetime value to be measured.
- **Customer behaviour** – shows direct marketing is a customer-oriented discipline. Good knowledge of your customer is fundamental to direct marketing planning.
- **Future strategies** – increasing the value of your customer database becomes a central objective of marketing planning, drives your business forward.
- **Developing long-term customer loyalty** – means that future customer retention will be achieved through increased goodwill and upgrading, cross-selling and reselling activities.
- **Continued profitable business growth** – which is achieved by expanding your base of loyal customers. The profit generated in this way will improve your company's ability to serve customers properly.

This definition views direct marketing as a continuing process of acquiring new customers, continuing to satisfy existing customers, and developing all customers so as to achieve greater loyalty and increased purchasing. This process is illustrated in Figure 1.1.

EXAMPLE

Frequent flyer programmes

Many of the world's major airlines now strive to maximize the value of their customer database, particular with respect to business travellers. Frequent flyer programmes are common. These identify the best customers on the database and reward them for their loyalty. The data generated on these customers is analyzed, and the airline learns from it, for example, what the profile of frequent flyers is, how best to develop a relationship with them and how to acquire new customers with similar characteristics. ○

Fig 1.1

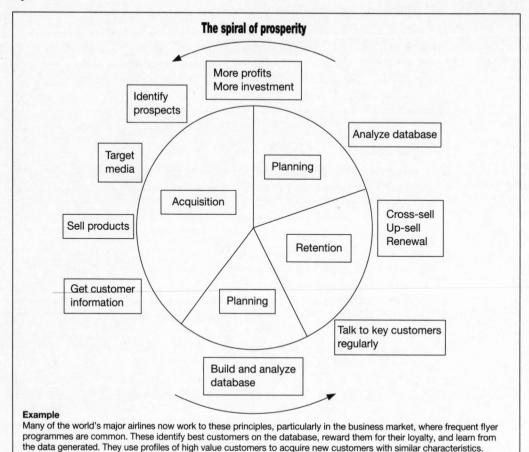

The spiral of prosperity

Example
Many of the world's major airlines now work to these principles, particularly in the business market, where frequent flyer programmes are common. These identify best customers on the database, reward them for their loyalty, and learn from the data generated. They use profiles of high value customers to acquire new customers with similar characteristics.

key benefits of direct marketing

DIRECT MARKETING APPLIES TO ALL BUSINESS SECTORS

There are three main modes of marketing:

- Through intermediaries.
- Directly to consumers.
- To other businesses or institutions.

MARKETING THROUGH INTERMEDIARIES

Many businesses work – at least partially – through intermediaries (wholesalers, retailers, dealers, distributors). Much marketing effort is expended moving the product along the channel. Here, you face two communication challenges – to market to the trade and to market directly to your final customer. Mass branding was traditionally the most powerful tool used to "pull" products through the trade.

However, using direct marketing, you can mount targeted sales promotion campaigns to encourage consumers to visit the retail outlets or dealerships. This is one way in which manufacturers deal with increasing retailer power, electronic checkout technologies and fragmenting media. Many packaged consumer goods companies are experimenting with targeted household mailings or leaflet drops to begin a dialogue to close the gap between themselves and their customers. Some have developed fully fledged customer databases and send them personalized money-off coupons which are scannable and trackable. Customers are encouraged to buy in the store, and measurement is based on coupon redemptions. Car manufacturers use similar techniques to persuade individuals to visit their local dealership.

At the same time, the above manufacturers collect customer information for planning. Manufacturers of consumer durables collect warranty and guarantee cards information. This information will be used for future business planning and communications. In the US, packaged goods companies offer samples and discount booklets off the television screen by asking viewers to call a toll free or even a 900 (pay for) telephone number.

Direct marketing can play an important role in trade marketing. Maximizing penetration of a market may be impossible with a limited salesforce. Direct marketing can extend your coverage to your entire distribution network. Often it is necessary to break barriers and communicate new programmes to the trade. Here you can use direct marketing to ensure that an identical message is delivered to the correct buyers at the right time. An example of this would be the Daily Mail reaching all large media buyers at home on Sunday with a pre-printed copy of the paper. Equally SmithKline Beecham has employed direct mail to motivate the trade for its Tabisco brand. In the US, packaged goods companies have employed high quality, high impact multiple promotions to reach and gain the attention of key retail buyers to persuade them of the value of retail sales promotion plans.

Some methods of collecting names and addresses:

- Money-off coupons in the media.
- Warranty guarantee cards.
- Customer satisfaction surveys.
- Loyalty cards and schemes.
- In-store credit cards.
- Off-the-page offers.

MARKETING DIRECT TO CONSUMERS

This is typically split into businesses using distribution channels for mail order and businesses selling through their own retail outlets (shops, service centres, showrooms). The former includes the major mail order companies such as Freemans, GUS, Littlewoods and Grattans, but also includes mail order publishers such as Book Club Associates, Time Life and The Readers' Digest. Businesses vary in size from bargain square operations to collectable companies like Franklin Mint.

In larger companies, there is usually more scope for controlled testing of products and communications. Retail outlets have the opportunity to develop their customer bases. Whether it be a national store chain or a local art gallery, customer contact means names and addresses with associated customer information can be collected. The opportunity here is to encourage retail visits, typically with incentive promotions for sales or preview evenings for privileged customers. An alternative is to offer a mail order facility through the store catalogue such as Habitat or Laura Ashley. Many larger retailers use their own store credit or loyalty card as a way of collecting customer data.

Service businesses, such as airlines, travel agents, personal finance companies, and hotels, have spearheaded the development of frequent buyer reward schemes for customers. As we saw earlier, all the major US airlines offer frequent flyer programmes. Barclaycard offers its Profiles scheme, rewarding its customers for use of the card. Sainsbury's Homebase Spend & Save scheme and BhS's Choice scheme are two further examples. Rewards range from gifts from a catalogue to discount vouchers.

BUSINESS TO BUSINESS MARKETING

Here, direct marketing is often used to generate leads for a sales force or dealer. Telemarketing is used to prospect for new business and service existing accounts. Catalogues are used to support marketing where the product range is wide. However, the field sales force is also a direct marketing medium, and many companies now subject their sales teams to direct marketing disciplines, asking them to work closely in conjunction with other direct marketing media and to carry out and record their activities in the same disciplined way.

DIRECT MARKETING INTEGRATES AND ADDS VALUE TO COMMUNICATION STRATEGIES

Direct marketing works best when deployed as part of an overall communication strategy. The addition of a response mechanism (telephone, reply address etc) does not dilute the creative impact of the advertising. As the pressure on advertising budgets increases, the need to measure the effectiveness of the contact is heightened.

Whilst an advertisement may heighten awareness and reinforce branding, if it can get the customer to respond, it can begin the process of collecting customer information, and the start of database marketing. Brand image is important to long-term preferences, but response can be vital to short- and long-term sales and loyalty building. Note, however, that direct mail can be used to convey general branding messages. Building goodwill, reinforcing purchase decisions, or saying "thank you" are all ways to reinforce branding and ensure future sales.

TRICKS OF THE TRADE

A money-saving tip!

The customer database generated by direct marketing enhances classic market research techniques, for example, by providing new sampling frames for research. Analysis of data on actual transactions should drive future research programmes. Some large companies have actually merged their market research and database departments so as to exploit information on the database better. Finally, the use of direct marketing should help media planning, as relative cost-effectiveness of different media becomes clearer.

DIRECT MARKETING COMMUNICATIONS CREATE INTERACTION WITH CUSTOMERS

For any communication to be effective it requires feedback to the sender. Mass marketing tends to be a continuous flow of one way messages. The purpose and one of the key components of direct marketing is the response or feedback mechanism. Two-way communication ensures the message has been received and assimilated. The more customer information flows back to you, the better targeted, more relevant and more personalized your messages to your customers can become.

WATCH OUT!

How do you know why your customers are contacting you?

Each message and medium is keyed with a unique publicity code to ensure the response can be tracked back to the original source. Every response device (eg leaflet with a questionnaire section) in direct marketing should have a unique code. This is vital to comply with data protection rules. It is the basis of the promotional record on the customer database. The added benefit is the ability to monitor different groups of customers who originally came via different sources over a period of time and assess their long-term value as customers. This can be used to plan future media selections.

DIRECT MARKETING IS MEASURABLE AND TESTABLE

Direct marketing is as near a science as marketing can ever hope to be. It allows you to carry out controlled experiments. Here, a universe or a representative (projectable) sample of that universe is split into equal parts. One part acts as a control to represent the current situation or norm. The other part(s) act as the test. In this way test results are compared to control results, the difference in response being attributed to the altered variable.

You can construct a trial which tests one variable or several at the same time. The key advantages of this are:

- It reduces your risk and saves you money if a sample can be tested first.
- It allows you to identify which aspects of the promotion have greatest impact on results (lists, offer, premium, format, copy and design).
- Testing relates to actual behaviour rather than likely or recalled behaviour, or attitudes (these are what you investigate through market research).
- Tests allow you to gauge the reactions by your customers to changes in marketing variables.
- Test results enable you to produce "what-if" models to simulate future business changes.

DIRECT MARKETING PERMITS MORE DIFFERENTIATED POSITIONING AND PRICING

With mass advertising for a product which aims to appeal to everyone, there may be only one viable positioning. Direct marketing allows you to reach identified market segments and tailor your positioning to individual customers' needs. Different pricing strategies can be employed for different market sectors.

the planning process of direct marketing

There are three key stages in direct marketing:

1. **Acquisition** (recruiting new customers).

2. **Database** (storing and manipulating customer information).

3. **Retention** (customer care/loyalty programmes to keep existing customers).

ACQUISITION

Acquisition involves:

- Deciding what kinds of customers you want.
- Finding out who they are, how many of them there are and where they are.
- Understanding what motivates them.
- Determining which media to use to talk to them.
- Developing communications and executing campaigns.
- Converting prospects to customers – the sale.

Often, the most likely prospects are targeted first as this represents the lowest cost per sale in acquisition terms.

DATABASE MARKETING

Database marketing involves:

- Obtaining relevant customer information.
- Storing the information in a usable, retrievable format.

- Enhancing this information over time.
- Analysis of the information.
- Selection of key target segments of customers for campaigns.
- Recording sales and response.
- Evaluating and measurement and future business planning.

RETENTION

Retention involves:

- Giving your customers service and product quality that meets or exceeds their expectations.
- Building loyalty over time.
- Maximizing the length and value of the relationship with customers.
- Communicating regularly to your customers, at the right time (right for them!).
- Deepening the relationship with your customers by encouraging them to buy different types of product, to upgrade and renew.
- Monitoring profitability.

lifetime value of customers

If customer transaction data is accumulated for a long enough period, you can calculate the *lifetime value of the customer*. This can be used for several purposes, such as:

- Making campaign decisions which *both* generate a profit and increase customer long-term value. Customer purchases have two effects. They generate revenue and also enhance the expected future value of the customer, since recent buyers are nearly always among the most frequent responders to additional offers.
- Setting levels of investment in both customer acquisition and in customer reactivation.
- Monitoring future business prospects. An increasingly valuable list indicates a solidly growing business, while a list whose value is deteriorating indicates a business with a problematic future.

applications of the customer database

Customer databases can be used in:

- Testing an offer or medium.
- Modelling the expected performance of potential customers for the offer, using test results.
- Analyzing the financial implications of promotion to different types of customers.

- Targeting narrowly defined market segments with specialized offers.
- Defining programmes for reactivating lapsed customers.
- Evaluating sources of new customers.
- Determining the optimal frequency of promotions.
- Quantifying the number of customers likely to buy new products or services and researching their needs.
- Testing new products or services.
- Measuring marketing effectiveness when multiple distribution channels exist – provided sales through different channels can be tracked accurately.
- Identifying groups of customers who are or will become loyal if a consistent communication programme is focused on them.

summary

In this chapter we have briefly reviewed the role of direct marketing and shown some of its uses.

DON'T FORGET!

The key benefits of direct marketing

○ It is applicable to all companies.

○ It is an integrative force in communications planning.

○ It offers new targetable media.

○ It encourages the building of customer relationships.

○ It offers scientific testing opportunities, based on measurement.

○ It reinforces distribution strategies and can add new distribution possibilities.

The cornerstone of direct marketing's strategic role is the control of customer information through the database, supporting the acquisition and retention programmes which should supply the life blood of your company's profits and growth. The reasons why you are almost certain to be relying on direct marketing to achieve profits and growth lie in our rapidly changing market environment, the subject of Chapter 2.

2

who's hitting the customer?

- The direct marketing industry's main customers include financial services, travel and leisure, utilities and charities.

- The industry's suppliers include direct marketing agencies, the media – such as delivery services, telephone networks, press, TV and radio, computer and telemarketing bureaux, systems and software suppliers, printers, paper merchants and response handling and fulfilment houses.

- These suppliers and customers work in an environment of increasing regulation, which adds to the already high level of technical competence required to succeed in direct marketing.

introduction

There are two basic types of customer:

- *Personal customers* – the consumers of the industry's products and services.
- *Business customers* – who buy products and services to sell on to personal customers or other businesses, or to use as inputs into their own businesses.

These two types of customer are the subject of Chapters 3 and 4. This chapter focuses on the direct marketing industry, its environmental influences and how you should take these influences into account in direct marketing planning. Let's start by having a look at who the main players are in the direct marketing game.

the players in the game

CLIENTS

Clients are companies who use direct marketing to influence their customers. Here are some of the main types of client.

Financial services

Financial services providers of one sort or another dominate the direct marketing league table spend. Traditionally, finance houses, unit trust companies and insurance companies have led the way. Now banks, building societies, credit card companies, investment houses and a whole range of financial intermediaries are also big users of direct marketing. The booming direct insurance industry is the best example of how direct marketing can transform an entire industry sector. Direct Line, the leader in this sector, has become a household name through its pioneering combination of direct marketing and classic branding.

Charities

Without direct marketing techniques, fundraising for charitable causes would itself be a lost cause. A large proportion of their income comes from direct marketing. In particular, direct mail and "off-the-page" advertisements are used to generate cash gifts, covenants and legacies for many charities.

Travel and tourism

This sector includes not only direct-sell travel companies, but many others, such as airlines. They use the direct route in combination with other communication and distribution channels and rely on travel agents to make the sale, using many media to bring customers into the travel agent.

AGENCIES

Direct marketing agencies are organized quite like advertising agencies, with account directors and executives, art directors, copy-writers, media specialists and so on. They can be big, small, specialist or full service. Some of the biggest are multinationals in their own right and many more are subsidiaries of international agencies. However, direct marketing agencies are required to perform to exacting technical standards and to create responses to advertising which are immediate and measurable.

The difference between direct marketing and advertising agencies lies mainly in the additional range of services supplied by some larger direct marketing agencies, such as:

- Database building and management.
- Data processing and analysis.
- Campaign planning and management.
- Campaign implementation (response handling, fulfilment and so on)

So, how should you choose between the variety of agencies on offer?

Much depends on how sophisticated you are as a client . If you are a newcomer, you may opt for a big, full-service agency, on the grounds that a full service will be required. You may not have the expertise to manage several different specialist agencies. If your company is large, or if you've been using direct marketing for some time, you might want to shop around, buying this service here, that service there. Or you might want to do it all yourself. The direct marketing process is extremely complex. A client mailing 10 or 11 pieces to millions of households over a three-month period may want the project management expertise of an agency that has often carried out such projects.

OTHER SUPPLIERS

These include media, mailing houses, computer bureaux, list brokers, paper and equipment suppliers and printers.

Media

The major media used in direct marketing are:

- *The broadcast and published media* – press, television and radio.
- *The distributed media* – eg leaflets, inserts, take-ones and free newspapers (also a published medium).
- *The direct response media* – eg mail, telephone, fax etc.
- *The new electronic media* – Internet, electronic mail, interactive cable TV (also a broadcast medium).

Press is still the most important medium. It includes national and regional dailies and Sundays, weekend supplements and the TV guides. Inserts are a distinct medium, which use press as a carrier.

Direct response TV advertising has not enjoyed the spectacular success in the UK that it has in the US, where the majority of TV advertisements carry a direct response device. Given the limited supply of TV time in the UK, direct response advertisers have to compete with the high spending, above the line advertisers. However, this is changing as satellite and cable TV increase their penetration of UK households.

Radio is fast improving as a direct response advertising medium. In particular, local radio serves local, highly targetable audiences. However, as a single-sense (hearing) medium, its ability to produce response is limited.

The medium most readily associated with direct marketing is mail. This medium gave birth to direct marketing and it still dominates direct marketing expenditure.

In the US, telemarketing is the most important direct marketing medium. In the UK, telemarketing expenditure is much lower per capita, but rising fast as new technologies, new suppliers and a new breed of telephone-oriented consumers come into the market. Suppliers of telephone services range from suppliers of equipment and lines to telemarketing agencies. The latter are very important, as without them much telemarketing would be impossible. As experience of telemarketing grows, more of it moves in-house, using specialist telemarketing systems and software available from many suppliers. But the independent supplier of such services will continue to prosper as telemarketing techniques become better understood and more widely employed.

Fig 2.1

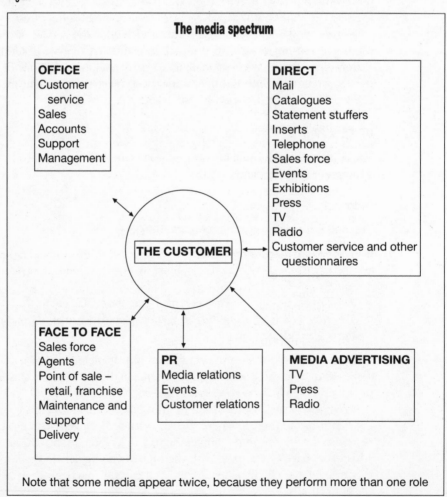

The media spectrum

OFFICE
Customer
  service
Sales
Accounts
Support
Management

DIRECT
Mail
Catalogues
Statement stuffers
Inserts
Telephone
Sales force
Events
Exhibitions
Press
TV
Radio
Customer service and other
  questionnaires

THE CUSTOMER

FACE TO FACE
Sales force
Agents
Point of sale –
  retail, franchise
Maintenance and
  support
Delivery

PR
Media relations
Events
Customer relations

MEDIA ADVERTISING
TV
Press
Radio

Note that some media appear twice, because they perform more than one role

Mailing houses

Mailing houses enjoy several different names eg lettershop, fulfilment house. They put printed material into envelopes and deliver them to the postal service, perhaps sorted by post-code to obtain Mailsort discounts. In its most sophisticated form, for very high volume or complicated mailings, this requires skill, experience and much expensive equipment.

Computer bureaux

Although some of the biggest clients and agencies have their own in-house data processing facilities, many more clients of all sizes and sectors use outside bureaux. These bureaux perform a range of tasks for clients, from list merging and purging to the design, construction and management of large databases supporting multiple applications.

List suppliers

List brokers act as an intermediary in the supply of lists of names and addresses from list owners (usually either clients that have built lists through transactions with their customers, or companies that have compiled lists specifically for the purpose of renting them) that can be used for direct marketing purposes. If you want to mail, you need a list of names and addresses. If you haven't got a list, then you may turn to outside lists and sources of list suppliers, probably a list broker.

A list is a perishable commodity which quickly dates, as people move homes and jobs. Whatever efforts are made to maintain the quality of a list, some names will inevitably not be accurate or usable. This is why a "net-names" agreement is usually employed. Here the broker will rent the list (usually for one-time use only) subject to payment for a specified percentage of names used (usually 85%). To protect the broker against the dishonesty of the client, "seeds" will be planted in the list. These may be employees of the list broking firm who will receive (unknown to the mailer) any subsequent mailings sent out by the company from the "once-only" list.

Paper and equipment suppliers and printers

These are the backbone of the direct mail industry. They vary from the largest paper companies to small print shops running off handbills and cheap inserts for local traders. Without paper, print and inserting machines, no mail-shot could be possible. But it is a particularly fragmented industry with local suppliers assuming considerable importance in many cases.

Types of supplier	What they can do
Mailing houses	● Send out the mailing. ● Ensure the mailing is sorted by postcode, to obtain Mailsort discount. ● Source any elements of the offer not provided by the client. ● Project manage the whole campaign. ● Provide a Freepost address for returns. ● Fulfil the offer.
Computer bureaux	● Hold client data. ● Clean client data. ● Produce mail-ready tapes.
List brokers and managers	● Sell lists. ● Advise on best possible use of lists. ● Act as an intermediary for the lists of other clients. ● Collect names and addresses to compile new lists.
Paper, equipment suppliers and printers	● Supply raw materials, such as paper and envelopes. ● Organize stuffing of envelopes. ● Organize deliveries and collections to clients, other suppliers and the Royal Mail. ● First proof-reader of mailing.
Direct marketing agencies	● Project manage all the above. ● Advise client on suppliers of above. ● Supply artwork and overall strategy. ● Final proof-reading.

the direct marketing environment

POLITICAL ENVIRONMENT

In the last decade in the UK, regulation of business gave way to deregulation and freedom to compete. The deregulation of the financial services industry affected the direct marketing industry because many companies turned to direct marketing as the most cost-effective means of penetrating new markets and launching new products. Privatization of the telecommunications industry created competition for BT, increased the latter's use of direct marketing and made it a more aggressive provider of services which support direct marketing. Media liberalization led to the arrival of new terrestrial TV channels, cable and satellite channels and local radio stations. But these developments have not been unrestricted.

There have been major changes in the legislative framework of the direct marketing industry.

The Data Protection Act, 1984, is perhaps the most significant piece of legislation. Guidance Note 19 (October 1988) requires computerized prospect lists to be compiled and used only with the prior notification (and consent) of data subjects on those lists. A company sending a mail-shot to someone who has not given consent to receive it may be subject to criminal prosecution and a large fine. The effect has been to end third party mailings to names selected from eg lists of catalogue buyers unless at the time of data collection the use is foreseen and explained to the data subject.

DON'T FORGET!

Data protection

○ *Always keep source data on the database.*

○ *Register the database with the Data Protection Agency, or the Data Protection Registrar will be after you!*

○ *Put seeds on the database, keep them up to date and ensure they go on every list you sell or swap.*

○ *Make sure that you have a process for keeping your data secure – a process which will make sense to the Registrar.*

○ *Consider the Mailing Preference Service (a computerized list of consumers who do not want to be mailed).*

○ *Be very careful if you are selling financial services.*

WATCH OUT!

A tough data protection law in Germany had a profound effect on the availability of lists. It reduced 2,500 lists five years ago to only 250 lists today. Ironically, companies rent fewer lists, target less well and therefore produce more "junk mail" rather than less!

The German position on data protection contrasts sharply with the US experience. In the US there are still no federal laws governing data protection, although some states have their own rules. The major piece of legislation is the Privacy Act of 1974. But the Mailing Preference Service, which dates from 1971, was lauded in the Privacy Protection Study Commission report. This service has given consumers an opportunity to be removed from (or added to) large numbers of mailing lists. Interestingly, three times more people have asked to have their names added than have asked to have them deleted from lists!

The UK Financial Services Act 1986 aimed to provide a fairer framework for personal investment. The Department of Trade and Industry delegated its regulatory powers to the SIB (Securities and Investments Board) which in turn established the SROs (Self Regulatory Organisations) to police the various branches of the investment industry. For direct marketers a key clause focuses on polarization, which requires sellers to be either wholly independent intermediaries selling a range of products or to sell only the products of the parent institution to which they are tied. This increased the use of direct mail and telemarketing, as alternatives to the traditional route of sales forces and agents.

The UK Building Societies Act, 1986, gives building societies more freedom to behave as banks, competing across a range of financial services. This also led to more direct marketing activity as building societies built databases and cross-sold a wider range of services through different media. However, their ability to link with third party providers of other investment services is limited by the Data Protection Act. Many are even nervous of using their lists for market research without a warning letter sent to targets prior to the questionnaire asking if they mind being contacted in this way.

THE ECONOMIC AND SOCIAL ENVIRONMENT

Markets consist of people with money to spend on goods and services. Growth will come from the same number of people spending more in real terms or from more people spending the same amount in real terms or some combination of the two. Given that there is little scope for substantial population increase in the next decade, marketers must look for areas of increase in real income and spending. The major variables which need to be understood include:

- Levels of unemployment/employment.
- Labour productivity.
- Inflation.
- Consumer/business spending.

- The savings ratio.
- Investment.
- The balance of payments.
- Life-style changes.

The 1980s saw a gradual (though not uninterrupted) increase in consumer spending across a wide range of durables and services. The stock market crash of 1987 was followed by reflation of the economy through low interest rates and taxes. This led to a rapid rise in inflation and imports, followed by rising interest rates to choke off demand. The speed with which these fluctuations took place caught many marketers unawares. Those that survived best were those who had cultivated their customers most assiduously during the good years.

It is often argued that direct marketing benefits in an economic down-swing as advertisers switch expenditure on advertising to direct marketing. Certainly at the end of the decade, TV advertising was much less buoyant than direct mail. In such circumstances, it is often the financial director who becomes the strongest advocate of direct marketing as the measurable benefits of it are strong compared to above the line advertising.

Perhaps the most significant changes in the social environment relate to demographic change, and the different behaviour of new generations of buyers. Today, children are much less likely to copy their parents' buying behaviour patterns. They are more likely to find their own way to major brands. For this reason, direct marketers court newer buyers with great assiduity. Fortunately, electoral rolls provide data on who is about to become an adult.

Technological environment

Technology – in the form of hugely improved databases and data processing and telecommunications systems – has enabled direct marketing to achieve so much of its potential. However, it is people's acceptance or rejection of technological advances that limits their application.

Key technological changes for direct marketers

- Development of increased computing and telecommunications power and sophistication.
- Electronic home shopping, although this may be limited by how much mass market consumers accept the technology required to order in this way.
- Satellite and cable TV, and proliferation of broadcast stations. The customer management chip gives satellite operators access to a constantly up-dated database containing the names and addresses of receivers.
- Further improvements in electronic design and printing technology, allowing mailings to be produced more quickly, to higher quality.

converting technology and technique to competitive advantage

Direct marketers must be more innovative in their thinking if they are to gain a competitive advantage based upon better products or superior communications strategies. The formula approach has so far worked well for many experienced direct marketers, but product (and corporate) life cycles are getting shorter – and direct marketers can no longer rely on their expertise.

WATCH OUT!

General marketers are waking up to direct response and are learning tools and techniques fast. Direct marketers need to learn from their above the line cousins that developing competitive advantage in a rapidly changing economic and social environment is as important as measuring the response rate on the last campaign.

Direct marketers must open their minds to new movements, to new issues, to new ways of defining old problems, and to shift from short-term to long-term thinking. Direct marketing has for too long been a tactical response to problems based on individual campaigns and their management, rather than on the achievement of long-term corporate goals or missions. Companies which have a clearly defined mission based upon an assessment of strengths, weaknesses, opportunities and threats, and the capacity to convert the mission into effective strategies and tactics, are better placed to survive and prosper.

summary

In this chapter, we've briefly described the structure of the direct marketing industry – clients, agencies and other suppliers. Each of these is a business in its own right. If you want to use direct marketing, you need to take on the campaign planning and implementation methodologies of classic direct marketing. But you also need to look outward, beyond the confines of the direct marketing industry, to the wider economic and social environment in which your campaigns will have to succeed. Political and legal changes may affect your market profoundly (eg financial services, utilities). You may be affected by economic and social change (eg charities), or by technological change. Computing and telecommunications developments are allowing so much more to be achieved, more quickly, at lower cost and with fewer staff. Consumers have so much more choice about how to get information about your products, how to obtain them and how to contact you afterwards to complain about them!

In the next two chapters, we show how these forces affect consumer and business buyers.

3

hitting the consumer

- Consumer direct marketing – like all marketing – depends for its success on your developing an in-depth understanding of your customers – who they are, what they think and how they buy.

- In particular, you must understand how they deal with the thousands of messages they may receive every day, if yours is to stand out from the crowd.

introduction

- Are your customers required to act immediately by sending a cash payment with the order form?
- Are your customers required to request further information?
- Should your customers request a demonstration of the product?
- Should your customers reply by mail, telephone or even personal visit?
- Is it vital they respond immediately or can they delay response for several days, perhaps even several weeks?
- Where should your customers respond – at home, in the office or at the store?
- Why should your customers bother to respond at all?
- What in the offer is likely to stimulate your customers to respond?
- Why will your customers respond to some offers and not others?

We started this chapter with these very basic questions, because direct marketing depends critically on this level of detail. Marketers play close attention to studies of consumer behaviour. Understanding consumers is the key to developing competitive advantage. The *quality* of such studies has grown – particularly in relation to concepts and empirical research techniques. Psychology, sociology, statistics, mathematics and information technology have all contributed to this. We can now say with confidence that some of the ideas produced in this way really do help you answer the tough practical questions posed above.

However, direct marketers have been slow to grasp the significance of these developments. When it comes to understanding customers, direct marketers tend to rely on their judgement and experience, derived from years of successful marketing. This is particularly so where this experience is based on wide-scale and systematic testing of direct marketing campaigns. For many, a huge database of test results is quite enough information to have about customers. It allows them to determine what techniques work and what techniques are less successful without having to determine *why* they work.

Even when direct marketers do want to know the reasons for the success or failure of the campaign, many believe it can be done by "modelling" the data. This involves using statistical techniques to identify and quantify the factors (eg the offer, the format, the creative approach or the list) which "determine" the response level.

This is not the right place to discuss the strengths and weaknesses of a wholly empirical approach to explaining consumer behaviour. However, as we are about to see, other approaches can add to and enrich your understanding of consumer decision processes. So this chapter shows the many different approaches to understanding decisions taken by consumers. The next chapter deals with the same issues for business buyers.

So far, words such as "consumer" and "customer" have been used fairly loosely and interchangeably. For most practical purposes this probably makes sense. But it is clear that the customer may be the buyer but someone else might be the consumer. Most family consumer behaviour is like that.

Mum or Dad might *buy* the groceries, but all the members of the family *consume* them. The word "behaviour" has also been used fairly loosely too, to imply *what* consumers do as well as *why* they do it.

There are times, for example in the gift market, when understanding the motives of the buyer and separating them from the motives of the receiver is vital to a complete understanding of consumer behaviour. In other cases, the decision-making process may be a group one, with each individual being a customer, consumer or both. For these reasons "consumer" and "customer" continue to be used interchangeably in this book.

Understand the customer as buyer and user

- Will your customer *be using* your product?
- Will your customer be *the sole user* of your product?
- Will your customer be *responsible for others* using your product?

types of consumer decision

HIGH INVOLVEMENT AND LOW INVOLVEMENT DECISIONS

Many purchases require little or no explanation. In many instances the purchase motivations are already understood. In others there is little that **needs** to be understood eg for routinely purchased products such as salt or sugar. It is clear **why** people buy salt and sugar – to improve the flavour of their food; and brand choice is for most consumers unimportant. If one brand is not available, then another or an own-label brand will do. Most consumers do not go into a store with strong brand preferences or knowledge. Selection is determined mainly by availability and shelf position. Price **might** matter, but rarely is there a big difference between the price of one brand of salt and another. Promotions may bring purchases forward, but are unlikely to influence how much is bought over a long period.

Low involvement products are usually basic commodities. They are bought for functional reasons and carry little or no symbolic meaning. Their unit price is low, whichever brand is selected. They are routinely purchased. There is not much economic, social or psychological risk of making the wrong brand choice.

However, not all low price, frequently purchased commodities are low involvement products. Take coffee, for example. It too is a commodity. It is bought about as often as salt or sugar. It is dearer, but not much more. Yet consumers exhibit much stronger brand preference for coffee than for salt. Why? After all, coffee is functional too. Isn't coffee drunk to quench thirst or to stimulate in the same way as sugar is used to sweeten it? Coffee *can* and *does* quench the thirst and stimulate, but whereas there are few alternatives to sugar as a sweetening agent (excepting substitute sweeteners such as Nutrasweet and Saccharin) there are many alternatives to coffee as a thirst quencher or stimulant – tea, water, fruit squashes and so on, many of which are either cheaper or more convenient to take than coffee.

Why do consumers demonstrate strong allegiance to the product (coffee), the product form (instant coffee or ground coffee) and the product brand (Nescafe or Maxwell House for instance)? It is because coffee is less a functional product than a symbolic product. It carries symbolic meaning of a highly personal (yet generalized) form. Brands of coffee define and differentiate this general meaning. Different brands therefore target groups of consumers for whom different attributes of coffee mean more (or less) than other attributes.

Some products offer more branding opportunities than others. Lager or even petrol, when stripped of their brand identity are clearly commodities. But all heavily branded products carry such symbolic meaning that consumers feel a high degree of psychological and social risk in making the wrong brand choice.

Products that we "wear" – not just clothes, but also cigarettes, alcohol, cars, books, home furnishings and the like – are **high** involvement products. Brands within each product class invoke and commit the consumer to such an extent that brand switching is seen as risky.

The rest of this chapter is devoted to high involvement decision-making, for it is this type of decision-making that is most relevant to direct marketers. Although some products that are marketed directly are relatively low involvement eg impulse purchases from low value merchandise catalogues, direct marketing is more strongly established, growing faster and offers greater future potential for high involvement products, such as financial services, charity fundraising, publishing, automobiles and retailing.

EXAMPLE

Charities

In charitable giving, consumers display strong allegiance to specific causes, often because of a strong personal involvement in the cause. For example, cancer charities receive most from people who have experienced cancer in their family. Fundraisers recognize this. Mass media and special interest magazines can identify potential donors to some extent (eg The Guardian is a better vehicle than The Financial Times for third world charities). However, direct mail, a highly targeted medium, offers more cost-effective coverage of high propensity donors, provided the charity has the *relevant* information. ○

THE HIGH INVOLVEMENT DECISION PROCESS

The more important the purchasing decision, the more thought the consumer is likely to devote to it. Of course, if the product is bought often (eg washing powder, beer), more thinking is likely to take place when the customer is considering switching brands. Once the new brand is established as a habit, purchases are likely to take place routinely, without much thought

Consumer purchasing decisions can be analyzed using the following framework.

- **Existence of the need** (whether or not the consumer realizes it).
- **Identification or realization of need** – the need comes to the "front of mind".
- **Problem recognition** – the need exists for a reason, typically a problem that needs to be solved (eg meeting a want).
- **Search for information** – about products and services which will solve the problem. This is triggered by the need for problem resolution – the dissonance (disharmony) that is felt when a problem is recognized triggers a drive or motivating force that leads the consumer to resolve the problem and restore the state of psychological balance or consonance.
- **Evaluation** – when all the relevant accessible information required to make the choice which will resolve the problem is gathered and analyzed. The consumer may or may not have established choice criteria. Even if they are already established, during evaluation they may change. Patterns of deliberation are also important. For instance some consumers rely more on personal advice than on information provided by suppliers. So the outcome of the evaluation will depend on various factors, varying from personality and past experience to the way different suppliers provide information
- **Choice** – some choices are purely impulsive, or at least seem so to others. But many choices are deliberate and rational, based upon reasonably systematic processing of information. Such processing leads first to the formation of an intention to purchase, which in turn, is determined by the formulation of beliefs about the product and its likely performance. Confidence in the individual's ability to judge and evaluate brand attributes and confidence in the brand itself play important parts in forming beliefs and purchase intentions. The more specific the required piece of behaviour and the closer choice is in time to the formation of a behavioural intention, the more likely it is that intention will lead to a decision to purchase.
- **Post-purchase review** – the consumer re-evaluates the decision in the light of any new information eg on product performance. Sometimes, consumers experience cognitive dissonance ie they are unhappy about what they now know. They experience doubt or anxiety if the product does not meet expectations. This may be resolved in various ways. Consumers look for information which supports their decision. They may focus on the "good deal" they got, to try to convince themselves they made the right decision. They may even ignore, avoid or distort incoming information which is inconsistent with what they want to believe.

This framework is presented in briefer form in Figure 3.1.

Fig 3.1

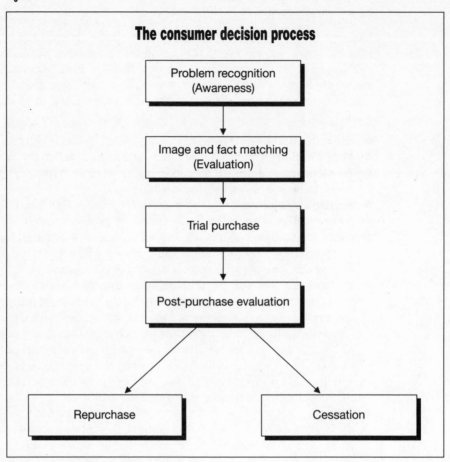

The consumer decision process

Problem recognition
(Awareness)

↓

Image and fact matching
(Evaluation)

↓

Trial purchase

↓

Post-purchase evaluation

Repurchase   Cessation

the determinants of consumer choice

Needs only trigger behaviour when the consumer **perceives** the need. At this point it makes sense to examine the process of **perception**.

> "**Perception**" is defined as "**the process of organizing sensory stimuli in a meaningful way**". Seeing is a purely neurological process and does not imply giving *meaning* to what is seen.

Marketers focus particularly on mental processing of external information, notably advertising messages. The direct marketer is also interested in this, as much direct marketing activity is essentially targeted advertising. Direct marketers usually see targeting as merely reaching particular target customers with a communication.

Targeting implies much more than this. It means identifying people who are psychologically receptive to the message.

This means much more than personalized direct mail, accurate post-coding and so on. It means identifying people who are less likely to screen out messages and more likely to be receptive to them, because they've perceived the importance and personal relevance of the message.

Most consumers remember very few of the 2,000 or so messages a day they are exposed to in the UK (in the US it is nearer 3,000 messages!). This is because they perceive very selectively.

WATCH OUT!

Selective perception is a function of two distinct but related forces: extrinsic and intrinsic forces. Extrinsic forces are outside the individual and potentially controllable by the marketer. They include:

- **Where** the consumer is exposed to a message.
  Television, for instance, is a particularly intrusive medium. If there are no other distractions in a room with the television turned on, the consumer is more likely to notice the advertisements than those placed, say, on billboards at a crowded sporting event. In this context the direct marketer should appreciate the value of inserts and direct mail. Both of these are highly intrusive media in the sense that the consumer cannot avoid handling them, even if it is only to throw them away.
- **When** the consumer is exposed to the message.
  Consumers are more likely to see and make sense of messages when they are mentally fresh and unlikely to be faced with distraction from other ads. For those who are freshest in the morning, direct mail is likely to be noticed.
- **What** the consumer is being exposed to.
  This is determined by factors such as the size, position, intensity and isolation of a communication. Obviously, larger advertisements are likely to capture more attention than smaller ones (though not in direct proportion to increases in size). The position of a press advertisement on a page affects attention: those on the upper half of the page seem to do better than those at the bottom of the page. Those on the left of a page do better than those on the right of a page. Intensity can come from sound and colour – the louder the sound or the brighter the colour, the more likely the consumer is to notice the advertisement. The degree of isolation of the communication affects perception too ie a mailing containing only one offer will gain more attention for that offer than one containing several offers.

PSYCHOLOGICAL DETERMINANTS

However, intrinsic forces are more important in determining what is perceived and how it is perceived. These include needs and social influence processes.

Needs

Needs may be functional eg the need to replace a faulty dishwasher or a super-annuated car. Such needs cause the consumer to pay more attention to communications about the product in question. Needs may be emotional. A consumer's eye may be caught by pictures of people of the same age and life-style. The consumer may identify with and relate to the subjects of the picture. Therefore, direct marketing works most effectively when messages address current needs.

Perceptual vigilance and defence

Consumers tend to recognize words or images that relate to their particular values more quickly than those which do not. For instance, if a particular consumer is a regular donor to charity, then that consumer will recognize and process very quickly words which connote values central to charity giving. "Cause", "help", "humanity", "suffering", "children" and so on will be recognized and absorbed more quickly than others. Words which tend to have a non-charitable connotation, for example "financial", may have negative meaning, causing the consumer to delay or avoid altogether processing the information.

Cognitive consistency

Perceptual processes are important in maintaining consumers' values and beliefs, even in the face of conflicting evidence. Consumers strive for cognitive balance. They try to maintain a consistent view of their world. Therefore, they accept messages that support their beliefs, rejecting those that threaten them. When threatened, consumers experience cognitive dissonance and the need to reduce it. Much of this dissonance or dissatisfaction occurs *after* purchase. In purely functional terms, products rarely perform as well as their advertising promised. Therefore, one of advertising's most important roles is to reassure recent purchasers.

When consumers experience cognitive dissonance, they seek out advertising messages which support their purchase decision and provide a prop for their now slightly dented self-concept. Direct marketers have an edge in this area because they can pinpoint more accurately those who are likely to feel let down and they can provide potentially more reassuring messages. "Welcome" and "thank you" letters are particularly effective in this respect. So, too, are "bounce-backs" ie further offers that are made following initial response or purchase.

Personality types and characteristics are likely to be linked to perception. For instance, deeply prejudiced types are likely not only to perceive selectively, but also to distort the meaning of what they see.

Motivation

Once consumers perceive a need, they are in a motivated condition. They are energized to seek to satisfy the need. In other words, motives link needs and their satisfaction. Motivation is therefore a *process* or a *state*. Some types of motivator are more common than others. The more common ones are of particular interest to marketers and include:

- Making money.
- Saving money.
- Helping the family.
- Saving time / effort.
- Feeling secure.
- Pleasure.
- Impressing others.
- Belonging.
- Self-improvement.

Many of these are the basis of famous direct response advertisements:
"Do you sincerely want to be rich ...?"
"How I made my first million in mail order ..."
"Cash if you die ... Cash if you don't "
"They laughed when I sat down at the piano, but when I started to play. ... "

Many so-called motivators are necessary to *maintain* behaviour rather than *increase* it. Their absence will demotivate but their presence will not motivate. These factors are called **"hygeine" factors** (the idea being that the presence of soap and clean towels will not motivate people to work *harder*, but their absence causes people to grumble and become dissatisfied).

Thus, the presence of an incentive may sustain consumers' interest in the promoted brand, whilst the absence of an incentive will cause them to choose a competitive brand. Offering consumers different ways to pay may not increase response, but their absence may well *reduce* response.

Learning

Motivational states lead to rewards (or "punishments"). These experiences – of motivation leading to behaviour followed by reward or punishment – form the basis for learning. In principle, we can measure, through experimentation, the reinforcers that produce behaviour. We can also measure the degree of connection between stimuli and the consequent behaviour. Applying this to marketing communication, it can be seen how consumers learn to associate the benefits of catalogue merchandise with the receipt of a new catalogue. The more frequently a particular offer is made, the more response behaviour is reinforced. Frequent offers are examples of what learning theorists call "schedules of reinforcement" and they depend for their effectiveness on regular repetition. However, consumers' response to stimuli is not unthinking. They usually consider their actions and may criticize them. The very idea of the Unique Selling Proposition (USP) rests on the consumer identifying and evaluating in a rational way the superior benefits of brand X over brand Y. The consumer's rationalization of competitive product attributes and benefits is an important attribute of high involvement decision-making.

Personality

Personality plays a key role in motivation and learning. Unfortunately, personality is easier to recognize than explain or even understand. Much work has been done on personality *traits* (sociability, gregariousness and aggression are examples of traits). In much consumer market segmentation, brand differentiation is based upon advertising's appeal to particular traits.

Attitudes

For cognitive theorists, attitudes are the outcome of learning and they are the predictor of behaviour. They suggest that attitude is a measurable concept and that reliable measurement produces (reasonably) reliable predictions of consumer behaviour. There are two attitudinal dimensions that shape behavioural intention – the attitude towards the object (ie the product or service) and the attitude towards the act (which is made up of purchase behaviour and use behaviour). This explains many apparent paradoxes. For instance, attitudes towards wet fish are positive, but wet fish sales continue to decline. Why? Because positive attitudes towards the attributes of wet fish are more than offset by negative attitudes towards the buying and preparing of wet fish.

The same distinction applies to direct marketing. Consumers may feel good about the products offered for sale through direct channels of communication, but may feel negative about the buying process through these channels. This may be reinforced through experience. For example, catalogue mail order returns are notoriously high (up to 50%). Poor experience with the medium may lead prospects and customers to form negative attitudes towards the advertised products, which may be strong enough to inhibit further mail order purchasing. Attention therefore needs to be shifted away from product selection to parts of the mail order process which consumers regard as negative eg slow delivery.

What are the psychological drivers of your direct marketing message?	What it means to the campaign
● Need	● Have you assessed the likelihood of your customer's need?
● Perceptual vigilance and defence	● Does your message fit the types of emotions which your customer will respond to?
● Cognitive consistency	● Will the message challenge their views, and produce negativity?
● Motivation	● Are there enough motivator words and messages to make customers want to buy?
● Personality	● Is the personality of the communication positive?

SOCIAL INFLUENCE PROCESSES

The above concepts relate to the psychological make-up of individual consumers. However, group behaviour also influences consumer choice, for example, the need to feel valued by groups we belong to, and this often leads to a desire for status.

EXAMPLE

Nothing less for American Express

For years, American Express mailings began with "Frankly, an American Express card isn't for everybody". You couldn't have a much more blatant appeal to status. ○

Status may imply power.

WATCH OUT!

Members of the higher grades of frequent flyer programmes (typically named after precious metals eg gold, platinum) have power which they can use to negotiate special benefits or deals. Moreover that power only works because they have been recognized as individuals by the airline. But it is important to identify whether the user is the buyer. For example, if a frequent flyer with a particular airline only flies with that airline because of a corporate deal, then their individual bargaining power is not so strong.

Conversely, some consumers need to conform rather than stand out from the crowd. To conform is to be "in", to be different is to be "out". This is a strong motivator. Direct marketers work hard to transform it into interest and buying. Hence the slogan: *Every home should have one!*

What are the social drivers of your direct marketing message?	What it means to the campaign
● Status	Will status appeals make your product (and customer) stand out from the crowd?
● Roles	Are role requirements clear? What are recipients of your message expected to do – buy, recommend etc?
● Conformity to norms	Have you told (threatened) your prospect what will happen if he/she doesn't buy?
● Power	Have you empowered your prospect? Remember, visible symbols of exalted position often work, such as special badges or cards.

summary

Effective direct marketing depends on a thorough understanding of consumer behaviour. Traditionally, direct marketers approached markets from an instinctive, experiential perspective and denied the need to understand consumer motivations, insisting that testing and modelling behaviour was enough. This approach is no longer adequate. Markets are too competitive to allow direct marketers this luxury.

High involvement decisions are the focus of much direct marketing activity. Such decisions occur where there is a high perceived risk of making the wrong brand or product choice. This risk may be financial, but psychological risk is a more powerful motivator. The high involvement process is made up of a series of mental and behavioural stages: problem recognition, search, evaluation, decision and post-purchase evaluation. Psychological and intra-personal forces determine the structure, extent and outcomes of this process. The major concepts involved are: needs, perception, motivation, learning, personality and attitudes. Social influence also exerts a powerful effect. The main social forces operating in groups are: status, power, roles, norms, and conformity. Conformity to the norms of the group is a particularly significant and powerful idea.

Now let us see what influences business buyers.

4

hitting the business to business customer

- In business to business markets, direct marketing is one of the most important marketing approaches, because it is a very cost-effective way of keeping customers informed and managing relationships with them, if you know your customers relatively well, and when the costs of other form of contract (eg the sales force) are very high.

- This applies both in marketing to trade buyers and other business customers.

- However, because direct marketing demands knowledge of who is buying (so you can contact them), you must understand your customers' "decision-making unit" if you are to use direct marketing effectively.

introduction

> **Business to business** marketing is marketing by one organization to others. In this chapter, we abbreviate it as "business marketing".

Much business marketing is direct marketing. Every time a business person picks up the phone and speaks to someone in another organization, every time a letter is sent, direct communication takes place. These kinds of communication call for a direct response – often immediately. Order taking may not be the objective, but some direct response usually is.

What's the difference between consumer and business marketing?

Many types of organizations are involved in business direct marketing: large and small; profit and non-profit; public sector and private sector; manufacturers, wholesalers and retailers. However, business direct marketing differs from consumer direct marketing because of the type of benefit that must be offered to business buyers. The latter are usually concerned with how to meet the needs of *their* organization's customers.

Business marketing is a key area for direct marketing. Advertising is less important than in consumer markets, typically taking up 10% or less of the marketing communications budget. More important are trade shows, sales promotions, sales incentives, sales force management and public relations.

Direct marketing typically takes up about a third of business marketing communications budgets. Telemarketing may be a large element of this – up to 50% – particularly if a business has many small customers. Direct campaigns are often run as part of a co-ordinated campaign with other media eg generating leads for the sales force, inviting customers to an exhibition, drawing attention to a new catalogue or to offers in the catalogue.

the importance of business direct marketing

Two key reasons for the importance of direct marketing in business markets are:

- Most companies' customer and prospect universe is small enough to permit and encourage precise targeting. Whereas consumer markets may consist of millions of individuals and households, most business markets have far fewer customers. Only the very largest business marketers have more than a million customers (eg utilities such as telecommunications and power, branch banks), and most have a few thousand.
- A field sales call is expensive. It includes basic salary, commissions, car, expenses, pension benefits, sales support costs and corporate overheads (which may be substantial if the sales person has an office and a team of support staff to help manage customers). As little as 42% of the 240 days a year a sales person has available to sell will actually be spent selling (the rest will be on prospecting, administration, sales meetings and conferences etc). It may

take many calls to make a sale. For this reason, many business marketers have been using direct marketing techniques to maximize exploitation of sales force time.

business buying

Much organizational buying is as routine as its consumer counterpart. For instance, the office manager's decision to restock the office cupboard with paper clips is likely to be as simple as the consumer's decision to restock with coffee or tea. In both cases, known suppliers with reliable brands will be chosen automatically. Such industrial purchases are called "straight rebuys". They are low involvement decisions taken by individuals with little or no search and evaluation of alternatives. In such cases, most purchasers rely on known suppliers. Only when the normal supplier is unreliable will a new supplier be sought. The arrival of a direct marketing communication from another supplier at the right time may be crucial in securing the switched business.

However, as the complexity of the buying task increases, the degree of search and evaluation increases. "New buy" situations occur when buyers depart from routines to learn more about alternatives. For instance, if a decision has been taken to replace all the computers in an office, then considerable search and evaluation may take place. The product form is sufficiently different to prompt research into the benefits of different machines and their suppliers. Moreover, several people may be involved. The purchasing department will have its say. So will the finance department and perhaps even the managing director and secretarial staff! Few similar business buying decisions are made by only one person.

THE DECISION-MAKING UNIT

Organizational buying of all but the most routine items is likely to be done by a "decision-making unit" (DMU). No matter how many individuals may be involved in the process, there are six clearly identifiable *roles* that individuals play (see Figure 4.1).

The gatekeeper

The gatekeeper's role is to screen incoming information. Typically, secretaries screen incoming mail and telephone calls. Rarely does the manager see the envelope containing the mailing piece, therefore. Nor may the manager see the contents if someone else deems them to be irrelevant. Similarly, incoming calls are often not recorded. The caller is merely asked to "call back later". The gatekeeper may be a junior executive who collects data on equipment and suppliers, or a senior technical expert who is not formally involved in decision-making. By filtering information, the gatekeeper's influence may be considerable.

The initiator

This role is performed by the person or group of persons who first perceives the need for the product or service.

Fig 4.1

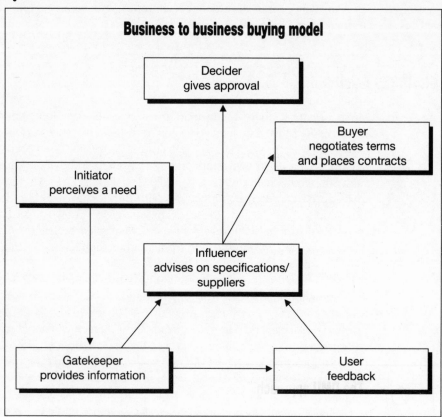

Business to business buying model

Decider
gives approval

Buyer
negotiates terms
and places contracts

Initiator
perceives a need

Influencer
advises on specifications/
suppliers

Gatekeeper
provides information

User
feedback

The influencer

This person may have either a formal or informal role and in the latter case may not be easily identifiable. Word of mouth influence may be very important, particularly in the later stages of the buying process.

The decider

Buying is a *group* process. Everyone in the group may contribute to the buying decision. Many members of the group may overestimate their role. Nevertheless, some members are usually more important than others, and these need to be identified.

The buyer

This person usually has formal authority to purchase and may be a member of the purchasing department. As the purchase becomes more important, the influence of the formal purchaser tends to diminish. For very large purchases, the formal buyer may do little more than send out the order requisition.

The user

This role requires little or no explanation. The importance of the user will vary according to an organization's characteristics. In one organization fork-lift truck operators will not be consulted when new trucks are being purchased; in another organization they might. But the selling task is made easier if the salesman (or direct marketer) knows which organization values the operators' opinions and which does not.

DON'T FORGET!

- *Will your communication get past the gatekeeper?*
- *What impact will it have on the initiator?*
- *Has it got the right messages to motivate the influencer?*
- *Are the messages strong enough to swing the decision?*
- *Is your sales administration easy to use and efficient?*
- *Does your product match up to the sales messages?*
- *Will your customer services department deliver?*

EXAMPLE

The DMU approach

A leading business direct marketing agency used the DMU approach to segment automobile fleet buyers. Research indicated that there were two key determinants of the decision – the product and the company. Some members of the DMU had a product focus. For example, sales-people cared about the model they were entitled to have, maintenance staff cared about the different models' mechanical specification and frequency and ease of maintenance. Others involved had a corporate focus. The finance directors cared about total cost of ownership, including resale values. These orientations are summarized in the table on the following page. ○

PURCHASE CRITERIA

It is one thing to know **who** is involved in buying: it is another to know **how** or **why** they buy. For instance, how important is price? Is reliable service more important? How do buyers react to interpersonal influences eg the personality of the sales-person? This information is best gathered from **focus group research**.

A **focus group** is a group of customers gathered together and moderated by a market research professional to talk expressly about a given subject. Focus groups are often the best way of discovering your customers' views and prejudices before investing heavily in a campaign.

Member of DMU	Role	Interest	Focus
Transport manager	Recommends vehicle policy	Residual values. Discounts. Warranties. Range of vehicles to fit different purposes. Reliability	Company focus. Product range as support
Senior management	User/chooser	One car. For self. Fit with self-image	Fitness for purpose
Finance director	Approver	Overall least cost for maximum benefit. Business efficiency	Company focus
Distribution manager	User/manager – commercial vehicles. Budget holder	Functionality of commercial vehicles. Reliability. Value	Product focus – commercial vehicles
Sales management	User/manager – sales vehicles. Budget holder	Functionality for sales purposes. Convenience. Motivation of staff	Product focus
Personnel	Influencer – benefits policy	Value vs fitness for purpose. Driver and user satisfaction. Safety. Image consonance	Company. Product range as support
Fleet maintenance manager	Initiator, user, influencer and gatekeeper	Ease of maintenance. Costs. Functionality	Product focus

THE STRUCTURE OF THE BUYING CENTRE

From a seller's perspective, it is also important to understand the pattern of communications within the buying centre. This, in turn, requires a clearer picture of the structure of the buying centre – hence the importance of research before deciding on the correct direct marketing approach.

CONFLICT WITHIN THE BUYING CENTRE

There is inevitably conflict within the buying centre. This conflict is likely to increase the involvement of other departments in the decision process. The seller must anticipate conflict between different departments and build into the offering benefits that will apply to all departments involved in the purchasing process.

MODELS OF ORGANIZATIONAL BUYING

One of the most influential models of organizational buyer behaviour was developed by Robinson, Faris and Wind. They identified eight **buyphases** and three **buyclasses**, from which they constructed a grid (Figure 4.2). This model indicates that the most complex buying situations occur in the top left portion of the grid. As one moves down and to the right, there is increasing commitment, with a diminishing likelihood of new suppliers gaining access to the buying centre.

Fig 4.2

The buygrid framework for industrial buying situations			
		Buyclasses	
Buyphases	New task	Modified rebuy	Straight rebuy
1. Anticipation, recognition of a problem or need			
2. Determination of characteristics and quantity of needed item			
3. Description of characteristics			
4. Search for potential sources			
5. Acquisition and analysis of proposals			
6. Evaluation of proposals and selection of suppliers			
7. Selection of an order routine			
8. Performance feedback and evaluation			

The most complex situations occur in the top left of the grid, the least complex in the bottom right.

(Source: PJ Robinson, CW Faris and Y Wind, *Industrial Buying and Creative Marketing*, Allyn & Bacon Inc., Boston 1967)

what is different about organizational buying?

Business to business buying has much in common with consumer family buying. The **problem-search-evaluation-decision** model for high involvement consumer purchases will often involve members of the family in the same way as business buying implicates members of the DMU. Family roles may also be initiator, influencer, user, decider and buyer. The family, too, is an organization! So, what are the differences?

One immediately observable difference is the absence of the gatekeeper in most family decision-making. Parents may deny young children access to media information, acting as gatekeepers. But in practice, this role is likely to be performed inconsistently and have little long-term impact. In business organizations, the gatekeeper role may be crucial, because business buying is more likely to be highly structured and formalized than consumer buying. This implies that purchasing agents will know more about the products they buy. There is also usually greater buyer-seller dependence than in consumer markets.

the role of direct marketing

As we stated earlier, the traditional tasks of business direct marketing have been lead generation and qualification, order taking and customer development. However, there are a number of problems that relate specifically to business market data.

LIST PROBLEMS

If you are working from externally sourced lists, you face several possible problems. External list availability and quality rarely matches the standard in consumer markets. Most business lists suffer in varying degrees from these problems. For example:

- Industrial codes (eg SIC) may not accurately describe the nature of the business.
- Address records are often inaccurate or duplicated.
- Smaller firms come into and go out of business quicker than data capture methods can keep pace with.
- Job titles and job descriptions may also be inaccurate and/or duplicated. The same individual may hold several job titles simultaneously, or titles may have been changed.
- Individuals change jobs relatively frequently. On average a householder moves every seven years; a jobholder moves on average every three years.
- It is harder to purge business lists of duplicates because the software rules are complex.
- The numbers of firms in some industries are so small that systematic testing is statistically impossible.

On the other hand, the relatively small size of the business universe makes list compilation, list maintenance and targeting relatively easy. Quality control, particularly telephone checking, is also likely to be more effective.

CONTACTING THE RIGHT PERSON

Although the buying process may be complex, the essential elements are captured in the useful mnemonic "**find the MAN**" – **the person with the Means,**

Authority and Need. There will be those who can afford to pay, those who need the product, and those who are authorized to pay.

A high-cost management development programme

EXAMPLE

To generate sufficient leads, you might need to contact the potential delegate (need), the delegate's manager (need), the personnel function (means/authority), and the financial function (means/authority). The level of manager to be contacted will depend on the size of the company. In large companies it could be the personnel manager and financial controller, in smaller companies the personnel director and financial director and in very small companies probably the managing director (who performs both authority and means roles). ◯

PERSONALIZING

The key part of personalization is to make all your communication relevant to the recipient. For instance, if your database holds details of prospects' lines of authority and responsibility, the number of employees in their charge, the size of their budgets, their purchasing limits, etc then it is possible to design letters, brochures and reply devices which make use of this information – greatly increasing the potential response rate.

With individuals changing jobs so often, personalizing direct communications is not always possible, or necessary. But without names, you'll have to find correct job titles – not easy either.

WATCH OUT!

Spud they liked!

EXAMPLE

A UK direct marketing agency was recently asked by a client to locate and communicate to all public sector potato buyers: schools, hospitals, care-centres, prisons, etc. No list of named potato buyers was available, unsurprisingly! Instead the pack was addressed to "The Potato Buyer"! The results of the campaign exceeded the client's expectations and clearly demonstrated that the packs were passed on to the appropriate individuals. ◯

EXAMPLE

The motor trade

In many industries, the partnership approach to managing dealers is now well-established eg the automotive trade. Here, database marketing is now an important link between the customer, the dealer and the supplier. The customer database indicates when a service or a purchase is likely to take place, and direct marketing techniques are used to encourage the consumer to come to the dealer. After the sale or service, mailings are often used to gain information on quality and to ensure customer satisfaction. Finally, "dialogue" programmes are now in place which keep up communication with owners of competitive makes, encouraging them to test drive the supplier's brand when replacement time comes. ○

summary

We have outlined the differences between consumer and business buying, and identified the DMU as a key concept. Selling to this unit involves identifying the roles its different members play and tailoring messages accordingly. Mass marketing communications have poor potential in this situation, but direct marketing – especially using mail and telephone – is very effective at reaching the right customer with the right message. Personalization is particularly important.

In the next chapter, we show you how to use this information about customers to good effect in planning your direct marketing.

5

the hit strategy

- Customer acquisition, development and retention provide the key to building your customer base through direct marketing.

- But you need to keep a close eye on customer attrition rates to prevent your business bleeding away.

- The secrets of attracting the right kind of customer lie in profiling your existing good customers and finding more like them.

- You may find that your best customers are the best recruiters of more like them, through "member get member" programmes.

- Once you've identified customers you want, you need to focus on getting them to make the first buy, and then welcoming them, up-selling, cross-selling and renewal.

- However, your inactive and lapsed customers may also provide an opportunity – after all, they once did business with you.

introduction

Because of its origins as a tactical weapon, especially as direct mail, direct marketing is often seen as an operational tactic, best expressed in the phrase: *"Let's do a mailshot"*, to which you should reply: *"Why, to whom, when, with what objectives, what will follow on, how will my relationship with my customers change etc?"*

Direct marketing's emergence as a topic in strategic planning is relatively new, and as yet not universally accepted. In strategic planning, direct marketing's key asset is collection, analysis and tracking of customer information. This information, maintained on your database, is clearly a corporate planning asset. Many companies are bought and sold on the knowledge they contain. On balance sheets this is shown as "goodwill" values, but in direct marketing terms it is an asset of tangible value – the name and address and all transactional and promotional information on all customers. The lifetime value of a customer is yet to appear on balance sheets but it will be an inevitable consequence of a better understanding of direct marketing.

What's in a name?

EXAMPLE

Next bought Grattan, a mail order company, largely for the value of its six million customer names. ○

Direct marketing permeates all levels of strategic and marketing planning. Enhanced customer knowledge means that you can enter new markets with greater degrees of certainty. You can identify customers under competitive threat and take steps to reinforce their loyalty. You understand more about particular markets. You can use the database to identify specific market and product range opportunities. You can derive and test product specifications and promotional options.

Different ways to use your database – examples from strategic to marketing planning

- Identify markets which have similar customers to those on your database.
- Identify customers who recently have bought less and research them to see if they are buying competitive products.
- Identify customers who are loyal and develop loyalty programmes to reinforce their loyalty and encourage them to buy more (greater volumes, wider product ranges etc) and recommend you.
- Identify customers who have bought particular products, and develop new products to suit these segments.
- Develop and test campaigns to get particular types of customers to buy more
- Test promotional ideas on a sample from your database.

the principles of acquisition and retention

Your "**customer attrition rate**" is the percentage of your customers at the beginning of a period who cease doing business with you during that period. A single figure is not always the best way of measuring it, as its significance depends upon factors such as the average length of the buying cycle – or frequency of purchase, and the range and value of products bought. For example, you might want to regard a customer as lost if they stop buying your highest value products products from you, and only buy your very low value products infrequently.

Your "**customer retention rate**" is the converse of your attrition rate ie the proportion of your customers that you had at the beginning of the period who are still doing business with you at the end of the period. For the same reasons, a single figure gives you only a rough guide to the situation.

Customer retention is similar to **loyalty**, but loyalty is strictly speaking a state of mind. A loyal customer may buy elsewhere because you don't happen to have the right product at the time.

"**Customer acquisition**" is the process or achievement of gaining new customers. **Customer retention** is the process or achievement of keeping them

Most objectives and strategies in direct marketing are based on the ideas of customer acquisition and retention. However good your marketing, you will always suffer some customer attrition. To stand still, you need to acquire more customers – the purpose of acquisition programmes.

ACQUISITION

There are usually six stages in an acquisition programme.

1. *Set objectives.*

2. *Profile the type of customers you wish to acquire* (usually similar to your existing best customers), by analyzing your database.

3. *Target those customers* – often using acquired lists.

4. *Media selection* – if the right lists aren't available at the right cost, use media which are targeted at the type of customer you want to acquire.

5. *Communication* – develop the communication that will attract those customers, through an offer designed to appeal to them, sent to them at the time it is most likely to appeal, and expressed in a way – copy, images etc – most likely to appeal to them.

6. *Sell to them.*

7. *Handle them properly after the sale*, to retain them, sell more to them, and sell a wider range to them.

Objectives

Perhaps surprisingly, the starting point for any acquisition programme is not analysis of the reasons why people come to you – or don't. It is a simple financial calculation.

"**Allowable marketing cost per acquisition**" is how much you can afford to spend to acquire a customer. It should be determined by the expected lifetime value of a customer, as opposed to short-term profit.

"**Lifetime value**" is the value (profit) you can expect from a given customer over the expected life of that customer with you. It increases the better your retention rate, the more you can sell up and sell across, and the more strongly you can get the customer to recommend you to others. Strictly speaking, it should be calculated using discounted cash flow techniques, but most direct marketers use much simpler approaches, such as the value of the first N years of purchase. How far ahead you should look depends upon how long you can expect a customer to be interested in your category of product and the length of the buying cycle.

Lifetime value

EXAMPLE

A parent is likely to be in the market for particularly high volumes of detergents for the period in which there are children at home. This can be for as long as 20-25 years. Acquiring a customer at the beginning of this period can yield a very high lifetime value if loyalty is managed successfully. However, keeping the customer loyal in such a highly competitive market is expensive, and many quite loyal customers will switch to try out competitive offers – the purchasing cycle is frequent enough for this to happen – and switch back later. This reduces the lifetime value even of loyal customers. ○

If you haven't got the data to calculate lifetime value, then various short-term measures can be used, such as:

● Cost of achieving the initial sale(s) to the newly acquired customer – this leads to a focus on finding low cost methods of acquisition (eg if the offer is price led, making it on a low-cost item)
● Return on investment from the initial sale(s).

However, the closer to lifetime value the measure is, the better it is as a criterion for targeting or selecting customers to be acquired. One reason why a good customer database is so valuable is that it allows you to track the longer-term buying patterns of your customers, and so calculate their lifetime value.

Acquisition and retention strategies differ according to your previous relationship with the customer. The key categories here are repeat customers, former customers, previous enquirers and new customers (see Figure 5.1 for more detail).

Fig 5.1

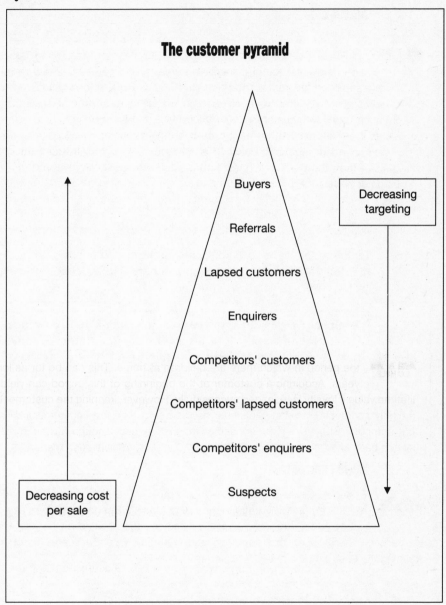

The customer pyramid

Buyers

Referrals

Lapsed customers

Enquirers

Competitors' customers

Competitors' lapsed customers

Competitors' enquirers

Suspects

Decreasing targeting

Decreasing cost per sale

Profiling

If your database contains data on individuals and their response and purchase histories, it is the right starting point for you to examine which media sources and communication strategies work best. Where little or no history exists, developing a profile of existing customers will help you target new customers. Many companies use customer satisfaction questionnaires for this purpose.

Air UK Ltd

EXAMPLE

Air UK Ltd developed a totally integrated system of monitoring their customers' opinion of the service and profiling the customer database. Using this method they cut complaints, found a totally accurate profile to use with future mailings and campaigns and used the data as part of a staff motivation and reward scheme. The system was developed in 1992 and has been used succesfully ever since. This approach is used in all communications with customers, always allowing them an opportunity to comment on the service as they perceive it. The response rates they achieve to mailings is between 30 and 80%, well ahead of industry norms. This demonstrates a critical point about marketing databases – they achieve their highest return when their use is highly focused – in this case on customer service. ○

Targeting

Targeting should be based on profiling the customer base. This is clearly the best way, but not always possible. Your aim here is to look for customers with similar characteristics to your best customers.

> **"Member Get Member" (MGM)** schemes are often used by membership and credit card organizations as a way of recruiting similar customers. Members tend to recruit similar people to themselves. If your database has not got enough good prospects and if relevant lists are hard to obtain, MGM should always be considered as an option. MGM is targeted word-of-mouth advocacy with a bonus built in for existing customers.

MGM campaigns

EXAMPLE

Preferred Direct is a direct selling motor insurer. For a two year period it relied exclusively on MGM campaigns, using Marks & Spencer vouchers as an incentive.

For years, American Express used a case of wine as an MGM incentive – perhaps on the grounds that any successful recruiter would assuage his or her guilt by splitting the case with the newly recruited member! ○

Media

When evaluating and selecting media, you must establish an allowable cost per sale. Your allowable cost per sale will increase if the lifetime value of customers is introduced into the calculations. Other variables to consider in the media plan for recruitment should include:

- *Size of audience to be reached* – the larger the audience, the more viable mass media will be.
- *Media cost* – which has to be weighed against the likelihood of response.

- *Media availability* – even with such a wide range of media available today, you may have to work hard to find the right combination for you.
- *Media accessibility* – do your prospects for recruitment pay enough attention to the medium for it to be a successful recruitment device?
- *Estimated effectiveness* – what is the likely response rate?
- *The number of stages of communication* required to achieve the right response (one stage or multiple, depending on the buying process). The more complex the product or service, the more complex the recruitment process is likely to be. For example, for some industrial equipment products, it may require two or three letters, a catalogue, two or three phone calls and several sales visits.

The "**law of diminishing media returns**" occurs in various forms, such as:

- A customer's responsiveness to a particular medium diminishes the more he or she is exposed to it.
- The more (frequently within a period, total period over which it is used) a particular advertisement is used, the lower the response.
- Doubling the size of advertisements, the weight of mailing packages, or their frequency, will less than double the response. This is often referred to as the "square root law", as doubling may lead to a response which is only about 40% higher (the square root of 2 being just over 1.4, or 40% greater than 1).

Multiple media campaigns are usually more cost effective as they are less liable to the law of diminishing returns. However, they are more difficult to co-ordinate. There is more chance of their going wrong. For example, if the timing of promotion through one medium slips (eg a letter which contains a reference to a television campaign), then the effect may be counterproductive.

Media sources can be ranked (from lowest to highest) according to the cost per sale. It is also possible to rank cost effectiveness within individual media such as direct mail (effectiveness of particular lists) and press (by individual publication). This highlights the requirement to source-code all promotions so that their individual performance in customer recruitment can be monitored and ranked over time. A high volume of sales from an advertisement in one particular newspaper may generate many customers. However, they may have no stamina (in other words, the drop out rate betwen enquiry and sale may be very high, or they may only buy once from you and never buy again) compared to those recruited by an identical advertisement in another paper.

In the past, many direct marketers focused on the immediate impact and results of any activity as opposed to the cumulative impact of several communications. As far as instant results are concerned, high, unduplicated (ie the same prospect is not hit twice) market coverage will normally outpull high frequency. This is in contrast to the philosophy of general advertisers, who prepare media plans based on reach (the total number of prospects covered) *and* frequency (how often the advertisement appears). However, if you want to focus on customer retention and lifetime value, you need to use both approaches to campaign planning to achieve a stable, high-yielding customer base. This principle is illustrated in Figure 5.2.

Fig 5.2

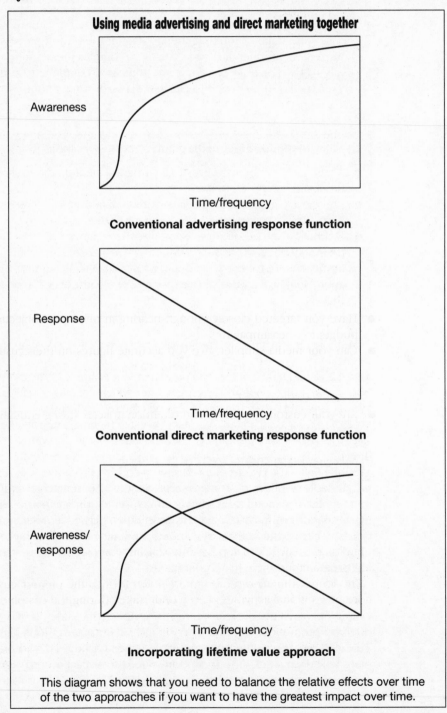

Using media advertising and direct marketing together

Awareness

Time/frequency

Conventional advertising response function

Response

Time/frequency

Conventional direct marketing response function

Awareness/
response

Time/frequency

Incorporating lifetime value approach

This diagram shows that you need to balance the relative effects over time of the two approaches if you want to have the greatest impact over time.

Communication

Creative treatment and offers made to potential new customers depend on your knowledge of buyer behaviour. Subject to the nature of your company's products or services, you may decide that you need immediate buyers, trial buyers, highly qualified enquirers or loosely qualified enquirers. These decisions will affect the creative treatment, offer, and the number of stages needed to complete the buying cycle. The creative treatment also depends on the brand personality of the promoted product or service. This determines, for example, whether a communication is product or offer led.

Sales

Once the sale is made, the process of managing and retaining your customer really begins. The obvious step is the need for a communication thanking your customer. Unfortunately, such an old-fashioned, small business norm has not yet permeated many large companies and this simple step is often forgotten.

Key questions for acquisition

- Have you set achievable, realistic objectives which will fit with the business's overall needs?
- Have you included a mechanism which will enable you to profile your database better in future, and have you made best use of the profiles available to you?
- Have you targeted closely enough bearing in mind your objectives and the budget for the campaign?
- Can your media supplier give you accurate figures on their customers' profiles, do they fit as closely as possible to yours?
- Does your communication leave the target market with the right messages about your product?
- Are your customer services and retention policies strong enough to support the campaign and a possible influx of customers?

KEEPING CUSTOMERS – THE PRINCIPLE OF RETENTION

The purpose of retention strategy is to maximize an individual's profitable lifetime value as a customer. Active customers can usually easily be identified from records of current transactions. The definition of lapsed and inactive customers varies by the average frequency of transaction in the market. To be cost-effective, retention strategies have to be planned in some detail and can result in quite complex programmes.

The longer the known lifetime or *potential* lifetime of your customer, the more promotional activities can be undertaken during the customer's life with your company. At the beginning, "welcoming" activities take place. These are followed by promotions encouraging the customer to upgrade or buy additional products or services. Finally, as the end of the product's life with the customer approaches (eg end of subscription, need to replace equipment), renewal activities are initiated.

Don't lose touch!

In merchandise mail order, a lapsed inactive customer might be defined as one who has not ordered for 12 months, an inactive customer as one who has not ordered for 24 months or more. But for goods with longer re-ordering cycles, these figures might be much higher. If the product is durable and replacement takes place every 10 years or so, then customers might consider themselves as loyal to a company even if they have not bought for five years. For this reason, companies with long replacement cycle products try to sell lower value items (service, support, parts etc) on a more regular basis. The main reason for this is to generate revenue, but it also works wonders as a way of keeping in touch with customers. ○

Welcome cycle

This is an opportunity to welcome and reassure customers, overcome any cognitive dissonance, build loyalty and gain additional customer information. It also opens up the opportunity of giving your customer initial benefits. Whether a welcome cycle is appropriate will be related to the length of life cycle of the customer.

Up-selling

Given a positive reaction to the product/service a natural next step would be to promote higher value product/services. In the case of a normal credit card, it could be a privileged customer gold card, in automobiles an upmarket model in the range or in recorded music a boxed set to appeal to a buyer of a single CD/cassette album. The timing of the offer can be determined by previous customer histories. Often this can be achieved by testing and then applying the test results using statistical analysis applied to the customer database, to give each customer record an individual score which indicates the likelihood of the customer to respond to such an offer.

Cross-selling

This is a conscious strategy to switch your customers across product categories. A credit card company could promote a home shopping service or wine club. An automobile company could promote the second car for the family. A book club could promote a music collection. In both up- and cross-selling, loyal customers should be given some incentive to remain loyal.

Renewal

The length of the renewal cycle should be tested to achieve the optimum results for the minimum expenditure. You need to find cost-effective inducements to reward loyal customers for continued patronage. Often a renewal cycle will mean a number of timed, relevant and personal communications before the date of renewal, on the date of renewal and after the date of renewal. Customers who pass the final renewal cycle date become "lapsed".

Lapsed customers

Reawakening lapsed customers is usually more cost-effective than recruiting totally new customers, unless they have lapsed because of a fundamental problem in the relationship (eg product or service quality) or because they have passed out of the target market (eg a different life stage, moving out of the relevant area). You may face problems with the quality of the information about lapsed customers. However, because data on lapsed customers is available to you from your database, its value can be tested, so the profitability on promotions to your lapsed customers does not have to be guessed.

Inactive customers

Here, cost-effectiveness is a more critical issue. Inactive customers have not bought or responded to a promotion for longer than lapsed customers. Again, however, the answer is to test and compare the results to the acquisition programme in terms of cost justification.

Making the most of your direct marketing

- Does your campaign have room for a "welcome" cycle when loyalty can be built up?
- Will the welcome cycle be used to up-sell? Have you formed alliances with other companies to allow for cross-selling, or does your company have enough interested customers for it to be valuable in an alliance with other companies?
- Is your new business section regenerating the database, and are you keeping the customers you recruited?
- Do you want to do anything about lapsed and inactive customers? Do you have sufficient budget to regenerate them? Is it cost-effective in your business?

ACQUISITION VS RETENTION

All company sales are made up from two groups, new customers and repeat customers. It is much more cost-effective to retain existing customers than attract new customers. Existing customers have known, identified needs which have been satisfied by your company's product. By focusing your marketing strategy on the profitable segments of your customer base, you will normally produce most of the required revenue and increase market share without investing in new customers. Acquisition is more expensive because it takes place in an unidentified universe where much of the campaign falls on hopeless causes. But once you succeed with acquisition, the maintenance of customer loyalty has additional benefits. Loyal customers not only repurchase, but advocate products and services to their friends, pay less attention to competitive brands and often buy product/service line extensions.

WATCH OUT!

*The critical issue in retention which is sometimes skimmed over by direct marketers is that **customer loyalty** is not merely created by cross-selling strategies or customer clubs. Loyalty is a state of mind, which is reinforced by how you manage your customers in the fullest sense , including service, communication and branding.*

To develop effective retention strategies, a company needs a thorough understanding of its customers' behaviour and needs. Loyalty is a physical and emotional commitment given by a customer in exchange for their needs being met. You should view your relationship with your customers from your customers' viewpoint. This should help you understand why you are getting your current level of loyalty, and how to reduce your customer attrition rate.

MBNA puts customer first

EXAMPLE MBNA, a loan and credit card company, reduced its defection rate from 10% to 5% pa and thereby increased its profits by 85%. It did it not by introducing a loyalty scheme, but by completely overhauling its service delivery system via business process re-engineering techniques. This means that it redesigned its systems and processes for managing customers to meet customers' requirements, rather than the functional requirements of different departments. Service quality went up, defections went down and profits soared. ○

Market research of existing customers is therefore an important contributor to planning retention marketing. Using market research or customer audits as the focus for this gives your staff an understanding not only of the customer, but of the need to understand them. If you are in an industry which can support using your staff as fieldworkers for research in customer satisfaction (eg retailing, travel and leisure, professional services) you will not only gain a cost-effective form of monitoring, but also their desire to use the information they have collected.

FAST TRACK

what creates loyalty?

The loyalty of your customers will be increased if you start to change how you manage your customers so as to meet their product quality, relationship, service, communication and brand needs.

What customers seek

- Convenience and easy access to your products or services.
- Appropriate contact and communication with your company.
- "Special" privileged status as a known customer.
- Recognition of their history with you.
- Effective and fast problem-solving.
- Appropriate anticipation of their needs.
- A professional, friendly two way dialogue

Using information on your customer database, there is no reason why a customer loyalty programme cannot be finely tuned to provide high levels of customer service to the majority of your customers.

STEPS IN A RETENTION STRATEGY

There are six steps in a retention strategy.

Identification

This is the first step – simply to identify and value your best customers against an agreed criterion of profitability. It may be that smaller, but regular buyers contribute a greater profit margin and lifetime value than one-time large purchasers.

Analysis

This is a detailed analysis of the profile of your best customers. A thorough profiling and tracking of their purchase histories (Frequency – how much, Recency – how recently, Amount – of what volume or value, and Category – what type: usually abbreviated as FRAC) and promotional responses and sources is vital here. It also helps you identify the potential market of similar customers for the acquisition programme. This is sometimes referred to as a direct marketing audit. Many financial institutions, when they have undertaken this activity, have been surprised to learn how many customers and families are multiple purchasers of their products.

Streaming for targeting

Once each customer's record has been properly analyzed and scored for its likely value to you, then it is accessible for selection. The criteria for selection include not only likely profitability, but also the customer's accessibility to you (whether by direct marketing or other techniques). At this stage, you should review all your potential contact points with customers for their usefulness in deepening the relationship.

Contact points represent two different targeting opportunities. One type is at a nominal cost to the organisation, whilst the other is paid for. The former opportunities are known as free rides and can include:

- Statement stuffers – promotional material in bills, along the lines of most credit card companies or direct print photographic companies.
- Product dispatch stuffers – promotional material enclosed with products such as mail order merchandise.
- Invoices and account letters – these are also promotional opportunities.
- Opening and closing letters.
- Catalogues.
- Calls from customers.
- Point of sale or service contact.

Contact strategies

The contact strategy is the type and sequence of promotional steps required to achieve the desired result, eg letter followed by telephone call and sales visit. This must reinforce the benefits of repeat purchasing. The aim is to reward customers' decisions to stay loyal and increase purchasing. You need to "bundle" different media according to their relative strengths in order to achieve the greatest effect.

For example, customers who are a long way off from buying (they may have just bought) may need a gentle mail prompt. Customers who are closer to rebuying may merit a telephone call or even a sales visit. With the cost of keeping a sales person on the road anything between £50,000 and £100,000, and the cost per visit between £120 and £240, this resource must be deployed carefully. This contrasts with an outbound telephone call at £6-£10 (depending on its length). So you need to assess whether the sales call is likely to be so many times more effective. The answer is that it will be for some customers, not for others. Your task is to find out which, and the best way to do this is to test it.

EXAMPLE

A number of very large companies, such as British Airways and BT, now use the contact strategy philosophy to determine the contact strategies for many different customer groups – particularly their best customers – pushing out the frontiers of customer service.

The idea of putting the customer in a privileged position is common to many contact strategies.

Testing and evaluation

Whatever stage of the life cycle a customer is at, it is always worth having a continued series of tests to establish optimum timing, frequency, offer and creative treatments. Without these, the profitability of loyalty programmes can be difficult to establish.

Understanding the customer base

Your customer base can present your market researchers with an excellent sampling frame, which is why the formal research process should be built into the contact strategy, involving the use of questionnaires and structured telephone interviews. Research can also form part of the customer care programme and if executed properly it will reinforce the brand and service values your company wishes to transmit to customers.

Customer retention

● Can you identify your best customers? What percentage of your total customer base are they?
● What particular features do they have in common? Can these be found in other customers?
● When is the best time to hit them with new services and offers?
● Are you communicating with them enough, or too much? Have you researched how they feel about this?
● How often do you talk to your customers and listen to their views, or run focus groups? Do you use this information to modify your profiling of best customers?

- Are you getting the right information from your customer database? Have you really used the market research element of it? Where are the gaps, and what can you do to fill them?

summary

Retention is more critical than acquisition as it is usually more cost-effective and profitable.

The communications employed in a retention cycle will vary according the nature of your business and your marketing objectives. By upgrading or cross-selling, your communications can include selective targeting of products, catalogue marketing, telephone upgrading, customer club, questionnaire, and customer care lines.

The objective of a retention programme must be to make it worthwhile for your customers to stay with you, which is why a thorough understanding of your customers' behaviour is vital. You will sometimes have to achieve a delicate balance between marginal income and customer irritation. In any retention programme, all possible contact points with your customers must be reviewed, competitive messages must be taken into account, optimal frequency must be tested, and your customers must receive the right products, customer service and quality.

DEVELOPING YOUR PLANS

All acquisition and retention strategies and programmes are ultimately driven by the customer database. All retention activities are geared to enhance the knowledge the database contains. Every element of the marketing plan should make a clear contribution to acquiring and/or retaining customers. In the next chapter a detailed methodology for developing direct marketing plans using your customer database is described.

6
planning the direct hit

- Direct marketing means more than just planning campaigns – it also means planning long-term relationships with customers.

- Direct marketing planning is similar to marketing planning, but this emphasis on customer relationship planning implies a stronger focus on customer acquisition, retention and lifetime values as planning criteria.

- A strong emphasis on efficiency is also important, as high volume mailings can be financially disastrous if response or purchase rates are too low.

what makes a good hit plan?

WATCH OUT!

Direct marketers' strong tactical heritage fills them with ideas about one-off campaigns that could achieve high response rates. To many direct marketers, a plan is just a string of good promotional ideas. But such a plan is unlikely to lead to long-term success in customer acquisition and retention. A good direct marketing plan is not simply a list of ideas, summary notes from meetings or sets of recommendations. It should be a structured series of initiatives, working to clear and quantified objectives, tightly targeted and (ideally) with the targeting, timing, offer and creative tested beforehand. Where the aim is to manage a group of customers to achieve increased loyalty, these initiatives should be aimed at building and/or reinforcing the relationship with them.

Planning itself is not simply about problem-solving, forecasting or making decisions, all of which are day-to-day management functions. Your direct marketing plan should be:

- A written, comprehensive and detailed document, prepared with the input of direct marketing professionals.
- The result of painstaking problem-solving and decision-making to specify the direction of your marketing operation for the coming year – or whatever period you are planning for.
- An integral part of your overall marketing and business planning process, and not a tactical afterthought.

Projects will have been evaluated, start and completion dates set, costs and priorities assigned. Activities will be quantified and evaluated according to how they contribute to revenue and profit. The plan will have been quantified from the customer perspective, showing how each group of customers is expected to perform, in their year of acquisition and over the lifetime of their relationship with you.

The benefits of a good direct marketing plan

- Allows specialists to identify and understand interfunctional relationships which might otherwise be missed.
- Stimulates tactical creativity.
- Allocates resources to their most profitable use.
- Creates benchmarks for future decisions.
- Improves staff quality control and deadline performance.
- Generates improved supplier performance.
- Enables faster rollouts of successful programmes and faster shutoff of failures.
- Saves substantial top and middle management time and stress during implementation stages.
- Facilitates learning by all staff involved – your own and suppliers.

To achieve this, your plan must:

- Be easy to understand.

- Be precise but detailed to avoid confusion.
- Be adaptable to change.
- Be realistic in application and goal achievement.
- Cover all significant market factors.
- Clearly identify responsibilities.

THE IMPORTANCE OF A SUMMARY

In companies with many products, operating in many markets and with many types of customer, marketing plans are complex. The result is that many people who **should read the plan do not**. If they do, they may not remember its details.

A good **management summary** expresses the dominant themes of the plan forcibly and clearly, and documents in summary form the resources involved, customers targeted, timings, budgets and expected results.

A good management summary means that no-one has the excuse that they do not know where you are heading. It is also a very helpful attachment to briefs to direct marketing agencies (subject to confidentiality). The summary should not, by its nature, go into much detail. It should concentrate on objectives, main target markets, opportunities and threats, and key strategies and timings.

WHAT EXPERTISE IS NEEDED?

Direct marketing planning requires a blend of the following types of expertise:

- Direct marketing strategic planning.
- Experience of achieving improvements in customer acquisition, retention and lifetime values.
- Knowledge of all relevant media.
- Creative expertise.
- Sound production experience coupled with knowledge of the latest techniques and processes.
- Systems specialists who understand database marketing.
- Manufacturing and fulfilment.
- Understanding of customers' service requirements, and trends in customer satisfaction.
- Buying and negotiating skills, to ensure budgets are used effectively.

the planning process

The key stages in direct marketing planning are similar to those in marketing planning, namely:

1. *Situation analysis* – customer, financial, competition etc.

2. *Setting business objectives.*

3. *Identifying, evaluating and choosing* strategic options.

4. *Developing action* plans.

5. *Financial analysis.*

SITUATION ANALYSIS

The first step here is defining the products or services to be marketed directly. This process is summarized below.

Product definition

> #### *The product definition process*
>
> 1. Select the product or service to be promoted – note that this may be a range of products or services, because your objective may be to manage a market segment using direct marketing (see "customer definition" below), rather than just a particular product line.
>
> 2. Identify the product(s) prime applications.
>
> 3. Carry out a "needs and wants" analysis leading to benefit evaluation, customer profile identification and market segmentation. This supports every aspect of campaign development, but particularly the targeting and the creative approach to be taken.
>
> 4. Identify the product or service benefits and USP. All the product features should be expressed into concise benefit statements. Each identified need and want can be stated in terms required of benefits. The same analysis should be carried out for competitive offerings, and a comparison undertaken. If a true USP exists, then it will provide clear differentiation from competition.

Customer definition

Together with product definition goes customer definition. The aim of this is to develop a customer/prospect customer profile. This process is summarized below.

The customer definition process

1. Identify the customers you wish to target.

2. Gather data – through research and database analysis – about how they buy.

3. Identify what they consider value to be.

4. Identify which of their needs your products or services satisfy.

5. Identify why prospects you want are not your customers, and what might make them yours.

6. Identify which of your existing customers are most "at risk", why, and which competitors they are most likely to go to, or why they might stop buying the product category altogether.

Once the customer profile is developed, you should rank your product or service benefits against the profiles of different types of customer. Your aim is to achieve best performance by defining customer profiles as accurately as possible, selecting segments of the total customer base with similar characteristics, and communicating effectively with them to maximize sales during the customer's lifetime. Transactional information gives you an accurate record of response and is a key discriminator. The best profiles are of those customers who have purchased recently, buy frequently, have a high monetary value and buy a variety of products. When you review an external list for its potential value, compare a sample of the list against your own database (often called the "house file"). The higher the correlation of names the more likely the list is to produce a good response.

Your ultimate aim is to score customer records for their propensity to purchase. Here standard statistical techniques such as factor analysis or regression analysis are employed. However, each segment identified through such techniques must be accessible cost-effectively. Isolating a segment which cannot be located at reasonable cost through existing media options or lists is not much help to you.

Financial performance

The key areas for financial analysis are:

- Sales turnover and profitability.
- Product analysis including unit costing and volumes.
- Media effectiveness, assuming response is trackable.
- Market performance.
- Distribution channel performance.
- Promotion and advertising budget effectiveness.

The six main performance measures direct marketers use are:

1. **Customer acquisition costs**. It is imperative to acquire customers at the lowest cost per sale and to know how much allowable marketing cost can be spent to acquire a customer.

2. **Break-even volumes**. What sales level is required to break even on campaigns to particular segments. Depending on how tight budgets are, you may or may not have the luxury of citing lifetime values in break-even calculations!

3. **Attrition rate**. This measures the rate at which customers are lost. Every company suffers customer losses, either through natural attrition (eg deaths, tired products), through poor customer service in the retention phase, or because the kind of customer attracted through a particular source had a low propensity to be loyal, perhaps being a cherry picker and always attracted to promotional offers.

4. **Lifetime values**. It is relatively simple for a sophisticated database with customer transaction histories to be programmed to compute the LTV figures.

5. **Profit potential**. What profit might be made by a programme.

6. **Resource allocation**. Which measures how all your marketing and service resources are deployed with particular customers, and the returns from each group of customers. Your resources must be deployed to produce long-term customer loyalty and satisfaction and profit. Only a profitable business will be able to service its customer base effectively and maintain growth through excellence in customer service and quality of products or services. There is little point producing more business if it cannot be serviced adequately.

These measures must be understood for your business as a whole and each market segment, because they will tell you where you should focus your direct marketing effort.

Reviewing your key resources

- Database facility – for storage capacity and processing speed.
- Distribution channels – for their efficiency at moving products to customers.
- Fulfilment operation from receipt of order to shipment and customer service procedures.
- Capital available to fund the business.
- Staff expertise in functional areas.
- Quality of the products and/or services.
- Your brand – and the consequent expectations associated with your company's reputation and name

WATCH OUT!

Being honest *about your company's* ***strengths and weaknesses*** *is vital for direct marketing planning. The failure of many direct marketing plans can be directly traced to lack of a solid review of strengths and weaknesses and a rose-tinted view of past performance.*

Competition

In monitoring the competition, the first step is to determine who competitors are and in what way they are competing. It is important to monitor market share movements, market trends and to gain knowledge of competitors' specific strengths and weaknesses.

What you should get from your situation analysis

- The wants and needs your products/services satisfy.
- Customer profiles which can be converted into market segments.
- The distinctive values your company provides to its customers.
- Emerging market segments, unsatisfied needs and competitive gaps.
- Your communication mix and distribution channels.
- Your company's real ability to service its customers.

SETTING BUSINESS OBJECTIVES

When you have reviewed your current market position thoroughly both internally and externally, you are in a good position to identify a feasible set of direct marketing objectives. Your objectives should be broad enough to maximize the identified market opportunities but narrow enough to ensure your resources can be realistically deployed to achieve them.

Make sure your objectives are sound

- Ensure every objective focuses on results.
- Quantify every objective (ROI, turnover, % market share etc).
- Where possible have a single theme for the objective.
- Ensure resources are realistic for achieving the objective.
- Ensure marketing objectives are directly tied to corporate goals and objectives.

IN THE REAL WORLD

Ranking objectives

1. Separate objectives that are measured in different ways from each other, and be clear about how you'll measure them in practice. Financial objectives will be measured by a combination of product profitability and database analysis. Increasing market awareness might be measured by recall research.

2. Rank the financial objectives and then the others, firstly in terms of their contribution to your current financial performance and secondly in terms of their contribution to longer-term lifetime value.

Now let's look at some specific direct marketing objectives.

Growing market share and volumes

Increasing sales volume within a category will grow market share. It is a typical option for those companies who live or die on market share, such as packaged consumer goods companies. For many direct marketing companies such as mail order operations, the same criteria may apply but may be combined with turnover increases, increasing customer cross-selling and upgrading, more frequent purchases and growth of the customer base. Increasing frequency of use is often the objective of loyalty programmes.

Increasing profit

There are three ways to achieve greater efficiency.

- **Improving the price and offer**. This is particularly relevant to direct marketers who have a large degree of flexibility in this area, because price can be adjusted to the market segment which is the target for the individual campaign. By changing the offer, you can increase price.
- **Improving the sales mix**. This can be achieved by discarding less profitable

lines. Mail order companies are very quick to delete unprofitable items. Concentrating on tested, proven, winners will yield a higher return.

- **Reducing costs**. This can be achieved by combining two offers in one, or reducing the quality of promotional material (though in both cases response rates might fall). It may be hazardous in the longer term, because of the risks to brand image.

STRATEGY OPTIONS AND EVALUATION

FAST TRACK

*Having determined where you wish to go, now's the time to determine **how** to get there! More formally, **strategy** is the art of devising a plan, using structured planning methods, to achieve a goal. Any strategy needs to be assessed against the product/service offer, the target market, the market place and competition, current distribution channels, media plan and mix, financial situation of the company, internal operational capabilities of the company. Part of the process of strategy formulation is to identify possible blocks to achieving the strategy, and then find ways to overcome them.*

What your direct marketing strategy should cover

- **Product strategy** – which products should be in your campaigns, and which not; which products must be successfully marketed using direct methods.
- **Positioning strategy** – how you want to position your company and your products in each target market.
- **Offer strategy** – what is going to make your customers respond to you at the right time.
- **Branding strategy** – how you will achieve consistency between your overall brand image and the one you present through direct marketing methods.
- **Pricing strategy** – overall and for each target market, and how to ensure that discounts targeted for one market do not bleed into another.
- **Target market** – the defining characteristics of the market segments you want to hit, and how you are going to apply them to generate lists of customers that match these definitions.
- **Sales force and channel strategy** – how your existing methods of managing customers are going to be integrated with your direct marketing methods.
- **Communication strategy** – how direct marketing is going to build up communication with customers, and how this build-up will be sustained by your other marketing communications approaches.
- **Fulfilment strategy** – how you will ensure that your customers will get the goods and services they have ordered and all intervening promotional material.
- **Customer relationship strategy** – which groups of customers you want to manage over the longer term using direct marketing methods – by themselves or in combination with other marketing approaches, what you want to achieve through this relationship management, and what you want your customers to experience.

- **Competitive strategy** – how you want to use direct marketing to fend off competitive challenges and make holes in your competitors' marketing achievement.
- **Acquisition and retention strategy** – how you expect to acquire new customers, and then retain them.
- **Database strategy** – how your database will support all your direct marketing activities, through data acquisition, maintenance and use.
- **Customer service strategy** – how your direct marketing achievements will be sustained by how you service customers in all other ways.
- **Marketing and sales information strategy** – how your customer data will be gathered and maintained through a comprehensive approach to marketing data management, affecting all modes of contact with customers.
- **Timing strategy** – how all the above activities will be co-ordinated to maximum effect.

To prioritize strategies, you may want to build models to forecast the consequences of implementing different strategies.

ACTION PLANS

These involve allocating specific resources to particular tasks within a framework defined by your overall strategy. This part of the planning process spells out the detailed actions that need to be implemented for your strategy to succeed. Responsibilities are allocated, budgets are set and timings agreed.

DON'T FORGET!

○ *Clear objectives for the overall plan and individual campaigns.*

○ *Assigned responsibilities – what, by whom, by when.*

○ *Controls in place to monitor progress, to plan for errors and document all actions.*

○ *Clear, concise briefs for all parties involved.*

Action plans cover:

- The products or service to be offered.
- The pricing and payment terms.
- The offer to target market segments.
- The promise.
- The positioning (generic or by segment).
- Production costs.
- Creative treatment (copy, graphic, etc).
- Timings.
- Fulfilment and returns handling.
- Payment processing.

Implementation plans should also include test designs (for media, timing, offer, format and creative execution). Testing is a sizeable investment of allocated budgets, so the key is to limit sample sizes to the minimum required to give significant results. The aim is to communicate to the majority of your customers and prospects with proven, profitable packages.

FINANCIAL ANALYSIS

Once you have drawn up implementation plans, and implementation has taken place, the next key planning task is to analyze results. Results analysis may include the following:

- Repeat order values (to monitor the lifetime value).
- Response values.
- Conversion values.
- Cost per order.
- Cost per enquiry.
- Average order values.
- Test results by cell.
- Response curves.
- Returns.
- ROI (the return on investment).

Financial analysis involves these steps:

1. Estimate required response rates, ideally based on past history.

2. Calculate return on investment.

3. Develop a P & L statement.

4. Infer customer lifetime values if appropriate.

DON'T FORGET!

○ *Have you got the correct mechanisms in place to monitor financial success?*

○ *Can you monitor success over the long-term as well as initial success? Will you know which customers stayed with you and how much they bought later on – ie their lifetime value?*

○ *Has everybody involved in the process agreed success and failure criteria before the campaign rolls out?*

○ *What measures are in place if the campaign fails?*

○ *How can you learn from the success or failure of the campaign?*

summary

This chapter has been concerned with direct marketing planning. If the direct marketing plan is too detailed, confused over planning terminology, not integrated into the marketing strategy, or lacks the support of line management, it is sure to lead to poor performance. When finalized the plan will provide a clear programme for the use of direct marketing. Concise objectives will be translated into specific operational objectives. Your plan will ensure commitment (if consultation has taken place) and the deployment of resources to the right areas at the right times. If you assign specific responsibilities, detailed schedules and budgets, monitoring of progress is made much easier.

In the next chapter, we describe how that critical resource – your customer database – can be built and deployed to support your direct marketing plan.

7

hitting through the database

- Through database marketing, computerized information on individual customers is translated into successful campaigns and long-term customer retention.

- But to achieve this requires a very systematic approach – not always a strong characteristic of marketers!

- Customer databases work best if they are designed in anticipation of marketing needs and not as an afterthought.

- This means deciding what information you think you will need to manage your campaigns and customer relationships, and organizing it into a useful database.

- Usually, the most important information is that on your customers and how to contact them, and on their past relationship with you – responses and purchases, and perhaps their service experience.

- If you start without customer data, you may need to rent and test lists.

what database marketing is and why direct marketing needs it

Direct marketing depends on customer information for its effectiveness. Managing a relationship with your customers over many contacts would simply be impossible were it not for recent developments in information technology – particularly telecommunications and database management.

"**Database marketing**" is an interactive approach to marketing, which uses individually addressable marketing media and channels (such as mail, telephone and the sales force):

- To extend help to a company's target audience.
- To stimulate their demand.
- To stay close to them by recording and keeping an electronic database memory of customer, prospect and all communication and commercial contacts, to help improve all future contacts and to ensure more realistic planning of all marketing.

---

how database marketing works

Database marketing relies on your creating a bank of information about individual customers (eg taken from orders, enquiries, customer service contacts, research questionnaires, external lists). You use this information to analyze your customers' buying and enquiry patterns. This analyzis, combined with the opportunity offered by the database to contact individual customers through a variety of media, allows you to achieve a number of different objectives. Database marketing helps you:

- Design products to meet the needs of identified customers.
- Target the marketing of products and services more accurately.
- Promote the benefits of brand loyalty to customers at risk from competition.
- Identify customers most likely to buy new products and services.
- Increase sales effectiveness.
- Support low-cost alternatives to traditional sales methods.
- Make your marketing function more accountable.
- Improve the link between advertising and sales promotion, product management and sales channels.
- Improve customer care, by making all relevant information available at the point of contact between your company and its customers, at any place or time, during service delivery.
- Co-ordinate different aspects of marketing as they affect the individual customer, to achieve full direct marketing potential.

THE KEY ATTRIBUTES OF DATABASE MARKETING

Companies come to database marketing in different ways and apply it to direct marketing in different ways, so not all the following characteristics are visible in all companies which use it. The attributes are:

1. Each actual or potential customer is identified as a record on your marketing database.

2. Each customer record contains information on:
   - Identification and access (eg name, address, telephone number)
   - Customer needs and characteristics (demographic and psychographic information about consumers, industry type and DMU information for industrial customers)
   - Campaign communications (whether the customer has been exposed to particular marketing communications campaigns)
   - Customer's past responses to communications which form part of the campaigns
   - Past transactions of customers (with you and possibly with competitors).

3. This information is used to identify likely purchasers of particular products and how they should be approached.

4. The information is available to you during the process of each communication with the customer. This enables you to decide how to respond to the customer's needs.

5. The database is used to record responses of customers to your marketing initiatives (eg marketing communications or sales campaigns).

6. The information is also available for your marketing planning. This enables you to decide:
   - Which target markets or segments are appropriate for each product or service.
   - What marketing mix (price, marketing communications, distribution channel, etc) is appropriate for each product in each target market.

7. If you are selling many different products to each customer, the database is used to ensure that the approach to the customer is co-ordinated (campaigns for different products do not clash) and consistent.

8. Your database may eventually replace large scale quantitative market research for your existing customers, though research will still be required for new products and markets, or for changes to your relationship with customers. You devise marketing campaigns so that customers' responses provide the information you need, possibly through questionnaires included in mailings or telemarketing campaigns.

9. You develop systematic processes to handle some key functions of marketing management, in particular analysis and project planning. Analysis must be systematized if it is to handle the vast volume of information generated by database marketing. It ensures that marketing opportunities and threats are identified more or less automatically, and that ways of capturing these opportunities and neutralizing these threats are also recommended. It makes higher quality information on marketing performance available to senior manage-

ment, allowing them to allocate marketing resources more effectively. It also allows management to identify situations in which direct marketing is failing. Project planning approaches are used to tighten up the management of campaigns, as database marketing involves a larger number of suppliers and much more complex actions than traditional advertising campaigns.

WHAT HAS HELPED DATABASE MARKETING GROW SO FAST?

The growth of database marketing has been facilitated by:

- The powerful processing capability and immense storage capacity of today's computers.
- The way telecommunications technology is being harnessed to make customer and market data available to the wide variety of staff involved in marketing and sales efforts.

Enabling technologies are developing fast. Most technologies, such as those which determine processing power and speed, memory and storage, are improving at least tenfold every 10 years. Speed of access (reading, writing) to stored data is growing more slowly. Communications technology, once slow to evolve, is accelerating. Software, once a barrier, is now easier to use and more reliable. Application packages (eg telemarketing) are more functional and flexible and capable of customization. Application development products have accelerated programmer productivity. End-user computing has created experience and even expertise in handling computers throughout organizations. PC based systems are available for the small user.

A wide range of tried and tested database packages are now available for all types of computer – mainframe, mid-range and PC. These have been used as the foundation to develop the specific packages required for database marketing: These include:

- Comprehensive customer databases.
- Mailing.
- Telemarketing (inbound – ie call receiving, and outbound – active calling of customers).
- Data analysis.

Suppliers of the underlying database software have also made it much easier for systems professionals to adapt this software to their own specific marketing use, by marketing a wide range of programming "tools". Our view is that today, the only area where technology can still pose a problem for database marketing is where the database is designed to be used in many locations (perhaps even worldwide), for planning, implementation and customer contact. Even here, the issue is more one of cost and the time it takes to develop, pilot and implement a system. The fact is that today, companies who experience problems with the development or implementation of a marketing database do so because of management problems, such as:

- Lack of agreement about the coverage and application of the database, and the related problem of overspecifying the first version of the system, so that it costs too much, takes too long to develop, and does not deliver benefits early enough.

● Lack of understanding that marketing databases only succeed if they are put to use and modified by practical experience – the data will grow, and along with it the knowledge of how to use it, once it is applied.

● Lack of attention paid to users' needs – for understanding, training and support during implementation.

These are problems that are common in all areas of business system development, not just in database marketing. They often occur because the path to database marketing is embarked upon without sufficient consultation with other companies who have been through the experience. A particular risk is it falling into the hands of consultants who overspecify the system because it enlarges their budget. Fortunately, at least in the US and UK, there are now enough training courses and professional groups where marketing managers can exchange experiences and avoid these obvious mistakes.

the strengths of database marketing

The strengths of database marketing are built on the solid foundations of direct marketing, as follows:

● **It is measurable**. Responses to campaigns are measured, enabling the effectiveness of different approaches to be checked.

● **It is testable**. The effectiveness of different elements of the approach – the product, the communications medium, the offer (how the product is packaged to appeal to the customer), the target market, and so on – can be tested. Tests can be carried out quickly, so quick action can be taken on the results. Test results can be used to forecast sales more precisely, helping manage inventory more effectively.

● **It is selective**. Campaigns can be focused accurately, because your communication is with specific customers, and can be attuned to their expected value (eg more expensive and frequent communications to higher value customers)

● Communications to each customer can easily be **personalized** by including details relevant only to them, drawn from the database.

● **It is flexible**. Campaigns can be timed to have their effect exactly when required.

the database

Information about customers and markets is one of your main marketing assets. The information on a marketing database has to come from somewhere. Database marketing is "learning by doing" – it provides most of the marketing information it needs. This is because database marketing campaigns ask for responses. Each response contains information – at least, it should do. It is up to you to make sure that this information is of value.

For example, if a customer responds by calling a toll free number, you may ask questions which:

- Qualify the lead for the product or service which is the subject of the campaign.
- Provide information which will help in future campaigns.

In this way, database marketing builds up a store of information about individual customers. You need to hold it in the most effective way. Unless it can be turned into profit, it is no use. So your database marketing system system is crucial for organizing the information and making it available.

Data use – two key questions

- Can you use your database to analyze and segment buyers and enquirers?
- Can you use your database to support list generation, lead generation and qualification, direct order fulfilment, direct mail, telemarketing?

If the answer to either is no, yours is no *marketing* database.

Question:	What databases hold customer details but are not marketing databases?
Answer:	Some databases are more likely to be *operations databases*, used for order processing (order taking, delivery, invoicing, etc) or after-sales service. They record what customers paid, and what they paid for, rather than helping to predict what they might like next!

data design

Computers work best with information that is well organized to start with. That is why database marketing puts a strong emphasis on the structured collection of data. For example, telemarketing scripts must be designed to get the maximum amount of high quality information possible from your customers, in a structured form. This allows you to add it to your database without too much further processing. The same applies to the design of forms to be completed by your customers.

Structured information gathering is essential. Unless you observe this discipline from the beginning, problems will emerge later on. To take a simple example, in business marketing, customers' financial year end is usually significant, either because they need to spend pre-allocated budgets, or because they are likely to be tightening their belts. So it is sensible to allocate a field on the database for this information and collect it in a structured way.

Database marketing can be put to many uses and applied in many sectors. So there is no general formula stating exactly which data should be included in the database. Each database is tailored to the needs of its users. But it is important to avoid the mistake of designing it on the basis of **past** requirements.

Data design – some key questions

- Is your data structured as efficently as possible?
- Are you using all cost-effective forms of data collection possible?
- Is there enough room on your database for the envisaged growth in the number of customers and the amount of detail you want to collect about them?
- Are you basing your database on future needs or on a view of the past?

sources of data

There are two types of data source, internal and external.

> **"Internal"** or **"proprietary"** data is data you already hold about your customers, usually arising out of your transactions with them. Your database marketing system should use most of information you have about customers. This data is one of your company's most valuable assets.
>
> External data is data you source from outside eg by renting a list, by exchanging data with another company

Data is often organized into lists.

> A **"list"** is the simplest form of marketing database. It is a set of names and how to contact them (eg addresses, telephone numbers).

A list may be:

- Bought or rented for use in campaigns or in building your database. Clever list buying is the key to many successful database marketing campaigns.
- Target customers drawn from your database for a particular campaign. Careful list selection is the key to high response at low cost.

INTERNAL DATA

Internal data includes:

- Customer files.
- Order records.
- Service reports, complaints, etc.
- Merchandise return records.
- Sales force records.
- Application forms (eg for credit, insurance).
- Responses to promotions.
- Market research.
- Enquiries.
- Warranty cards.

EXTERNAL DATA

External data include compiled and direct response lists from sources outside your company. Also included are classificatory data (eg census and post-code data, data from credit reference agencies, and their derivations), which can enhance other external and internal data.

data selection

You should decide which data to put on your database according to its cost and its potential to make money for you.

Only put data on your database which will help you answer these questions:

- Who are or will be your customers, and how can you contact them?
- What will they buy from you or your competitors? How can you motivate them to buy more from you?
- Will they maintain a dialogue with your company, and which medium do they prefer to do it through?
- How can they be retained? Do they have any propensity to be loyal to suppliers in your market sector?
- Where can others like them be found?
- When are they most receptive to your comunications, and when are they most likely to buy from you?

If a data item does not help you answer these questions in a way that clearly leads to revenue defence and/or growth, then it should not be included.

types of information on the database

This may include:

- **Customer or prospect** ie information on how to access your customers (eg address, telephone number) and on the nature and general behaviour of customers (psychographic and behavioural data).
- **Transaction** ie information on commercial transactions between you and the customer eg orders, returns.
- **Promotional** ie information on what campaigns (tests and roll outs) have been launched, who has responded to them, what the final results have been, in terms of contacts, sales and profits.
- **Product** ie information on which products have been involved in promotion, who has bought them, when and from where.
- **Geodemographics** ie information about the areas where customers live and the social or business category they belong to.

These types of data are considered in more detail below.

CUSTOMER DATA

If you are marketing to consumers, you might hold these items about customers on your database:

- First name.
- Last name.
- Title.
- Salutation.
- Name of spouse.
- Address (in meaningful format, three or four lines).
- Gender.
- Age.
- Income.
- Marital status.
- Number of children.
- Names of children.
- Length of residence in current abode.
- Type of abode and tenure.
- Whether recent or anticipated home mover.
- Telephone number.
- Internet address.
- Special markers (VIP customer, do not promote, shareholder, frequent complainer).
- Responses to questionnaires.
- Customer service history.
- Geodemographic coding.

If you are marketing to businesses, you might hold:

- Company name.
- Addresses of head office and other relevant sites.
- Telephone, fax and telex numbers, possibly mobile and voicemail numbers of key contacts.
- E-mail address.
- Account number(s).
- Names of buyer(s).
- Names of contacts and influencers.
- Purchasing process.
- Links with other companies.
- Revenue and profits – size and growth.
- Type of company (industrial classification code).
- Number of employees.
- Site structure.
- Responses to questionnaires.

TRANSACTION DATA

Past transactions are one of the most important indicators of likely future transactions.

The use of **"FRAC (Frequency, Recency, Amount and Category)"** in direct marketing is based on years of experience of finding that these variables dominate most explanations of buying behaviour for existing products. Your transaction data must include enough detail to allow FRAC information to be extracted for each customer. It is tempting to summarize past purchasing history, but in summarizing it, you may lose vital FRAC detail.

So the details of each purchase for each customer must be logged. This includes not only the obvious "identifying" details (who bought or returned what, when, how, etc), but also the associated marketing data (at what price, from which promotion).

In consumer markets, transaction data is usually much more effective as a basis for selection for promotions than geodemographic variables. However, the widespread availability of geodemographic data which is matchable to individual customer data means that a consumer products company with limited or no transaction data available can start with a campaign based mainly on geodemographic data. This will normally be organized in a national file based on the electoral roll enhanced with postal coding and possibly telephone numbers. Census information will usually be used to enhance the file further and provide some of the basis for demographic classification. If you are in this position, your key objective is to learn very quickly which customers respond the best, and focus future promotions on them, as promoting to national files is very expensive. To do this, you should start with a test, and find out which kinds of customer respond the best, "score" them and focus future promotions on customers with good scores.

You give customers a **"score"** by identifying their characteristics are correlating them with their likelihood to respond, buy etc. This allows you to create a **"scoring module"** or "directory" for selecting target customers from any larger file. Scores are usually derived from tests. This is based on the idea that when a customer is identified as belonging to a particular group, it can usually be assumed that the customer has the same likelihood as other members of the group of buying a particular product. The score given a customer in relation to a given product is determined by:

● Analysis of all the customer's characteristics.
● Assessment as to whether those characteristics, when they appear in whole groups of customers, make those customers likely to buy.

Once the characteristics that are important have been identified, a scoring method can be devised to be applied instantly, by the computer. This score indicates the likelihood that the customer will buy. This information is combined with campaign objectives to determine a priority for the response.

Your campaign should create transaction data fairly quickly. This transaction data is likely to come to dominate your selection criteria, but geodemographic data may continue to be useful. The emergence of companies offering comprehensive data services (list validation, data pooling, matching to other files) means that few new users of database marketing have to start from scratch.

PRODUCT DATA

In a one-product company, this raises no problem – each transaction is either a sale or a return. In companies with very wide product ranges, product classification may be a problem, and a numbering system to suit the requirements of database marketing may have to be adopted. Such a system must allow like products to be grouped easily.

PROMOTION DATA

Documentation of past and present promotions in some detail (right down to which customers were subject to them, and the media and contact strategy used) is essential if you are to measure the effectiveness of your promotions and if your promotional planning is to benefit from analysis of the past.

holding the data

WATCH OUT!

Care must be taken about which data is kept for quick access, or the system will drown in useless information. So another characteristic of database marketing systems is the constant check kept on which information is useful, and which data are "nice to know", but not very useful. This latter data can be archived and retrieved if necessary. However, due to the rapid advances in computer storage and retrieval technology, this problem is not as serious as it used to be.

Merging external data with proprietary data, or merging data from different proprietary sources, can be a problem. Special computer programs are normally used to "deduplicate" data sources.

> The need for deduplication arises when an individual or company is listed in different ways in different databases (or even in the same one). If the different databases are combined, customers may be listed more than once. The databases or lists must be **"deduplicated"** against each other, so that duplicate records are removed, while valuable data (which may be spread over more than one record of the same customer) is not lost.

Deduplication can be computerized. However, some human intervention may be necessary, as the computer can only deduplicate within certain tolerances. Depending on how important deduplication is, the computer may be asked to list entries where duplicate entry is suspected, for manual correction. However, you should bear in mind that the law of diminishing returns applies here. So the costs of further deduplication should be weighed against its benefits. These benefits are:

- Savings in costs of duplicated contacts.
- Avoiding alienating customers by contacting them more than once for the same reason.

DATA QUALITY AND MAINTENANCE

WATCH OUT!

*Data does not stay fresh. It becomes stale, as the contacts on which it is based recede into the past. So special exercises are required to check the validity of data and/or update it. This **maintenance** of your database is very important.*

Databases **get out of date quickly**. People change addresses and jobs. Companies move, new companies are set up and companies go out of existence. Errors in fulfilment records occur, through commission and omission. This is why audits must be undertaken.

A **"data audit"** takes a sample of your customer records, and analyzes when the different data items were entered, what their quality is, and how accurate they are. Accuracy may be checked by:

- Comparing the data with a source which is known to be accurate.
- Asking the customer (or customer contact staff) to confirm accuracy.

Data quality is measured by the results of the last audit. You can carry out quality checks via testing. Questionnaire mailing can be an effective but costly way of improving data quality, so questionnaires are usually combined with some other promotional initiative.

The quality of the data drawn from your database depends mainly on:

- How up-to-date your source data is.
- Whether it contains the detail needed to access the right individuals (names, addresses, telephone numbers, job titles).

The quality of information depends partly on customer-contact staff (sales, telemarketing, retail branch, etc) understanding the value of high quality information and the importance of their feedback in improving its quality. You should take **every** opportunity **to improve data quality**, during every contact with your customer. These contacts may be with sales staff, over the telephone, in showrooms and dealer outlets, on service calls, in shops and at exhibitions, by return of guarantees, via competitions and through past customer records. Lists can be traded with relevant businesses to help here. But the advantage of using your own database is that it consists of people who:

- Have done and are doing business with you.
- Trust you.
- Will therefore respond better to you.

WATCH OUT!

If information on your customers' contacts with your company is not entered on your database, you may suffer in two ways:

○ *You may approach the same customer in successive days (or worse, on the same day) with different messages (or the same message delivered twice). This cannot be avoided – a customer may read an advertisement and receive a mail shot on the same day. But wastefulness can be reduced by ensuring different direct approaches are co-ordinated.*

○ *Without a history of contact, you will have no idea where the customer is in the "buying cycle". This information is needed to determine when you should write, telephone or schedule a sales visit.*

external lists

These are often classified into *responsive* and *compiled*. Mail or telephone responsive lists consist of anyone who uses the post or telephone for transactions which could be carried out in some other way eg mail order customers. Compiled lists are those compiled to cover particular kinds of people (eg conference attendees, product buyers, small businesses). Lists can be sourced from list brokers who often act as agents for list owners. They may also be sourced from directories and by research.

techniques for merging and purging data

Merging databases and purging them of errors and duplicates saves costs and prevents customers being alienated by being contacted more than once with the same objective. Deduplication of many items may need to be undertaken, so merging and purging of large databases requires sophisticated computer software.

To ensure that you can merge and purge, make sure that:

- All data is entered in standard format.
- Matching rules are used which recognize duplicates.
- Efficient fulfilment procedures exist, so all transactions are recorded and customers are helped to signal any duplicates or errors (eg by asking them to confirm details).
- Different ways of selecting customers are available.
- Auditing procedures exist.

Software is available to carry out the following:

- The filing of all customers and prospects together with their relevant data (eg type and date of purchasing activity).

- Merging of bought or rented lists with in-house lists.
- Identification and purging of duplicates.
- Matching and merging of data which relate to the same customer.
- Post-coding of addresses, for ease of access to census data, accuracy of targeting and easier sorting for postal rebates.
- Validation of names against relevant official or national standard files, or telephone company directories, to ensure that prospective customers are actually resident at the stated address.

Investment in merge/purge software is often required to set up a useful database. But the investment is well worthwhile, and pays considerable dividends in terms of reduced marketing costs, increased revenue and enhanced customer satisfaction. You can use bureaux to do this, but if you find you are having to use a bureau too often, you should consider acquiring the software. However, remember that you need more than software – you also need expertise and time. If you haven't got it, stick with the bureau.

using the database

Your database gives you a measure of a company's success in moving a prospect through a sales cycle. For example, you could produce a list of customers in a particular market sector with a particular product who have not responded to the last mail shot on the subject. These could either be followed up more forcefully (eg by telephone), or (if there were other priorities) be omitted from a telephone prospecting campaign, because lack of response (perhaps after second mailing) demonstrated lack of interest.

The history of your direct contact with customers can be used to calculate the costs and benefits of acquiring particular kinds of customers, not just for the first sale, but over their lifetime with you. Thus, if the database shows that customers who buy product X are 50 per cent more likely to buy product Y than other customers, then the benefits of acquiring a customer for X extend beyond the profit made on X. This helps you take a more comprehensive view of the viability of particular campaigns.

summary

In this chapter, we have focused on the central role of the database in direct marketing. We have examined the raw material of direct marketing – information about customers and your relationship with them – and shown how important it is that this data be chosen and used for its predictive power. This applies particularly to transaction data - always remember your FRAC! We showed that scoring is the key to using data precisely. We also emphasized the importance of keeping data fresh, of finding out how fresh it is through audits and testing, and taking every opportunity to update it – ie every contact with customers. We also considered the need to get rid of duplicate records, through merging databases and purging them of duplicates.

In our next chapter, we show you how databases are used in practice.

8

who's using a database to make the hit - and how?

- Most sectors that use database marketing are finding recent technological changes a boon.

- Charities, automotive companies, retailers and other consumer service providers eg airlines, hotels, leisure clubs have latched onto card technology as a means of identifying their customers, rewarding them and extending credit to them.

- In all markets, computing and telecommunications developments have enabled much higher quality to be obtained when managing customers "over the wires".

the start of the story

Database marketing often grows out of a direct marketing department or section, set up to carry out tactical sales promotions, provide higher quality leads for a sales force, or support an in-house credit or loyalty card operation. However, there are many more potential users:

- Telemarketing operations, which may use the database to manage, enter and track customer data and target customers for calls.
- Field sales support, where the database is used to target customers for campaigns and measure their effectiveness.
- Customer service, particularly in companies marketing complex equipment or those in consumer services, where the database is used as the key to managing the full range of service activity – before and after the sale.
- Credit collection, where credit/debit status of the customer is used as a key criterion for relationship management, adding an additional weapon to the credit collector's armoury.

which industries are using databases

Database marketing tends to progress in waves, with particular industries making rapid progress and then going through a period of consolidation. This is where the action is likely to be for the next few years.

POWER AND WATER UTILITIES

The utilities' use of their customer databases range from **"bill-sweetening"** stuffers explaining the nature and benefits of the service being provided, through targeting high-value users for offers and loyalty programmes, to equipment and maintenance service marketing. The utilities benefit from strong coverage of potential markets – they started with operational databases of practically every household and business in their area. Their strength as marketing entities derives from their regular billing arrangements.

WATCH OUT!

Pressure to allow more direct debiting and less frequent communication with customers may reduce the strength of customer dialogue. Paradoxically, direct debiting has been treated by some as a customer loyalty exercise, because it locks in customers. But it also results in much less attention being paid to the supplier, so utilities have been developing aggressive programmes of mailings and telemarketing to defend and develop their customer base.

FINANCIAL SERVICES

Companies in the "**financial sector**" provide ways for customers to manage their assets and liabilities (including cash), to achieve their desired income and expenditure over their lifetimes. The sector includes marketers of insurance, pensions, savings and credit, credit and charge cards, banking and mortgage services.

This sector presents some of the greatest opportunities for database marketing. The underlying growth rate of this sector, relative to the economy, seems assured. The factors driving this include:

- Rising incomes (which generate larger absolute amounts of saving).
- Increasing longevity and earlier retirement (and the need to fund a longer retirement).
- The risk of longer periods of unemployment.
- Uncertain involvement of the state in providing for eventualities.
- Awareness (stimulated by suppliers, media comment, government and personal experience) of the need for improved management of personal financial affairs.

Coupled with these demand-side factors are supply-side factors. One of these is the increasing level of competition as companies traditionally confined to one sector start to market other services, freed by liberalization. UK building societies are the best example of this. As a result, marketing staff in these companies have nearly all been on courses on database or direct marketing, and are now seeking ways to implement their ideas. In addition, rising staff and real estate costs have driven the search for different ways of managing relationships with customers other than through traditional agents and branches. These different ways are being made possible by the development of telecommunications and computing technology – First Direct and Direct Line being the best examples of new companies which have sprung up based entirely on the database approach.

So the whole sector is moving heavily into true database marketing. Many companies have accepted the idea of **customer lifetime value** as a key variable in the acquisition equation. Once the customer is acquired, the central objective is to sell more than just the initial product – a common fault in earlier financial services marketing. Now, these companies are aiming to keep customers longer and raise their average number of "**relationships per customer**" – a piece of jargon which puts the focus not on the number of different products sold to each customer, but on whether each product relationship endures – this is because switching and early cancellation are endemic in the sector.

Credit cards have been a vital tool for parts of the financial services industry. From a database marketing perspective, they are just a customer identification technology, which happens to facilitate transactions and credit. **Smart cards** are an emerging addition to the technological portfolio. Cards create postal and electronic traffic and hence opportunities of selling direct. More importantly, they also lead to the creation of a coherent picture of customer behaviour and needs, a prerequisite of true database marketing.

LEISURE AND TRAVEL SERVICES

> The **"leisure and travel services"** sector includes all suppliers of personal transport (rail, air, coach, shipping, car hire, etc), of accommodation (hotels, timeshare, etc), of packaged and tailor-made holidays, travel agents, motoring organizations, leisure operators (bingo, gambling clubs, betting shops, theme parks, and the like), photographic processors, theatres and cinemas, political parties, charities and publishers.

With so much information potentially (and actually, in some cases) available to suppliers about customer behaviour and preferences, the penetration of even primitive direct marketing into some areas of this sector (eg hotels) has been surprisingly slow. This contrasts with other areas (eg airlines, certain holiday companies and cruise operators), where the value of a long-term relationship with customers is well appreciated and exploited through a continuing dialogue, and their marketing strategies are based on **customer relationships** (eg frequent flyer packages, special sea cruises for previous customers).

This category of expenditure looks very robust for the long term. The average size of companies is growing through mergers and take-overs. So the potential for database marketing is immense. There are also good cross-selling opportunities within this sector.

NON-PROFIT INSTITUTIONS

> **"Non-profit institutions"** include public sector organizations (eg local authorities, educational establishments, government agencies), charities, political parties, professional and trade associations and other pressure groups.

Political parties and charities will see a considerable widening of the use of database marketing, in recruiting members and influencing voting. Charities are heavy users of direct mail, and understand the characteristics of more generous givers, and also their tendency to give to several different charities – hence list exchanging between them. Trade unions are using database marketing techniques to organize elections. The same applies to many professional bodies and societies. Educational institutions are using their databases of past students (alumni) to raise money as public funding tightens. Many of these types of institution have introduced "affinity group credit cards" as an additional service to their members. The credit and transaction fees they raise add to their funds, while the database operations are usually facilities-managed by the credit card providers.

Governments are considering ways of using database marketing techniques – whether in disseminating information, such as people's rights, or in tax collection (eg profiling of likely fraudsters or late payers).

MARKETERS OF PHYSICAL PRODUCTS

This group includes all companies which have a physical product to sell, such as household durables, cars, home improvement products and fast moving consumer goods, such as food. They have the following attributes:

- The processes of manufacturing and physical distribution, which increase the time and costs involved in adjusting supply to demand. Stocks are present in the system, and this creates a strong pressure to find customers for them. However well these companies forecast demand, there will always be this pressure.
- The presence (in many cases) of retailers or distributors between the supplier and the customer, making their own merchandise selection and marketing policies and with (in some cases) a strong hold on customers and customer information.

In general, these suppliers were slow to awaken to the opportunities of database marketing. One exception to this is the motor industry, which uses it to **sustain dialogue after purchase**, and for prospecting. Domestic appliance manufacturers have long tussled with the question of how to maintain a cost-effective dialogue with customers when replacement for a given appliance is typically once every seven-10 years. They usually resort to retail display and occasional media bursts. Computer suppliers such as Microsoft and Compaq are now working hard to develop customer loyalty using database techniques.

Enhanced ability to segment and access particular groups of customers will help them solve this problem. However, they will still need to move away from an advertising emphasis to total database marketing if they are to be able to explore the full potential of their (usually multi-product) relationship with customers. For example, a typical household might have as many as 10 or 15 large and small appliances, many of which could have been sourced from one manufacturer.

Fast moving consumer goods are a source of much controversy in database marketing circles. Some hold that the contribution of database marketing is bound to be limited. However, some families may well be spending hundreds of pounds a year on products from a given manufacturer. If cross-product branding is nurtured, these customers become good prospects for database marketing. Their lifetime value is greater than that for many financial products. The potential competitive pay-off to successful database marketing in this area, where the only alternative is massive media spend, is clearly great, and has been realized by leading US companies, such as Heinz and Procter and Gamble. They have built massive databases and are sending personalized coupons to their consumers. These are giving such suppliers a good indication of which of their customers are highest value and therefore worth investing in to keep.

Meanwhile, the tactical promotional use of database marketing is receiving more attention from companies in this sector. Many promotions currently being mounted are single product promotions which yield consumer lists as a by-product. Many are toll free telephone campaigns. The interactive Tango campaigns take this idea further, so that the consumer is clearly interacting with the brand and not just responding to an incentive to call.

Here are some examples of incentives to call in (and to buy the product in the first place, of course):

- To find out if the consumer has won the prize described on the pack.
- To answer questions on the product, receive a coupon and perhaps a prize.
- To listen to a commercial, receive a coupon and a free gift.
- To listen to a pop star's promotional message for a record.
- To have any problems resolved (the Careline approach).

PRODUCT RETAILERS

**IN THE
REAL WORLD**

What are retailers?

Retail marketing used to be considered very different from the marketing of most of the above sectors. Now, they are converging, and database marketing is one of the factors causing this convergence. Retailers are nearly utility companies for some consumers – a source of the basics – food and clothing. They play a key role in financial transactions, representing the destination of most cash. Retailers are used at least as frequently as banks (and some, such as Marks & Spencer, now provide a wide range of financial services). They are providers of a service (halfway between leisure and work), but they are also product marketers in their own right, as some of them now have strong brands of their own (eg Sainsbury's Novon).

The main difference between product marketers and multiple retailers is the sheer volume of data about customer needs that they can collect because of frequent and direct contact. This makes them prime candidates for database marketing. Initially slow to take up marketing, let alone database marketing, most large retailers have developed their marketing resources and skills quickly in the last few years. This is partly because of competitive pressure that is internal to the sector, visible in the many mergers, take-overs, extension of product lines and regional extensions of operations. Retail management is now much more aware of the lifetime values of their customers and of how database marketing can provide ways of keeping customers. The retail credit card and loyalty scheme gives them a strong weapon in their competitive armoury. Retailers already realize the tactical value of these techniques. But they are now understanding their strategic value – as evidenced by the success of the BhS Choice and Homebase Spend & Save schemes, now imitated by the Tesco Clubcard. Members of these schemes are targeted for promotions aimed at getting them to visit more often, broaden their buying range, and introduce new members to the scheme.

MAIL ORDER HOUSES

Mail order houses are one of the largest users of direct mail. Their databases are now used for agent recruitment, promotions and also third party promotions. The use of specialized catalogues is becoming widespread. The question these companies must ask themselves is what their role will be when everyone else becomes a database marketer! In some cases, (such as the Next/Grattan merger), the answer has been to help a product retailer go into mail order. Within Littlewoods, the mail order experience was the starting point for a chain of catalogue stores.

the demand for database marketing

The demand for database marketing will continue to be driven by these factors:

- **Increased fragmentation** of consumer markets, partly as a result of more database marketing being used. This leads to increased ability on the part of suppliers to meet the needs of small groups of consumers, which puts pressure on non-users of database marketing to start using it, causing existing users to improve their use of it, and so on. In many consumer markets, companies will find it necessary not only to target their communications more precisely and manage their relationship with customers in a more "personal" way, but also to plan their business using the ever more detailed information accumulated about their customers, and the ever more sophisticated tools available for them to do this planning.
- **Further fragmentation** of business markets may also occur, for similar reasons. Other factors putting more pressure on industrial marketers to target their marketing more precisely include the steadily increasing professionalism and knowledge of industrial decision-making units and the pressure that customers' managers are increasingly put under to make more effective use of their time and resources.
- In consumer and industrial markets, **increased awareness** of the absolute and competitive benefits of using computer and communications technology to manage customers. In many markets, companies are keeping a watchful eye on their competitors' attempts to implement particular facets of database marketing. This applies especially in its use for marketing planning, where developments are kept very close to the chest. In its use for marketing communications, secrecy is obviously more difficult.
- In all markets, increased emphasis on "**getting closer to the customer**". In the 1980s, many supposedly marketing-oriented companies were chastened by their marketing experiences. Thinking that the information provided by relatively infrequent and superficial market research gave them good understanding of their customers, some companies were distressed to find that their customers' loyalty was less strong than they supposed, or that they were wrong about the kind of customers they had. In the 1990s, they have resolved not to make the same mistake again.
- In many businesses, the presence of one of a **small but increasing band of professionals** with direct marketing or similar backgrounds. These managers are demanding that their companies seize the best that database marketing has to offer, not just in marketing communications, but in all marketing.
- In many public sector organisations, **greater sensitivity to the needs of "customers"** (patients, users, consumers, ratepayers, etc). This is emerging not

only in the "attitude" training being undertaken by many organizations, but also in the kinds of information technology being installed to give better service to "customers". Some of them are actively looking to improve communication with their "customers". Government pressures (eg Citizens Charter) have added fuel to this fire.

● In charities, political organizations and pressure groups, increased **striving to influence people** and reach them first and/or more effectively. Many charities are expert users of direct marketing in competing for their share of the donor's budget.

DON'T FORGET!

Effective use of your database marketing techniques

○ *Does your database marketing address the increased fragmentation of your customer base, both now and in the future?*

○ *How does your database marketing address the "new professionals" in purchasing and their demands?*

○ *Are you continually creative in the way you address your customers?*

○ *Can you identify your most loyal customers and do you address them differently?*

○ *Do you try new ideas and approaches to database marketing regularly?*

○ *Does the tone and message of your database marketing fit with the overall corporate culture?*

○ *Are you trying to influence your customers or just keep them happy?*

○ *Does your use of database marketing fit with your current corporate objectives and strategies?*

the supply of database marketing services

The above trends spell radically increased opportunities for companies serving the database marketing market. The leading edge suppliers in this market form a new group of specialist companies, which work to turn the most advanced technology and marketing concepts into useable database marketing systems.

The "supply-side" factors encouraging increased use of database marketing include:

● Further advances in computing and telecommunications which make it easier and cheaper to hold more complex information about individual customers or users. This information can then be analyzed more comprehensively, accurately and quickly, and analyses can be integrated more immediately into policy. Relationships with your customers can be managed more professionally, using the information held on your database or generated during each step in the relationship.

- Relative increases in the costs of other more labour or media intensive modes of marketing, and relative weakness in performance. In the US, the lack of national and often regional broadcast and printed media and the relative cheapness of classical direct marketing media (post and telephone) may have been factors in the dramatically higher usage of the latter for marketing purposes than in the UK. In the UK, the situation may never rival that in the US, but the same trend is evident.

Many suppliers are broadening out the range of services supplied. Direct marketing agencies are offering fulfilment and database services. Database bureaux are offering mailing and fulfilment services. With this rapidly developing supply of services, no company which needs to stay in touch with its customers has the excuse that it does not know how to use database marketing.

summary

Database marketing has its roots in the world of direct marketing, where the needs of "mass communication", broadly defined, led to the use of computerized marketing systems. However, this mass marketing is not to be confused with mass prospecting for new customers. Most direct mail and telemarketing activity takes place between companies and their regular customers. As database marketing professionalism improves, there has been a rapid increase in the use of database marketing for prospecting, but there is a limit. Success in prospecting depends not just on the effectiveness of prospecting tools, but also on successful defence of existing customers by "incumbents", who can also be presumed to be increasing their professionalism.

In this chapter, we have seen that database marketing started as an offspring of direct marketing. Now, the relationship is the other way round in many companies, with the database driving direct marketing developments. In this chapter, we have seen how many types of company are using database marketing, and what they are doing with it. We have also seen why database marketing continues to grow – mainly because of fragmentation and competitiveness in markets, the need to manage customers better and influence them more strongly, and the improved supply of database services.

In the next chapter, we examine in more detail how customer databases are applied competitively.

the competitive hit -
via the database

- Database marketing can be used to cut marketing costs, restore neglected customers, and improve customer loyalty.

- If you have developed a high quality database, holding information about your customers' past behaviour and current needs, use of it can lead to one of the most effective barriers to competitive entry.

strategic vs tactical use of your database

You can use your customer database just to improve your tactics eg to find customers who are the best prospects for a one-time hit. However, database marketing is more effective when used strategically, to transform the way you do business. Here are some ways you could transform your business:

- Take a more methodical approach to conquest selling eg by regular mailings to competitors' customers, asking for information about needs. This information can then be used to design products and marketing programmes. In consumer markets, data on competitors' customers is now readily available from companies who have built proprietary lifestyle and similar databases (eg CMT, NDL, ICD). Fords' Talkback programme (involving a regular magazine and a range of promotional benefits) was specifically designed to target competitors' customers.
- Take a comprehensive approach to customer retention, with long-term programmes designed to maximize customer lifetime value
- Make your marketing function more accountable for its expenditure. This has great appeal for finance directors. Marketing results can be traced back to activities and benefits set against costs. Measurability makes it easier to test the effectiveness of different approaches, giving the marketing function the tools to improve results.

WATCH OUT!

*Accountability **creates pressures** within marketing. In many companies, the marketing function is not truly accountable for all its policies. It may be accountable in a general sense, but the information may simply not be available to hold it accountable for particular policies. For example, the results of a change in promotional policy or in sales force compensation may not be accurately measurable. Database marketing changes this. It should lead to greater professionalism in marketing planning, for example, and create a stronger culture of analyzing what worked in the past – a culture that is usually missing in marketing departments.*

cutting field selling costs

In many industries, the field sales-person can only make between two and five calls per day (although in some industries the norm is 10 or more). A telemarketer can make between 20 and 50 decision-maker contacts per day. The optimum competitive policy is to use your field sales and telemarketing according to their relative strengths, using a customer database to co-ordinate the two.

When to use the sales force rather than telemarketing

- Personal service is considered essential.
- An important new contact is being made
- A difficult and sensitive problem needs to be solved.

- A complex presentation needs to be made.
- In-depth diagnostic work needs to be carried out.
- When the customer's purchasing patterns need to be reinforced or developed (provided the customer's value is high enough for the required investment of time).
- The customer asks for a sales visit.

A telemarketing team working off your customer database can be used for all other calls. Eventually, with appropriate teamwork between your field sales force, the telemarketing team *and the customer* (whose time is also valuable and therefore who wants to be contacted by the most effective means for each call), more complex objectives can be handled by the telemarketing team. The telemarketer may become a full account manager. This approach increases the quantity and quality of contact between the sales force and customers, without increasing the cost. It also provides greater flexibility, enabling sales effort to be redeployed more quickly to meet competitive challenges. The discipline with which your sales effort is managed can be increased. For example, you can focus your sales force on mounting attacks on competitors whose customers are known to be dissatisfied. For example, an automotive manufacturer could target owners of a make with reliability problems.

putting an end to neglected customers

WATCH OUT!

Neglected customers are a problem for most businesses. In many industrial product or service markets, neglected small business customers may be neglected. In consumer markets, neglected customers may be isolated households or households with low purchasing frequencies. For both groups, the costs of traditional sales channels may preclude frequent enough contact. The customer may eventually switch to competitive products, assuming that competitors have not fallen into the same trap!

Database marketing can help here. For example, in the small business market for certain types of office equipment (eg facsimile, copiers, personal computers and telephones), the direct response advertisement and the catalogue, co-ordinated through the customer database is becoming the industry standard for reaching the customer. Once the prospect has become a customer, database marketing can be used to maintain the dialogue, while supplies and upgrades are bought, until the equipment needs replacing.

product launches

Database marketing can be used to improve your relationships with customers. It can be particularly effective in establishing the new customer relationships needed to ensure the success of a new product launch. In many companies, the product development function uses market research to determine the features, functions, applications, advantages and benefits required by customers. Much later on, the product emerges, and the contribution made by the customers who were researched is forgotten.

Yet, in many industrial markets, the most successful innovations are those where potential customers were in close contact with the company from the earliest stage of product conception. Indeed, many successful innovations are actually made by customers! But if the research was driven from the customer database, after the initial product development research, a company could use database marketing to contact potential customers for a product and create and sustain a dialogue with them from product conception through to launch. This approach can lead to better designed products and high quality services and is likely to lead to higher customer satisfaction, as customers involved in this way in the launch of a successful product will feel greater commitment to its supplier.

building loyalty

For existing products, database marketing provides an ideal way of building loyalty and maximizing revenue. For example, the quality of customer service may be checked by a questionnaire to all customers. This could monitor customer satisfaction and intention to purchase next time. The results of the questionnaire could be used to identify problems and ensure that dissatisfied customers do not become ex-customers. Such a questionnaire could also be used to structure campaigns aimed at managing the replacement cycle. Mailings could be sent just after purchase, half-way through the expected life of the product, and close to replacement decision time.

alternative sales channels

Many businesses find that their ability to serve their customers' needs is constrained by the cost of accessing them – the cost of the sale. So they are turning to database marketing to solve this supply problem. As we have seen, database marketing can lower the cost of sales, through applications such as telemarketing, mail order, enquiry management, and the like. In some industries, mail order has taken over many of the traditional functions of the sales representative, eg the insurance industry.

In some companies, whole product divisions are using database marketing as their main process for handling the sale. This applies to the "supplies" (consumables and user-replaceable parts) divisions of many manufacturers of complex equipment.

Customer information centres

Many companies are using customer information centres to reduce costs of handling enquiries and to enable sales offices to focus on the next stage of the sale. Idle enquirers and less interested customers are screened out and given other treatment, ensuring that they remain satisfied without incurring the cost of a sales call. In all these examples, the key to success is to match the cost of sales with the value of the customer. One automated test equipment company which chose this route discovered that so much of its sales time was being wasted that when it moved to this approach it was able to reduce its staffing throughout Europe (saving millions of pounds), and the remaining staff benefited by being much closer to their (best) customers. ○

barriers to market entry

If you don't have a good customer database, you may find yourself unable to enter a market, if faced with competitors who have high quality databases and use them effectively. They may have realized that the cost of setting up such a database may make entry difficult or impossible for other contenders. Conversely, possession of a database marketing capability may be the key to entering new markets. Thus, database marketers from other industries (eg automobile service associations, retail credit card operators) have used their capability to break into the financial services industry.

To some, mainly service businesses, the database has become the company's greatest asset. Perhaps the saddest example of this value is that when ILG – the Intasun to Air Europe leisure group – went bankrupt, the database was sold off to help cover the debts of the company! ○

new products and services

Information is a product in its own right – and the information on customer databases is no exception. Strategic alliances between database marketers have been formed. Banks, automobile manufacturers, financial services companies and publishers are planning new joint venture businesses, pooling the data that each possesses to build a comprehensive picture of their customers. In these markets, a number of services are already being provided, such as:

● Data vending and enhancement.
● Data laundry services eg cleaning up addresses and adding other third party data to existing customer data.
● Data management – the creation, updating and maintenance of a database.

Telemarketing agencies can be used here, to create a qualified customer information base by starting with cold lists, calling to qualify them, and managing sales campaigns through them.

● Electronic shopping.

Several companies have put together a comprehensive package of services for database marketers, such as:

● Creative services.
● Credit checking.
● Credit card application handling, processing, and administration.
● Data verification and management.
● Data pooling between clients.
● Data rental.
● Comprehensive geodemographic consumer classification systems.
● Mail services.
● Telemarketing.
● Household distribution.
● Statistical, analytical and consultancy services.

identifying opportunities

In competitive strategy formulation, database marketing is most frequently used to achieve one or both of the following objectives:

● Revenue defence and development (including sale or rent of customer information – subject to conformity with legal requirements).
● Cost reduction.

EXAMPLE

It can save you money

Where customers are remote and scattered or diffused throughout the population, or the service offered is used by only a small percentage of the market, database marketing may be the most cost-effective way of reaching customers. This is why airlines have taken the discipline seriously. Only 3.5% of the population fly regularly on business. Television advertising informs 96.5% of the population who will never use this service. Database marketing, therefore, offers a big saving on marketing communications costs. ○

Many of the changes produced have a short **and** a long-term-dimension. For example, telemarketing may produce cost savings and revenue increases which arise relatively quickly through reducing the cost of contacting and selling to customers and by increasing market coverage. However, greater market coverage and reduced cost of coverage may allow you to enter different product markets. You may be able to sell a wider product range to existing customers. These are longer-term gains which also need to be taken into account.

quantifying the gain

You need to identify the revenue and cost changes that result from applying database marketing and quantify them. This can be done in many ways:

- By category of customer.
- By category of product.
- By application introduced (eg sales force support, inbound or outbound tele-marketing, direct mail).
- By category of change (ie whether it is cost saving, revenue defence or growth).
- By time period (short, medium or long-term).
- By category of staff, function or marketing channel (eg impact on field sales force, sales offices, retail outlets, physical distribution, marketing communication, market research).

Here are some examples of the types of gain you need to quantify.

COST SAVING

Field sales force

- Reduction in number needed for given market coverage, perhaps through a more efficient calling pattern and less time spent identifying prospects and obtaining prospect information.
- Reduced staff support required, due to higher quality information available to sales staff.
- Reduced systems support, due to unification of possible variety of support systems.
- Reduced sales force turnover due to quality of support and consequent higher motivation.
- Possibly broader span of management control and reduced number of reporting levels feasible. This would be due to a better standard of information on activities and effectiveness of field sales staff, leading to lower management costs.

Sales office

- Reduced number of staff required to deal with a given number of customers or support a given number of field sales staff. This would be due to reduction in time spent obtaining and collating information and more efficient prospecting systems.
- Reduced costs of handling customer enquiries due to improved structuring of response handling mechanism, so that customer enquiries go to the relevant destination more smoothly without passing through irrelevant hands.
- Lower staff turnover due to higher level of support and consequent improved morale.
- Broader span of control and reduced number of reporting levels feasible, due to better standard of information on activities and effectiveness of office sales staff, leading to lower management costs.

- Reduction in number of branch offices due to ability to cover market better and more "remotely".

Market research

- Lower expenditure on external research, due to higher quality and relevance of information available on customers and prospects.

Marketing and business planning

- Reduced costs of information collection and management, due to availability of higher quality, more relevant and updated information on customers and prospects, leading to possible reduction in numbers of planning staff or in planning component of other jobs.

Retail

- Improved site planning, due to ability to match customer profiles to area profiles more accurately. This might lead to a reduction in the number of outlets to attain given revenue targets.
- Lower surplus inventory, due to ability to target the marketing of "sale" merchandise
- Higher utilization of space, due to ability to market special in-store events to database.

Product/brand marketing

- Reduced costs of selling, due to better attunement of existing and new channels – some of which are only possible using database marketing – to customer needs.

Marketing communications

- Lower costs for achieving any given task, due to greater accountability and to improved ability to identify targets for communication and make communication relevant and therefore more effective.

Inventory

- Reduced write-offs due to reduced frequency of launch of inappropriate products and to earlier termination of dying products.
- General improved forecastability of marketing campaigns, leading to reduced temporary inventory peaks for given products.

REVENUE DEFENDING OR INCREASING

Field sales force and sales office

- Higher revenue due to ability of sales staff to concentrate calling on higher revenue prospects.
- Less lost business and fewer lost customers due to improved customer care, as database marketing provides improved channels for customers to signal needs.

- Enhanced new product revenues due to improved ability to target customers for new products and eventually greater ease of launching new products.
- Greater ability of sales force to handle broader product portfolio, due to deployment of response handling system to inform relevant customers prior to the sales call.

Market research

- Greater ability to identify potential for increased revenue among existing customers.

Business and marketing planning

- More coherent plans to address new revenue opportunities, due to higher quality and relevance of information, leading to higher success rate with launch of new products, greater matching of distribution channels to customer needs, etc.

Retail

- Ability to market additional products to existing retail customers, whether at retail or through mail order, due to quality of customer information.
- Higher sales volumes of existing products due to ability to target promotions.

Marketing communications

- Greater effectiveness of communicating with customers and prospects, leading to higher revenue for given cost.

Product marketing

- Reduced costs of selling, due to better attunement of channels to customer needs, leading to ability to capture higher market share through lower prices or improved offers.

Inventory

- Lower stock-outs and therefore quicker inflow of revenue and reduced loss of sales to competition due to improved sales forecasting.

quantification

TARGET OPPORTUNITIES

Draw up a list of target opportunities. This is best done in a management workshop, perhaps supplemented by interviews and discussions.

FAST TRACK

You'll find that many of the best ideas are usually present in your company – and have just been looking for an outlet. They may not have been allowed to emerge because of the way in which policies are planned and implemented. After all, many database marketing applications are the implementation of commonsense ideas through the use of modern information technology. The outcome of this step is a statement of the target opportunities. This provides the focus for the rest of the analysis.

INCREMENTAL REVENUE FROM DATABASE MARKETING

Review current marketing plans to identify long-term revenue growth objectives and to clarify the basis for revenue growth plans.

FAST TRACK

Revenue growth plans may be based on factors such as overall market growth, specific marketing strategies (product range, price, distribution, advertising, etc), or anticipated competitive changes. This analysis will indicate the areas where database marketing may generate revenue growth through improving the effectiveness of policies that are already planned.

QUANTIFICATION OF COST EFFECTS

Quantifying the cost savings from implementing database marketing before implementation is not easy. It is more difficult if your existing marketing information is not well organized. If you have only recently adhered to the marketing creed, the information to quantify cost effects may have to be estimated. This may require "reconstruction of figures" (ie answering the question – "what if we had done it this way?") plus pilot studies.

WATCH OUT!

Typically, a comprehensive exercise to gather and analyze cost information is required. It will normally cover every channel of communicating with and distributing products and services to customers, such as sales force, sales offices operating by telephone and mail, retail outlets, media advertising, and direct mail. The aim is to quantify costs which may be changed by database marketing approaches.

To do this properly, use interviews, questionnaires, and analysis of financial and operating information relating to your channels of communication and distribution. This should be done by market sector and product line as well as for your whole business.

FAST TRACK

CONTACT STRATEGIES

FAST TRACK

Document clearly how you contact your customers today. Then identify contact strategy options, using database marketing, and assess:

○ *The capability of existing channels to support revenue growth targets and the cost of resourcing those channels to achieve them.*

○ *The incremental cost of the database marketing strategy needed to support the revenue growth target.*

REVENUE AND COST REVIEW

FAST TRACK

A summary of marketing activity over the period of the plan should then be prepared.

This should show the effect on costs and revenues of employing existing methods to achieve targets, and compare it with the costs and revenues implied by the use of database marketing. This should show the areas where database marketing is more effective.

WATCH OUT!

If the analysis indicates the need for distribution channel change underpinned by database marketing, the result might be a wholesale change in the revenue/cost profile. Whole categories of cost may disappear (eg the abolition of sales branches) and new ones appear (eg their replacement by a central sales co-ordination unit). Distribution channel change may create further strategic marketing opportunities, such as the ability to address whole new markets or launch completely different types of product.

EXAMPLE

A major high street loans company recently re-evaluated its route to market, and decided to close its retail operations and move to a telemarketing-led databased operation. ○

However, the change may be less revolutionary eg the refocusing of a calling sales force on larger customers and the replacement of their efforts by a telemarketing operation.

DON'T FORGET!

○ Have you assessed opportunities to use database marketing to change how you manage your customer relationships, including restructuring your route to market?

○ Are your remaining sales force trained to use the necessary IT, enabling you to reduce back-office support?

○ Have you consulted your customers about any proposed change to your relationship with them?

○ Have you used your database to reduce your market research budget?

○ Are you up to date with the technology required to use your database as a planning tool?

○ Have you kept all departments of your company up to date with developments on the database and sold its capabilities in-house?

○ Have you created a user group for your database?

○ Are your marketing suppliers – particularly your advertising agency – comfortable with the database and its uses?

○ Have you worked hard to introduce the culture of honest assessment of campaign results?

Database marketing may afford many opportunities for increasing revenue and reducing costs, but unless these opportunities are **firmly built into operating plans as targets**, they are unlikely to be achieved.

WATCH OUT!

Make sure you involve every function affected by the introduction of database marketing, as functions outside sales and marketing can determine whether the approach succeeds eg customer service, credit control.

summary

In this chapter, we've focused on the strategic uses and benefits of database marketing. We've stressed particularly the cost and revenue benefits that flow from planned use of a marketing database. We've also argued that this approach can give you significant competitive advantage. But you must understand that few competitive advantages can be sustained for ever. What you do today, your competitors can imitate tomorrow. This is particularly true of database marketing. The techniques and processes to make database marketing work are becoming widely known. So you need to stay ahead of your competition. Just having your customer database is not enough. Staying ahead of your competitors depends upon the applications supported by the database – the subject of our next chapter.

10

applications - the key to the database hit

- A customer database, by itself, can do very little.

- It needs a variety of "applications" if it is to be used to generate revenue and long-term customer value.

- Management applications – campaign planning, co-ordination and tracking systems – are necessary for you to deliver campaigns and find out what worked.

- You must also have a management process to control your activity, or you may find that your database marketing activities become unmanageable.

introduction

This chapter shows you how to create cost-effective, competitive and strategically significant applications for your customer database. These applications are the answer to the question "How can I use computerized customer data to support a significant and profitable dialogue with my customers – now and in the future?"

what types of application are there?

Customer database applications can be split into two categories – customer applications and management applications. A third category – dialogue application – is effectively a combination of the two.

CUSTOMER APPLICATIONS

> **"Customer applications"** are those uses of the database which involve the creation and maintenance of contacts and relationships with customers.

The main customer applications of a marketing database are:

- *Direct mail* (using the system to select customers to receive relevant mailings).
- *Response handling and fulfilment* (using the system to record your customers' responses and manage the next step in the contact strategy – fulfilment).
- *Telemarketing* (using the telephone to manage your customers, by contacting them or allowing them to contact the company, recording the results of the dialogue and initiating the required next contact).
- *Dealer, distributor or agent management systems* (providing data to them, helping them meet their customers' needs better, monitoring their performance in so doing).
- *Club or user group marketing* (creating an "inner circle" of your customers, who receive special additional benefits in return for their loyalty).
- *Consumer promotions* (eg coupon distribution and redemption).
- *Business promotions* (eg sales force incentive schemes, competitions).
- *Credit card management* (using the system to recruit credit card customers, record their transactions, invoice them and promote to them).
- *Targeted branding* (using the system to deliver branding messages to individuals identified either as being specially receptive to them or as being at risk from competitive actions).
- *Data marketing* (selling or renting the customer data on the system).
- *Any other dialogue application* (ie one which involves a sustained series of communications with a target market).

Listed in this way, these applications look very familiar. However, as we shall see, making them work is quite a task.

MANAGEMENT APPLICATIONS

> "**Management applications**" are those applications which change the way marketing management plan, implement and assess their marketing activities.

Management applications include:

- *Campaign planning* (using the system to select customers with specific needs and to identify the kind of offers to which they will respond).
- *Campaign co-ordination* (using the system to ensure that campaigns fit into a logical sequence and lead to the establishment of a sensible dialogue with customers, rather than clashing and inconsistent messages).
- *Project management* (using the system to manage the delivery of communications projects).
- *Campaign performance and marketing mix productivity analysis* (using the system to identify which elements of the mix are best for managing different kinds of customers and which campaigns are most successful).
- *Campaign monitoring* (using the system to provide interim data on campaign performance, so remedial actions can be taken where necessary).

WATCH OUT!
Which applications you implement should be determined by marketing strategy. They should not be chosen simply because they are possible once the customer database has been created. In fact, it is best to plan the database and applications as an integral proposition. The fact that this is so rarely done gives you a competitive opportunity. If you plan your applications from the outset, you'll get much better results from your database. But if you rush ahead with customer applications and don't pay attention to management applications, your use of your database is likely to be very inefficient.

EXAMPLE
A major retailer with one of the best known and productive customer loyalty schemes in the business spent very large amounts on bringing its data in-house from a bureau. Just before the completion of this project, it discovered that it had no management process for developing strategic use of the database. Rather, it was used whenever the company decided a tactical campaign was necessary. The result was that large groups of very loyal users were effectively unmanaged by the company.

Another retailer with a similarly strong database discovered that it had no process or software for analyzing its database, other than through guesswork (eg "let's see how many customers behave like X"). ○

In both these examples, the company had focused on the customer applications, leaving the management applications trailing behind. Much potential profit was lost because they were not able to use the right customer applications. This in turn was due to failure to develop the right management applications.

dialogue applications

A **"dialogue"** is defined as a structured series of contacts – involving you contacting the customer and the customer responding – giving information, making purchases etc. The concept of dialogue is central to maximizing profit from customer data. A dialogue is more effective than a monologue – a one-way series of contacts with no response, or than a single conversation (a one-off promotional contact).

In a dialogue, you ask your customer questions such as "When do you intend to buy?", "When will you next need help?" and "What other products might interest you?" You effectively programme your database system to analyze these responses, and the outcome of the analysis is the triggering of future contacts – of a type and timing the customer wants. This is how you develop a dialogue with your customers. The aim of this dialogue is to:

● Move your customers towards purchase.
● Keep them satisfied after the purchase.
● Ensure they buy additional or replacement products later on.

Without this, the result is a one-way flow of promotional literature, most of which is wasted.

Your database system is essential in ensuring that the right communication reaches the right customer at the right time. It selects the initial contacts. It analyzes the customer response pattern. It plans the follow up. Your aim should be to develop contact strategies and dialogue applications that suit all your target customers and prospects, and to have management applications that ensure that you are able to do this properly.

strategic issues

FAST TRACK

*Your first step – one that many companies forget to take – is to turn your customer information into a customer database. For example, if you sell to customers directly (eg via a field sales force), you are likely to have a reasonably high quality **customer file** already, and possibly several, containing details about your customers. You will almost certainly have a **transactions file**, showing which customers have bought what and when. You need to turn these into a **marketing database**. Remember, a marketing database contains more than just customer records – it also holds details of:*

  ○ *The marketing and sales campaigns you run.*

  ○ *The resulting contacts with your customers.*

  ○ *The outcomes of these contacts.*

Your transactions file may contain useful source data on frequency, recency, amount and category. But it may not be stored in the right way, so that you can use it to target customers and find out what purchasing histories are associated with high potential for future purchases. Other information which indicates likely customer needs (organizational, psychographic, etc) may not have been collected methodically or at all. You may need to enhance the database through imported or questionnaire data.

FAST TRACK

If you have no direct contact with customers, you have three main options in database and application development, which you can pursue simultaneously:

1. *Compile, through list purchasing, testing and research, a database of those likely to be buyers of your products.*

2. *Create marketing applications which by themselves generate the data through direct contacts, often through "plastic" (credit cards, club membership, promotional entitlement cards), etc.*

3. *Switch (partially or wholly) to channels of distribution which do involve direct contact.*

With indirect sales, critical transactions data (on frequency, recency, amount and category, or FRAC) will not be available (except through customer questionnaires or if your bargaining position is strong enough to enable you extract the data from third parties eg automotive suppliers).

The problem of getting the right data is often compounded by the fact that companies often go into database marketing at times of strategic uncertainty. They may not be sure which products they will be marketing to whom over the next few years. This means that it is not easy to determine which data will be needed. If this is your situation, your best strategy may be to start a programme of testing the importance of different variables in explaining buying behaviour for different kinds of products, combined with data reduction (see below) and profiling wherever possible, to simplify the data set, which could otherwise get out of hand.

data acquisition and development

A **data acquisition and development strategy** is needed. This strategy determines:

● Which data you need to support your marketing strategies.
● How sources of data are to be identified, qualified and tested (including different questionnaire programmes).
● How the data is to be maintained.

You need this strategy whether or not you have started with a customer file, and whether or not your aim is to sell more to existing customers or to recruit more customers.

For example, you may use a long questionnaire to find out whether your cus-

---

"**Data reduction**" is the science of finding a few variables to explain a complex set of data. This is done by statistical techniques.

---

tomers are satisfied with their relationship with you, and use statistical techniques to find out which questions account for most of the difference between customers. Or you may wish to segment your customers for targeting purposes. Again, you might use a questionnaire on buying attitudes and behaviour, and find which questions enable you to divide your customers most neatly into different groups. Data reduction is important because unless you use it, you could find yourself collecting masses of data which prove very unwieldy to use.

There are so many new data sources these days that it is important to keep informed about what lists and databases are available. Although the golden rule is still that your own data is best of all, there is always room to enhance it – particularly if you are moving into new areas (eg recruitment of a different kind of customer, launch of a radically new product).

Some database marketing users are investing in **profiling approaches**, to give convenient measures of customer characteristics/susceptibilities. The idea is to develop (usually from an analysis of your existing data) one or more profiles (eg of a type of customer the company would like more of). Credit scoring is the "home" of this kind of work – where it is used to develop profiles of customers that are definitely not wanted! The benefit of this approach is that it provides score-cards or directories which can then be applied to any file, provided that the latter contains the variables which the scoring technique uses. For example, in credit scoring, these variables include income levels, home ownership and credit card history. This reduces the volume of testing required and increases the response rates of campaigns. However, campaigns may be required just to bring in the right data.

maintaining the database

If you have a customer database, you need to maintain it.

Best practice is that the database should be largely self-maintaining through the applications run on it. But the paradox is that databases which are easiest to update may be the least valuable. If all competitors are in monthly direct dialogue with their customers (eg in the credit card market), data on monthly purchasing patterns and repayments is plentiful. Competitive advantage will come not from having data but turning it into a form that can be used for marketing purposes. Dialogue applications – ones in which you are informing and selling to customers, and they are responding with information and orders – provide the best data, but are the most expensive to create and manage.

Once the database is in order, it is worth **re-examining objectives** to see whether the database still supports them or justifies **more aggressive** objectives.

EXAMPLE

A branded durable goods company which develops a database to target promotions more accurately may discover that some of its customers want to buy by mail order (they may already be buying from another mail order company). A small catalogue may be in order, with carefully timed promotions against it. The company may discover that its list is valuable and start to market it. Service contract marketing may prove viable. Related products may be marketed. Having a good marketing database can open up new lines of policy. But all this should be judged against the strategic objectives of the company and the costs of running the database. ○

making applications work

In most large companies, the database user community is larger than just straightforward direct marketing users. The database is used by marketing analysts, sales managers, retail planners, brand managers, and so on. The marketing applications they need could be any combination of those mentioned earlier.

WATCH OUT!

Because of the variety of possible applications, database marketing can be a destabilizing influence, when introduced into a complex marketing and sales organization, if the changes which result from its introduction are not understood beforehand and managed proactively. It helps if database marketing policy (campaigns, support resources, systems capabilities) is developed together with marketing planning and organization policy.

Developing the applications plan means aligning database plans with strategic marketing plans. If you have a large number of customers who buy moderate amounts from you but not enough to justify a field sales call, the first applications you are likely to need are direct mail and telemarketing. On the other hand, if you want to use the system to gather information about customers buying your products through retailers, then the first applications needed may be high-volume, low-cost coupon processing and questionnaire management.

How to determine which applications you need

1. Identify the kinds of contact you have with your customers (pre and post-sales) – this is called the contact audit.

2. Identify whether there is a requirement for more frequent or different contact, and what the benefits of these contacts might be.

3. Produce a list of possible marketing applications (as detailed earlier – plus any others that are relevant to you).

4. Identify the combination of applications which is most likely to be cost-effective, using standard techniques of cost-benefit analysis.

using management applications

Once the database and its marketing applications are set up, a process is required to make the database work as a management tool. Here is such a process.

Step 1 – Formulate your marketing strategy, including considering the different ways (channels, products etc) of relating to (now known) customers. This is critical to making the database deliver value to general users. The management application should include ways of extracting data about different groups of customers and how your company has performed with each of them. It should also enable you to model the effects of different strategies.

Step 2 – Develop a clear view on the kinds of campaign to be run, and whether they will follow particular themes. Develop a structured approach to maximizing learning and effectiveness, minimizing costs and reducing conflict. Different kinds of campaigns have different pay-offs, use different kinds of data, and have different priorities. The further you progress with database marketing, the more your campaigns will increase in sophistication, placing a greater load on marketing, statistical and systems services. Without a proper medium-term campaign plan, you may run into bottlenecks or worse, conflicts. Your management applications should enable you to run simulations of individual campaigns and of several campaigns together. This will help you evaluate different options.

Step 3 – Co-ordinate campaign plans, to ensure maximum effectiveness and minimum overlap. Make sure that campaigns make sense in terms of the dialogue with individual customers. A campaign planning and co-ordination application, which shows what campaigns are planned when, and to whom, will help ensure this. In some parts of the "classic" direct marketing industry, rolling campaign plans – from one to five years' duration – are used. In some companies, the database system has a full management process application attached to it. This shows not only what campaigns are planned to be run when, but what are the different stages in getting these campaigns to market ie a project management application.

DEVELOPING ACCOUNTABILITY THROUGH APPLICATIONS

As soon as you start to use your marketing database to sell to customers, you may run into a series of ownership and accountability problems.

WATCH OUT!

Companies with a territory sales force, regional marketing teams and product or brand managers, may find that all these groups want to contact the same (usually the most loyal) customers and claim the benefits of resulting sales.

FAST TRACK

*The solution to this problem is partly political – your senior management must make it clear that the company as a whole owns the data, and accountability is therefore **shared**. But the effectiveness of the campaigns run by different centres of marketing power should be measured and compared! Your database should make performance achievement much clearer. Eventually, it should become the foundation for a marketing mix evaluation application. This shows which elements of the marketing mix are being used cost-effectively, by comparing spend with results.*

One area where financial evaluation is particularly important is the media mix. Database marketing provides more accurate data on media effectiveness. It provides a firmer basis for the development of a media usage strategy, overall and for particular market and segments.

WATCH OUT!

Your financial evaluation may show that no media are cost-effective for accessing a particular market. You may need to develop new media to access it (eg your own newsletter, a customer helpline). The development of a media analysis application (which simply means that the data on media effectiveness must be gathered, through coding of all response vehicles, and analyzed properly) can lead to dramatic savings in advertising budgets.

DON'T FORGET!

Using your database effectively

○ *Is your marketing strategy developed in consultation with all potential users of the database?*

○ *Does your direct marketing campaign plan lock in with your advertising campaigns and field sales initiatives?*

○ *Will all your campaigns sustain your brand image?*

○ *Have all your campaign plans been "sold in" to your staff? Will they benefit the whole company?*

○ *Does the timing of your campaigns clash with any other communications going out from your company – like renewal notices, safety warnings?*

○ *Have you taken all the steps you can to reassure other departments about the database's use and its benefits, including external suppliers like advertising agencies?*

SUPPORTING DECISIONS

The system holding your database must have an executive system/decision support element, which makes manipulation of data for analytical (research, analysis of effectiveness) and policy purposes much easier.

DAY TO DAY WORKING APPLICATIONS

Your database must be *internalized*. That is to say, a clear view must be developed of how it will be used in practice, by the many kinds of staff who will want to use it.

When your users feel happy about the value of the database, they will be happier about using it more proactively to manage customer relationships.

You must identify how users can incorporate the database into their traditional disciplines, their planning processes and their day to day working, with clear benefit to them. This may mean building a number of simple reporting applications into the system, so that it produces the outputs required by different kinds of staff to fulfil their jobs. You may need to combine data from the system with output from your other systems. It may cost more in terms of programming, maintaining data compatibility and sustaining data links, but if it achieves the objective of making the database approach a way of life, it may be worthwhile.

sophisticated statistical applications

These are not a "must" at the beginning. The initial benefits of having a customer database are straightforward – ie you know what your customers want and what effect your marketing is having on them. However, as experience accumulates, sophistication of use increases, and your staff become familiar with management processes, a good "history" of properly mounted campaigns is accumulated. So carefully and regularly presented reports on these campaigns can really help sell the benefits of using database marketing internally. A good statistical capability becomes essential for understanding the true determinants of effectiveness (eg through new ways of segmenting, targeting, and managing contact strategies via scoring).

Strategies for testing are particularly important for prospecting programmes, in which it is easy to invest a lot of resource for little return. Testing is also vital to establish which contact strategies are right for different customers.

WATCH OUT!

Too much experimentation too early can lead to waste of resources on statistical analysis before the fundamental characteristics and quality of the database are understood. You'll best understand how your customers react to your marketing efforts by exposing them to a consistent series of communications, not a few, one-off, poorly co-ordinated promotions.

phasing the applications in

How you phase in use of your database depends very much on your company's structure and strategy. Take the example of an integrated company with a structure of local branches/offices in which some marketing and most selling is done, and which has a central marketing unit. This company might start with central outbound calling and mailing combined with central response handling and fulfilment. This is not really relationship marketing or long-term investment. There is low involvement of local sales and marketing staff. Contact strategies may be very simple, scoring may not be used and offers may be just one type per campaign. Later, local outbound telemarketing may be introduced, to generate local leads. Then more advanced, central campaigns may be introduced, involving local fulfilment – integrated with central or local response handling, but still not as part of a long-term relationship. Campaigns will still be product-based, but better co-ordinated. But this is still not relationship marketing. Eventually, the company may move to fully integrated local and national **"virtual account management"**. More complex contact strategies will be used, their design driven by a scoring capability. Offers will be much more varied to suit different customer types. For some companies, the ideal will be when the database is used by *real* account managers, contacting customers on a regular calling cycle, using database marketing disciplines. Campaigns for particular products and services are then treated as a highlight to the relationship, helping focus customer attention on additional benefits.

the fully integrated system and its applications

At the centre of your database marketing system is your customer database. If your organization is multi-branch or multinational, then this database may have central and local elements. Where these are and how they are used depends on the degree of variation between local and central campaigns, the costs of communicating data and of distributing computing equipment to handle local databases. Specialist support staff will need to work with company management to plan and help implement campaigns. Leads generated by the system will need to be passed out to the appropriate channels. Lists of various kinds may be needed to build the database. Further lists are generated from it as the basis for tests and full campaigns. Leads and enquiries from various sources (eg mail, telephone, branch customer service) are handled using pre-tested contact strategies, and the results placed on the database, which leads to firm orders being placed with the distribution function. Marketing analysis is carried out to show the profitability of different approaches and to allow tactical changes to be made to campaigns currently being undertaken. This is depicted in Figure 10.1.

Fig 10.1

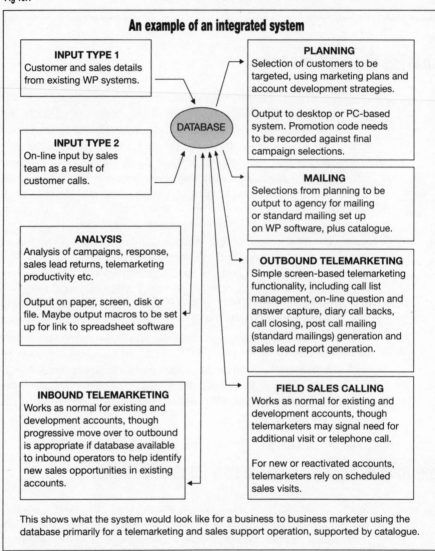

An example of an integrated system

INPUT TYPE 1
Customer and sales details from existing WP systems.

INPUT TYPE 2
On-line input by sales team as a result of customer calls.

ANALYSIS
Analysis of campaigns, response, sales lead returns, telemarketing productivity etc.

Output on paper, screen, disk or file. Maybe output macros to be set up for link to spreadsheet software

INBOUND TELEMARKETING
Works as normal for existing and development accounts, though progressive move over to outbound is appropriate if database available to inbound operators to help identify new sales opportunities in existing accounts.

DATABASE

PLANNING
Selection of customers to be targeted, using marketing plans and account development strategies.

Output to desktop or PC-based system. Promotion code needs to be recorded against final campaign selections.

MAILING
Selections from planning to be output to agency for mailing or standard mailing set up on WP software, plus catalogue.

OUTBOUND TELEMARKETING
Simple screen-based telemarketing functionality, including call list management, on-line question and answer capture, diary call backs, call closing, post call mailing (standard mailings) generation and sales lead report generation.

FIELD SALES CALLING
Works as normal for existing and development accounts, though telemarketers may signal need for additional visit or telephone call.

For new or reactivated accounts, telemarketers rely on scheduled sales visits.

This shows what the system would look like for a business to business marketer using the database primarily for a telemarketing and sales support operation, supported by catalogue.

stepping through your system

One of the main justifications for database marketing is that it serves the needs of marketing managers who have responsibility for particular groups of customers (or the entire market) or for particular products. These are the "internal customers" of database marketing. One way to understand how a fully fledged database marketing system works to serve the needs of "internal marketing customers" is to go through the steps by which a campaign is designed and implemented. The following description does just that. The channel of distribution being used is a direct sales force.

1. A **marketing plan for a brand, product or sector** is formulated. It identifies the need for one or more marketing campaigns. Preliminary work is carried out to identify which kinds of campaign are likely to be most successful for the product or sector, and which customers should be targeted in them.

2. A **campaign brief** is drawn up, including campaign objectives, targeting, timing, the precise nature of the product or service to be promoted, the offer to be made to the customers, the benefits, how the campaign will help build company brand values, the resources required to implement the campaign, the way in which the campaign's success will be measured and the expected returns. This brief is the basis on which all work is carried out and ultimately executed.

3. The brief is used to derive a **campaign specification**, which is entered into a computerized campaign co-ordination system. This co-ordinates the planning, execution and implementation of all marketing campaigns. It ensures that the approach to customers is co-ordinated and prioritized, taking into account the importance of different target markets, budget availability and the need to avoid clashes. One of its principal outputs is an agreed schedule of campaigns to be run. Without this, databased account management is impossible.

4. A **campaign is designed** to achieve the marketing objectives within the permitted budgets. Data about customers and past campaigns are used to define the target market more closely and to identify which broad kinds of campaign are likely to be most successful for the product or sector.

5. Campaigns are devised to **test the different elements** of the design on statistically significant sample lists extracted from the database. Testing normally covers the main elements of the campaign, ie which customers are targeted, which offers they receive, the timing of contacts with them, how they are to be reached and how their responses are to be handled.

6. The test campaigns are **implemented and the results are analyzed** to determine which campaign elements (eg media, contact strategies) produced the best results.

7. The detailed design of the **campaign is developed**. As the contact strategy determines a high proportion of the costs of a campaign, contact strategies should be tested very thoroughly and prioritized. The tests provide the basis for prioritizing. This occurs in various ways, eg by including some customers in the campaign and excluding others, by handling customers in different ways.

8. The **details of the campaign** are agreed and an outbound list is selected. This determines which customers will be contacted in the first step in the contact strategy. The list is selected using a formula derived from analysis of tests.

9. The **main campaign runs**. The customer receives a communication which is part of the campaign. This prompts a response eg by coupon or telephone. If the response is to an inbound telemarketing set up, the operator at the latter finds out which campaign or "offer" the customer is interested in. The

operator, cued by a sequence of on-screen displays, asks the customer a series of questions. These include confirmation of the customer's identity (possibly including telephone number, address and job title), specific needs concerning the product or service in question, and the customer's needs for further contact. The operator enters the answers into the computer. If the enquiry is by mail, the respondent is contacted by an outbound telemarketing call and a similar process takes place.

10. The **enquiry information** gathered from the customer is matched to the existing customer file (if any) and merged with other information on the database.

11. The computer uses rules derived from tests and agreed with the campaign originator and project manager, to prioritize the enquiry according to the likelihood of a customer ordering. These rules are based partly on pre-determined campaign profiles (ie the kind of customer the company is trying to attract) and may use the **data gathered** during the customer's response.

12. A particular **contact strategy is recommended**, based on the type of product and on the priority.

13. **The fulfilment organization receives information** indicating, among other things, what kind of letter and additional material should be sent to the customer or, if the product is mail order, what product should be sent.

14. **Local sales offices, sales staff or dealer outlets receive information** about the enquiry on their computers, follow up enquiries, and feed the results of the follow up back to the database.

15. The results of all enquiries and responses are analyzed to provide regular reports on the **effectiveness of activities** and to help improve the effectiveness of future campaigns. Detailed performance data plus expenditure data from financial systems are used to evaluate financial performance and plan new campaigns.

summary

The road to database marketing begins by defining the applications your database is to support. We've shown that there are two types – customer applications, or what you want to do with customers, and management applications, which help you structure these customer-facing activities and ensure that they take place efficiently. A key issue for both sets of applications is how you aim to acquire, use and maintain your data. We also showed what happens when you leave consideration of applications until after you've built your database.

Database building is a process which doesn't take place overnight. It is a phased activity, which never ends, as your data grows and improves the more you use it as your foundation for contacting customers. This was shown through the description of the development of a databased direct marketing campaign.

Having covered all the infrastructural issues involved in setting yourself up for direct marketing, we now move to the point at which you can start your data collection and analysis – through market research and segmentation.

11

understanding where to hit - with segmentation and research

- Segmentation is the key to understanding where to hit.

- There are many ways you can segment a market, but the key is to find segments that respond well to you, and buy a lot.

- For this reason, the most important variables in segmentation are those which describe the frequency, recency, amount and category of your customers' buying.

- Statistical techniques are widely used in segmentation, particularly in applying the conclusions of your segmentation analysis to individual customers to decide whether they should be selected as a target for your campaign.

introduction

Chapters 3 and 4 showed that markets are classified into consumer and organizational or industrial markets, with the main differences between the two being:

- The influences on the individual (objectives, buying power etc).
- How the individual functions as part of a buying unit (family or organization).

In fact, the difference between the two is not hard and fast – they shade into each other. In some markets, the behaviour of individuals as consumers overlaps with their behaviour as organizational buyers (eg motor cars, telecommunications).

In most markets for consumer goods and services, consumers are too numerous to research or understand as individuals. They tend to be researched on a sample basis, to identify what types of consumer exist and what the behaviour of different groups is. We then aggregate this information to make sense of the market.

This type of research includes:

- **Buying behaviour or audit research** – investigating what customers buy, when and how.
- **Usage and attitude surveys** – investigating customer and prospect perceptions and attitudes and relating them to their buying decisions.
- **Tracking studies** – studying trends in either of the above over time.

Today, this research-based approach to understanding customers is disappearing in industries which can profitably sustain direct access to their customers, using direct marketing techniques. This depends on whether the average frequency and size of transaction is enough to justify direct contact, and on whether the type of transaction is such as to facilitate or even require the capturing of individual details (eg banking).

what is segmentation?

"**Segmentation**" is just a technical term for classifying consumers. To segment customers is merely to group them by shared characteristics. Your aim is to find segments whose members are as similar as possible to each other in some respect (eg attitudes, perceptions, buying behaviour, location, responsibility) and as different as possible from members of other segments. You do this because if you find such segments, you can predict their behaviour more accurately.

Consumer market segmentation approaches

- *Demographic* – age, social class, marital status, number of children.
- *Socio-economic* – occupation, income, assets (eg house).
- *Geographical* – location (physical and relative to people with specific socio-econo-demographic characteristics).

- *General behavioural* (shopping, leisure, etc); or
- *Behaviour in relation to product/category* (whether or not user, frequency of use, loyalty etc).
- *Psychographic* (eg extrovert-introvert, optimist-pessimist, planner- improviser, consumer-saver)

standard classification methods

The most widely used and simple classification is that produced by JICNARS – the Joint Industry Committee for National Readership Surveys. They are called "social grade definitions", and are as follows:

Grade – Status	Typical occupations
A – Upper middle	Higher managerial, administrative and professional (eg judges, board directors of large plcs, very senior Civil Service administrators)
B – Middle	Intermediate managerial, administrative (eg lawyers, doctors, lecturers, middle managers)
C1 – Lower middle	Supervisory, clerical, junior management/administration etc.
C2 – Skilled worker	Skilled manual
D – Working	Semi- and unskilled workers
E – Near subsistence	Pensioners, widows, casual and lowest grade workers, those at lowest subsistence level

The classification gives a rough indication of purchasing power plus behaviour patterns in relation to media. The shortcomings of this simple system are obvious.

EXAMPLE

The media behaviour of students is close to that of group B, while many self-employed businessmen in group B identify themselves quite closely with C2, and have the same media behaviour. However, the system gives you a useful initial classification. ○

geodemographic segmentation

Many more sophisticated approaches to segmentation are now used. Several specialist data suppliers have produced advanced socio-demographic classifications, based on a mixture of census, electoral roll, credit and other data. The classifications give up to 50 or more types, and data is available down to the lowest post-code level (group of houses – the average number is 15 per post-code).

Neighbourhood classification data falls into three categories:

1. **Demographic** – how many people live in a household, their ages, and family structure.

2. **Socio-economic** – value of house, income of household, occupations of household members.

3. **Physical** – type of dwelling (house or flat), size (eg number of rooms).

This has proved particularly useful for direct marketing companies. It allows them to enhance their customer files (which usually cover names, addresses, telephone numbers, response to promotions, and purchases) with other data relatively cheaply and quickly.

psychographic analysis

Another development has been the trend to more advanced psychographic analysis, using data on customers' attitudes, interests and opinions. This started with basic psychological categories, but has developed much further. It provides useful categories to use when analyzing purchazing behaviour in relation to new products or new channels of distribution. You can also develop categories which are completely specific to your products and services.

life-style questionnaires

> **"Life-style questionnaires"** are sent out to millions of consumers. They gather data on their media and buying habits. In exchange for this data, consumers are mailed coupons giving reductions on the kind of products they say they like.

The data is then sold to direct marketing companies who either use it as a promotional list or to enhance their files. The sheer volume and depth of data produced in this way can make it excellent source material for segmentation. It also makes it much easier for companies getting started in consumer direct marketing to obtain data on their target markets.

WATCH OUT!

Many potential customers are becoming wise to the nature of these questionnaires and the information contained in them can be unreliable, because consumers fill them out just to get the coupons. Treat them with great care and test the value of the information by running campaigns using this information alongside campaigns using data from other sources.

combining sources

Many data supplying agencies now supply combinations of the main marketing data sets. They started by combining census, post-code, and credit data. Now, they combine their original data with life-style surveys, media surveys (eg readership surveys) and shopping data from retail audits, to give much greater depth of information on customers of particular types. This combined data also shows companies how to reach customers of particular kinds through published and broadcast media (eg for "hand-raising campaigns" to get prospects to identify themselves, or for branding campaigns to provide a positive context for direct marketing campaigns), and what coupons to distribute in which areas to encourage the purchase of their products through retailers.

other sources of segmentation data

Some of the agencies who provide data and analysis also provide forecasts of social, economic and market change. Larger consumer goods companies use forecasts of the impact of changing demographic and social patterns as input for their strategic plans. The factors highlighted include ageing, home-centredness, changing shopping habits, and the growing computer and telecommunications culture.

FAST TRACK

This kind of data is most likely to be useful if you want to look beyond the horizon that current buying data imposes, to what the state of your database will be in three to five years time.

response-based segmentation

The advantage of using direct marketing is that it routinely generates the data required for market segmentation. The response data includes:

- Information your customers have given during the response eg answers to a questionnaire. This includes the simple facts about who they are and (if the address was not known beforehand) where they live.
- The fact that they have responded to a particular approach.
- Where appropriate, the fact that they have bought.

What this data can tell you

- What products and services your customers have bought and when – and what they have not bought, and so by implication what they are most likely to buy in the future, and when they are likely to buy it.
- What kinds of promotion they have responded to, and by implication are most likely to respond to in the future.
- How they paid (or not) – type and timing, and by implication whether a customer constitutes a credit risk.

Although you might like to customize your entire communication to individual customers – the market segment of one – in practice this is rarely possible (except for **personalization** – addressing the customer by name). Products and offers must normally be designed to meet the needs of groups of customers. You will find it very expensive to customize both your communications and your products and services to individuals. Letters must be mailed and advertisements shown such that they reach cost-effectively the groups of customers most likely to respond and/or buy. So your aim is to find the best groups – the ones most likely to respond, buy and pay. Fortunately, years of direct marketing experience have shown that customers' needs are not all that varied, so we can confidently expect to be able to group our customers according to their needs.

how to define segments

Much segmentation aims at finding variables whose values are associated with each other in different groups, for example:

- Finding that people who live in one area have a greater chance of liking a particular product than people who live in another area.
- Finding that people who buy product X are more likely to respond to a mailing on product Y than people who buy product Z.

To target as precisely as possible, you may be interested in finding associations between several variables.

EXAMPLE

You might, through analyzing your database, find that people who bought product X last year and product Y this year, who live in upper income areas, are very likely to respond to a promotion on product Z. ○

purchasing variables

In direct marketing, the key segmentation variables are purchasing variables. We have already introduced the FRAC variables. Now let's look at them in more detail, and a few other variables which are absolutely essential to track.

FREQUENCY

"**Frequency**" is defined as how often the customer buys. This is not a single figure, although the average figure over a period may be used eg once a year. Just as important is the **trend** in frequency ie is it rising or falling? Imagine two customers with the same very recent purchasing behaviour, but one's purchasing frequency is rising and the other's is falling. The former is likely to be of more interest to you than the latter, other things being equal.

WATCH OUT!

Frequency depends upon how frequently you promote to a customer. Even if the customer is a catalogue customer, promotions may still be used to stimulate purchase from the catalogue. So, any analysis of frequency must take into account promotions history. Where customers receive varying numbers of promotion, a better statistic to use might be average frequency of response per promotion, measured for each time period eg last half year, half year before that.

RECENCY

This measures **when the customer last bought**. Again, this depends on promotional factors, ie when the last few promotions took place. Other things being equal, more recent purchasers have greater value.

Small changes in recency may be a harbinger of doom – or great success. If you find recency increasing ie your customers are on average waiting longer before rebuying, you must urgently find out which customers this is happening to, and why. Are your promotions failing in their objective because of problems with the offer, or have you got a problem with your product or service?

AMOUNT

This measures **how much** the customer bought – usually in value terms. It may be defined for individual products, or for your whole product range. This latter definition usually only makes sense if the customer knows that the products come from the same supplier.

The points made about frequency apply here. For example, a customer could be buying with the same frequency, but the average value of purchase might be falling. You need to find out whether this is due to factors you can't control eg the customer's income is falling, or whether it's due to your marketing or product failures.

CATEGORY

Category defines the **type of product** bought. The point made above about amount bought per customer applies here. Cross-selling as a concept only makes sense – from a measurement point of view – if the customer knows that the product is coming from the same source.

EXAMPLE

In financial services, as companies from different sectors move into each other's territory, and the market becomes more competitive, the cost of acquiring new customers is rising. So the key to success is the number of different product relationships maintained, ie how many categories the customer is buying. ○

SPEED OF ORDER FOLLOWING PROMOTION

This can be an important variable.

FAST TRACK

Fast orderers may be very interested in new offers and keen to try them. So it pays to find out the characteristics of fast orderers, profile them using whatever data you have about them, and apply this profile to other data sets to try to find more fast orderers. If fast orderers can only be identified through psychological variables, then you may need to use lifestyle questionnaires to identify them.

MODE OF PAYMENT

Unless all payment is by the same method, the mode of payment can be a very important discriminator. Credit card payers may be regarded as safer, because there is no risk of default (unless the card is stolen).

modelling

Modelling involves specifying assumptions about the relationships between the different factors at work in a situation. These include internal factors as well as market factors.

> Typically, **a model** will cover:
>
> - The variables involved, distinguishing between variables which are dependent ie their values are determined within the modelled situation, and independent ie their values are determined outside the modelled situation.
> - How they relate to each other (which ones affect each other, the direction and timing of the relationship).

For example, you may need to model the relationship between purchasing frequency, income, type of housing, frequency of response to past promotions, and so on.

Often, different models of a situation must be tested. Statistical analysis is used to find out more about how the variables inter-relate, and which model best explains the behaviour of customers. The model is then used to predict future behaviour, provided that any independent variables can be forecast. In direct marketing, these independent variables may be the ones you control eg price, timing of mailing.

IN THE REAL WORLD

We have already encountered one of the best known modelling processes used in direct marketing – "scoring". Initially derived from credit markets, the aim was to give customers a score according to their likelihood of default (eg on credit card payments). A number of variables are normally analyzed, such as past credit record (in particular whether any previous defaulting took place), court judgements against customers (if any), type of housing, mode of house possession (rent, mortgage etc), whether a bank account is possessed, and so on. A customer is allocated a better score the better the values of the individual variables. This scoring approach has provided the foundation for much direct marketing modelling. In some sectors, such as direct insurance, a company's scoring module is considered the source of competitive advantage. Get customer scoring right, and you'll lose less money through bad debt.

statistical methods for finding segments

Once upon a time, market segmentation was a matter of creative guesswork, based on deep experience of the market. Tables of data would be pored over to find links in behaviour. Today, statistical methodologies are available to do most segmentation work automatically. Some methods produce transparent results – meaning that you can see why the segment behaves as it does, but others are less transparent. The details of these techniques would take a complete textbook to explain.

FAST TRACK

Here, we content ourselves with one simple rule – if a technique helps you identify that a particular group of consumers is good eg has a high response rate, buys a lot, but you cannot in practice select that group as a target (eg because you can't predict who'll be members of that group, or find a group that is quite similar to the group you've identified), then the result is not very useful for direct marketing purposes. But if you can target the group in practice, then target it again and again, because the more you concentrate your efforts on that segment, the stronger your presence will become, and although you may find yourself subject to the law of diminishing returns, you'll be putting up a barrier to entry which your competitors will find tough to overcome.

using market research in direct marketing

Compared to traditional methods of marketing consumer goods and services, direct marketing has under-used marketing research. The question for direct marketers is whether market research can add anything to their understanding of customers, given the rich data provided by their customer databases. Research should be used to find the link between information on your database and the emotions behind customer behaviour. Qualitative groups, possibly using a viewing facility, so all personnel using the database can attend, will bring to life the reports and statistics produced by the database. They may also produce ideas about campaign design – who to target, with which products and service, and with what offer and creative.

WHY DIRECT MARKETERS DO NOT USE MARKET RESEARCH

There are several reasons why direct marketers have been slow to use marketing research.

- In the past, the direct marketing industry was dominated by a large number of small entrepreneurs who knew how to make quick money out of a mailing. They had lots of good product ideas. They did not really care why a product sold, or what customer needs they satisfied. All they wanted to know was whether the product sold. If it sold, they went on selling it. If it did not sell, they tried another. Direct mail entrepreneurs succeeded because of their ability to act quickly, based on their own judgement of a product's saleability. They moved from one product to another at great speed. Long-term planning and the idea of customer acquisition were largely foreign to them.
- With such a mentality dominating, research is seen as a cost rather than as an investment which can lead to higher response rates, fewer test failures and less

waste of resources. Given the low costs of setting up a simple direct mailing operation, the costs of research looked very large beside the profit to be obtained on a single mailing. Without the perspective of customer acquisition and development, it is difficult to justify customer research. It is even more difficult when a test mailing costs so much less than thorough research – and the research will not even tell the entrepreneur whether the mailing is going to succeed! Even today, direct marketers see research as synonymous with testing.

Only the longer range planners are researching their direct marketing as it should be researched, and these are very often the larger operators. The larger the mailing, the more important it is to get it right first time, particularly if there is no relevant past experience on which to base the test concepts. If the test is the wrong test, then you may be sacrificing very large potential profits if you do not research the test concepts properly. So, for your largest campaigns, don't go ahead without at least a few focus groups.

FAST TRACK

WHY DIRECT MARKETERS ARE STARTING TO USE RESEARCH

The new wave of direct marketers is composed partly of companies which formerly marketed entirely by brand marketing techniques, which are very research-intensive. They have always wanted to know not just **whether** a concept worked, but **why** it worked. The largest of these companies are also very concerned about their public image and the standards of customer care that they achieve. Their degree of success in these areas is normally measured using market research techniques. So they would no more launch a major direct marketing campaign without researching the concept than they would launch an advertising campaign or a new product without research.

where research can be used

There are a number of areas where you can use research, as follows:

- **Product/concept testing** – to get an idea of the viability and acceptability of a new product or concept, before investing money on producing it and test marketing it.
- **Product features** – to find out which product features are important to customers, and what advantages and benefits they provide.
- **Creative guidance** – to direct the creative effort by obtaining a current reading on the market. This enables you to understand whether its message is being understood, whether it is using the correct wording, whether consumers have hidden objections, or whether opportunities are being missed.
- **Missing features** – to uncover hidden emotion and feelings behind customer response.

So research, by creating a true understanding of the awareness, attitude and interests of customers can help to focus testing programmes and avoid some test failures. When deciding how to use research in direct marketing you could consider the following.

DON'T FORGET!

○ Are you launching a totally new product or service? If so, do you understand why customers might buy it?

○ Is your modelling data available, provable and reliable?

○ Do you understand the reasons for the response rates you are getting to your campaigns?

○ Will it help you and your colleagues to get closer to your customers and understand what motivates them?

○ Are you convinced that your creative execution will motivate your customers?

UNDERSTANDING CUSTOMERS

The results of your tests and full campaigns will give you a lot of information about who responds and to what degree they respond. However, *why* customers respond in a certain way can only be inferred. Why customers do not respond is extremely difficult to infer, as they have provided no additional data except the fact that they did not respond. Lack of response may be due to:

● Poor product.
● Poor offer design – customers wanted the general concept but not the way it was embodied in the offer.
● Poor targeting.
● Competitors providing better offers.
● Poor company image – consumers liked the offer but didn't trust you as a supplier, because your image was poor or non-existent.

A research programme can answer these questions.

main techniques direct marketers use in research

GROUP DISCUSSIONS

Group discussions are commonly used as a pre-testing technique. They are usually externally moderated by a research professional and cover a range of pre-decided topics. The results of this research are presented, and then usually argued over in order to establish what are the implications for campaign design and relationship management. They are used for other purposes, including:

- Basic need studies for new product idea generation.
- New product idea or concept exploration.
- Product positioning studies.
- Advertising and communication studies.
- Background studies on consumers' frames of reference.
- Establishing the vocabulary consumers use, as a preliminary stage in questionnaire development.
- Determination of attitudes and behaviour.

DEPTH INTERVIEWS

Depth interviews are usually used to find out why individuals buy various products and what buying, owning and using means to them. The interview can last anything from a few minutes to two hours or more. This method can uncover basic predispositions eg why a consumer does not order through the post. People's attitudes can be probed and their cause, intensity and implications can be uncovered. If the subject is sensitive, personal or complex, depth interviews can be better than group discussions. This applies particularly in business marketing, where topics being researched may include complex buying procedures.

MAIL QUESTIONNAIRES

Mail questionnaires are just that – questionnaires which are mailed to customers for them to complete by themselves.

They are used widely in direct marketing, usually when you want a large enough sample to derive a statistically valid result. They are also used to gain additional information about customers already on a database. If qualitative information is required, this can be elicited through more detailed questions about why they respond in particular ways to particular questions. Some responses may be triggers for action for you eg when a customer indicates an immediate need or raises a customer service problem.

WATCH OUT!

If you ask open-ended questions they will add significantly to the cost of analysis. So the best approach is to carry out a few focus groups to identify what customers' needs and concerns are likely to be, and the language they express them in, and then structure the questionnaire so that it can cope with most of the likely variations in customers' responses.

Mail questionnaires have these advantages:

- They are more economical and convenient than personal interviews.
- They avoid interviewer bias.
- They give people time to consider their answers.
- They can be anonymous.

They have these disadvantages:

- The questions need to be very straightforward if the response is to be valid.
- Answers must be taken as final.
- Respondents see the whole questionnaire before answering it.
- It is impossible to be sure that the right person answers it.

The main problem with mail questionnaires is non-response and the consequent likelihood that non-responders will be different from responders. The higher the response rate, the more valid the result. The only way to check this is by chasing up a sample of responders.

How to encourage response

- Use a covering letter explaining what the survey is doing, how the respondent's name was selected, and why he or she should reply.
- Tell the respondent the benefits of replying.
- Explain why the survey is important
- Enclose a stamped, addressed or business reply envelope.
- Give a premium for responding.
- Follow up.

FAST TRACK

When your research results are returned, one of the best ways of having them analyzed is by using a specialist market research data processing agency. Ideally, you should consult them before you design your research strategy. They can advise you on questionnaire design, sampling and how best to analyze and use the results. Off-the-shelf analysis packages are unable to offer the depth of knowledge of a reputable research data processing agency.

TELEPHONE QUESTIONNAIRES

Telephone questionnaires are used in very similar contexts to mail questionnaires, with the notable addition of questionnaires administered when customers telephone in, eg to respond to a promotion or to contact a Helpline.

Telephone surveys are normally more accurate than mail surveys. They combine many of the advantages of mail questionnaires and in-depth interviews. Their strengths are:

- They are one to one.
- The consumer cannot see the whole questionnaire.
- Any problems of understanding can be dealt with.
- Careful scripting helps avoid interview bias.
- Computerized routing of questionnaires allows for complex patterns of behaviour to be captured.
- Response rates are higher – customers can be called until they reply.
- Costs are lower than personal interviews.
- The telephone is a way of life to business.

- Speed – telephones get higher priority than post, and the results are immediately available.

Their disadvantages are that:

- Some consumers object to the approach.
- The call is at your convenience and not the customer's. This can produce a negative response from the customer. For this reason telephone is often not the best medium for customer satisfaction work. However, if you have a long questionnaire to administer, you can overcome this problem by scheduling the call at a time agreed with the respondent.
- The costs of setting up a telephone questionnaire can be high.
- Calling costs are higher than postal costs.
- It is a voice medium only, so customers' reactions cannot be seen.

USING MARKET RESEARCH IN POST-TESTING

Post-testing, which uses the same techniques as pre-testing, is used to find out why things went as they did. Typical questions include:

- Why do particular kinds of consumers order or not order a catalogue or a product?
- Why are members cancelling?
- Why is the conversion rate low or high?

summary

Market segmentation is the essence of direct marketing. But not all the data used in direct marketing arises from campaigns. Market research has got a particularly valuable role to play in backing up the customer data and in exploring areas which cannot be covered by customer data. It is also vital if you are to use direct marketing to position your products or services – the subject of our next chapter.

12

positioning through direct marketing

- Positioning is the best way to give customers a short cut to valuing your brands.

- Customers who value your brands are more likely to respond to your direct marketing.

- Direct marketing can by itself help mould customers' perceptions of your brands.

- But direct marketing also works very well when you use media advertising to position your brands.

introduction

Modern society is an over-communicated society. Your customers are exposed daily to thousands of messages. Most messages compete for their attention without involving them personally. This "noise" or "clutter" in the market-place means that few messages register with your customers, and even fewer mean anything to them. It's no use making a direct hit if the arrow falls to the floor afterwards! So, how can you make sure that it lodges properly in its target? What does make a message succeed?

FAST TRACK

You've got to give your customer a short cut. Your poor customer cannot constantly process information to make a sensible choice. Customers need a short cut. This short cut is the product's positioning – the subject of this chapter. Unless you create strong positioning for your product and perhaps for your company – one that is right for you and your customers – your arrow will fall to the floor!

positioning explained

The origins of the idea lie in the packaged goods industry, where the concept was called product positioning. This referred to the product's attributes and functional features and how they compared with competitive products. In the 1950s, positioning meant finding some USP and communicating it in order to gain competitive advantage. Thus, for instance, Daz had the "blue whitener" and Esso petrol put "a tiger in your tank". However, the search for new features in highly competitive markets with many similar products proved to be increasingly difficult and ineffective. Words like "new" and "improved" lost their value. When product development staff really did come up with an improvement, it was much harder work for advertising to make the claim credible.

The response to this problem came from David Ogilvy, who coined the term "image" and translated it into highly effective advertising for products as different as shirts and cars. The "image era" dawned and the mid-1960s was the heyday of the image-makers.

WATCH OUT!

Just as the "me-too" products killed the product era, "me-too" companies killed the image era. Companies with similar offerings found that the "noise" they had created was deafening customers. It was just as difficult as it had ever been to establish a permanent, profitable position. It was not uncommon for consumers exposed to an advertisement from one company to believe that it came from another.

"Positioning" is not defined in relation to your actual company or product attributes. It is defined as the way these attributes are perceived in the consumer's mind. For advertisers, this means that the results of a campaign depend less on how advertising is written than on how the product and/or supplying company is positioned.

The implication of this view of positioning is that challenging companies with dominant market positions with a head-to-head confrontational strategy is doomed to failure, because it means changing deeply entrenched customer perceptions. The best route is to create an alternative, unique position in the consumer's mind. The mind screens out most information, accepting only that which is consistent with prior knowledge and experience. Telling the customer "change your mind – you got it wrong before" is not a good idea. Offering them another image – one which relates to their needs but does not tell them "you made the wrong choice" is a much more fruitful strategy.

However, the mind cannot deal with too much information at a time. Most consumers cannot recall more than a few brands in a product field. The lower the involvement, the fewer the brands that the consumer will remember.

WATCH OUT!

To cope with the *complexity*, people reduce everything to its utmost simplicity. Moreover, they rank everything, putting objects on ladders. This is done for products, too, otherwise consumers could not cope with the bewildering variety of choice they are faced with. Each rung of the ladder is a space or position.

So, if you are to increase brand preference you must move your product up the ladder, which can be difficult if the brands above are strongly entrenched and no positioning strategy is applied against them.

FAST TRACK

If you are a new entrant to a market, you are in a particularly difficult position. You must either accept the bottom position on the ladder or try to force your way in by pushing someone else off. But it's much better to carry in a new ladder! This means that if your new product is to be seen as number one, you must help customers see products from a different point of view ie use a different scale to rank products.

One of the ways detergent manufacturers compete with each other is to offer consumers something else to think about. One supplier gains an advantage by focusing on whiteness, the other responds by getting consumers to focus on the good smell of clean washing. ○

EXAMPLE

These examples illustrate a central problem in positioning – and a solution to it. Consumers learn in two ways: by **generalization** and **discrimination**. First they learn about products and then to discriminate between brand attributes. If the new product entrant is radically different from the market's perception of the nearest competitor, it will struggle to penetrate the mind of the prospect. If consumers define a car as having four wheels, then a car with five wheels is not a car! Consumers will have no label to attach to this strange new arrival. Therefore it will not register in consumer consciousness.

FAST TRACK

*So, if you are to succeed in creating a new ladder with yourself at the top, you must offer a proposition which is closely related to accepted products or brands. This will enable the consumer to label it. In this way, consumers use existing labels to generalize. So the recommendation for marketers is, **be different, but not too different!***

EXAMPLE

Direct Line motor insurance is positioned clearly as motor insurance, but with the difference that the mode of access to the brand has itself been positioned – the telephone. It has been strongly branded too – as a red telephone. It has now transferred this positioning to several other financial services products.○

product and real positioning

The concept of positioning described so far is psychological, ie the process creates customer perceptions of product attributes which are internalized and evaluated against competitive attributes. "Positioning is what you do to the mind of the prospect." However, there are other definitions of positioning, including:

● Product positioning.
● Real positioning.

Product positioning is the oldest and crudest form of positioning. It emphasizes particular product attributes eg size, shape, quality, speed, taste. It uses advertising to communicate the message.

Real positioning takes objective attributes of the product and converts them into consumer perceptions. However, instead of relying on advertising, it uses all aspects of the marketing mix to create an overall message.

Fitting the features to the message

EXAMPLE

In the china collectable market, a very competitive market where direct marketing techniques dominate, it is important to establish strong positioning. This is done in different ways by different suppliers. Some target home lovers, others aesthetes, status-seekers or investors. In so doing they select messages which appeal to these markets. The important point about the messages is that all the product features are developed to fit the message. The complete marketing mix is then employed to deliver the message – not merely advertising. For example, an exclusive limited edition porcelain promotion would feature:

○ A high price.

○ Copy referring to a limited number of discerning buyers.

○ Up-market packaging and other fulfilment material.

In short, everything about the product and the communication would say "premium quality". All the marketing mix elements are combined to affirm and reaffirm that message. ○

developing a positioning strategy

Whatever type of positioning is being considered, there are several possible positioning strategies and particular stages that should be gone through to achieve them.

ATTRIBUTE POSITIONING

Here the product is associated with one or other of its major attributes, eg "Ford gives you more".

PRICE/QUALITY POSITIONING

Here the attribute, price, is singled out and associated with quality. A high price signals high quality, a low price signals a cheap, value-for-money product.

USE/APPLICATION POSITIONING

Here the product is associated with a particular use or application, eg *"More"* cigarettes were positioned as the weekend alternative to the normal brand of cigarette.

PRODUCT USER POSITIONING

This strategy associates the product with a particular user or class of users. For instance the Renault 5 was positioned as *the woman's car*.

PRODUCT CLASS POSITIONING

Here a product associates itself with another product. The classic example is 7-

Up, the "*un-cola*". This positioned it against the dominant cola brands, Coke and Pepsi. The Audi A4 is positioned against the BMW 3 series as a car bought by someone with all the achievements of the typical 3-series buyer, but who does not have the need to state achievement in a crude way. The positioning is "understated achievement".

COMPETITOR POSITIONING

Here brand is positioned against brand. Avis ("we try harder" – implicitly than Hertz), Coke and Pepsi, McDonald's and Burger King, Apple and IBM in the early days of personal computers, are all good examples of this. Note that most good examples are of total company positioning, rather than of individual products.

steps in the positioning process

DON'T FORGET!

- ○ *What position, if any, do you already own in the prospect's mind?*
- ○ *What position in the prospect's mind do you desire?*
- ○ *What companies must be overcome to achieve that position?*
- ○ *Is enough money available to occupy and hold that position?*
- ○ *Do you have the stamina to stick with one positioning concept?*
- ○ *Does your creative approach match your positioning strategy?*

These questions provide the framework for the following positioning process:

1. Obtain a measure of your brand's present position.
2. Initiate a positioning/repositioning campaign.
3. Obtain a measure of your brand's position after the campaign.
4. Determine whether your brand's position has significantly changed in the desired direction.

WATCH OUT!

The techniques for doing this are beyond the scope of this book. Just note that a product, service or company with unresearched positioning and with unclear positioning objectives may perform very badly in direct marketing campaigns even if the direct marketing itself is excellent!

key requirements for successful positioning

Here are some rules you should follow in positioning:

- Positioning strategies must be customer-oriented. In other words, you must begin with solid research facts about people's perceptions of key attributes. Use market research to find out what people think of the product and how they use it.
- Recognize that customers' perceptions are *real* perceptions – to them.
- Avoid unthinking "creativity" in advertising – just because you're dealing with perceptions. It may be more expensive and difficult to build symbolic differentiation than to create genuine feature differentiation.
- Positioning strategies are the end-result of the positioning *process* that should co-ordinate all the marketing functions – not simply new product development and advertising.

IN THE
REAL WORLD

Positioning works. You should use it at both the micro and macro marketing levels. You can use it to position single brands in single market segments, or to position your entire corporation worldwide. Where both the brand and your company are "visible" to the consumer, both should be positioned.

applications of positioning in direct marketing

Positioning as a concept, a process and a strategy is inextricably linked with image advertising in published and broadcast media. Almost all classic positioning and repositioning strategies have depended wholly on using media advertising to build the required levels of awareness and involvement that positioning strategies inevitably require.

How, then, can direct marketing play a part in positioning or repositioning a brand, a product, or a company? Is there a role for direct marketing?

The answer is definitely "yes". Here's how you can use direct marketing in positioning:

1. Elements of the direct marketing system can be added as a product feature or attribute, thereby creating opportunities to reposition an existing company. For instance, a database can be built as an aid to market research. Questionnaires can be mailed to prospects and customers. Research results can be passed back to respondents, clearly creating a sense of relationship. This relationship-building can then be incorporated into media messages: "X – the company that learns from the customers", a believable claim because there is real evidence that this company is indeed in tune with customer needs.

EXAMPLE

Air UK Ltd used this approach in their campaign "You told us where to go" supporting their new route launches. ○

2. A complete direct marketing system can be incorporated into your marketing mix, thereby allowing a company to say that it offers more choice or variety than its competitors. A retail operation, for instance, might add a catalogue, as

Next did with its Next Directory. Such additions can change customers' perception of your company relative to the competition. (In the case of Next it did much more than that, as shown below.)

3. Direct communication can be used to support a positioning strategy. *For example, direct mail can be used to support television or press; the telephone can do a similar job*.

4. Direct distribution can be used to reposition existing products or position new ones. For example, insurance companies now use direct distribution to reach particular groups of customers with particular types of products. The distribution system is itself a positioning statement.

5. Direct marketing can become the positioning statement. For instance, direct banking's generic benefit is that it is direct, one-to-one banking. The benefits of direct banking will vary from segment to segment but a saving in time is a benefit with potentially universal appeal. The direct route can be used to give credibility to the time-saving theme.

positioning via direct marketing

Next Directory

EXAMPLE

In the UK catalogue shopping has always had a down-market image and a relatively down-market customer profile; and in the early to mid-1980s the market itself had become depressed as increasing affluence led consumers to express themselves more individually than had hitherto been possible. One of the main beneficiaries of this trend had been the Next retail store group which had been at the forefront of developments from which it was already benefiting. The company had conducted extensive research which showed a gap in the catalogue shopping market:

1. Demographically, ABC1.
2. Existing catalogue shoppers currently dissatisfied with the quality of service and merchandise.
3. Non-catalogue shoppers unattracted by traditional catalogue offerings.

The strategy was to offer Next merchandise direct to these segments via an exciting, visually stimulating catalogue and a 48-hour fulfilment operation. Product samples ("swatches") were included in the catalogues which were not distributed free, but had to be paid for.

At the launch in January 1988 the target had been 500,000 enquirers in the first season. In fact, this target was exceeded by 50% – with 90% of the orders taken by telephone. By the end of the second season, sales had reached £65 million and a competitive reaction had been stimulated. For instance, Freemans, one of the "big five" catalogue operators launched "Mia", aimed at women in the 30 plus age and also incorporated Miss Selfridge into the main catalogue.

Although the launch of the Next Directory is an example of a repositioning strategy through the addition of a direct marketing channel, it achieved much more than that for Next. The company is now perceived as a "paper store retailer" which pioneered exciting new concepts in catalogue shopping. It is not the largest catalogue operation – but it is certainly number one in the minds of those for whom, until the launch of the Next Directory, catalogues were a highly unattractive shopping medium. ○

Bullworker

For years the Bullworker had been positioned as the muscle-man's friend – an indispensable aid to a bigger, stronger body. But the shift away from muscle-building to fitness which gained pace in the 1980s amongst young men had, by 1988, seen a sharp reduction in the sales of the Bullworker. Quite clearly a major repositioning of the Bullworker was necessary. So Odhams Leisure Group, which bought Bullworker from Leisure Arts in 1983, decided to change the product's image to make it reflect the kind of all-round fitness important to modern young people. As a result, former world boxing champion, Barry McGuigan was recruited to promote the new "healthy family fitness look" that was to be the core value of the revamped Bullworker.

Direct response press advertisements featured the line: "Even a professional sportsman like me finds it all too easy to get out of condition between fights. That is why my Bullworker is invaluable".

In addition, retail outlets were mailed with a telegram which was followed up with a fuller mail-shot one month later detailing the Bullworker hot-line number for 24-hour orders and offering a competition with a personal appearance by McGuigan for the winning three stores. This immediately increased retail penetration by 60%, an increase of 150 additional independent outlets. This use of an existing direct marketing medium allied to a new use for direct mail had a dramatic impact on the Bullworker's image in the minds of the target market, moving it off the macho-male rung of the positioning ladder and onto the family fitness rung. Note that nothing about the product had changed. What had changed was people's perceptions of the product – thanks to direct marketing. ○

The Worldwide Fund for Nature (WWFN)

The WWFN was for long regarded as a charity which only supported wildlife species. However, there was a huge attitudinal shift in the late 1980s as more and more supporters of the charity realized the relevance of environmental issues to species' survival. So the WWFN's interests had to change. Rather than concentrating on the survival of one species, it re-focused its concentration on habitats and the earth's environment as a whole – and even changed its name to the Worldwide Fund for Nature from the World Wildlife Fund.

Like all major charities, the WWFN was already a heavy user of direct marketing, regularly mailing its 200,000 strong member database three or four times a year. However, the positioning shift the WWFN were looking for could not be achieved simply by communicating with the existing file. New recruits had to be acquired – and to this end teachers were targeted as prime educational influencers in environmental issues. Moreover, in June 1989, an 18 million door drop was tried for the first time.

Further innovations current and future, include an affinity credit with National Westminster Bank, corporate advertising and television advertising – as the rules governing charity advertising have been relaxed.

▶

> ► This repositioning of the WWFN was not merely an image exercise. The "product" really had changed and those changes needed to be communicated in order to reshuffle the charity pack. Existing environmental charities (eg Friends of the Earth) were now being challenged, but not head-on. The link between environmental protection and specific species prote. ion is at once both logical and unique, allowing the WWFN to occupy a discrete position in the donor and prospect donor's mind. ○

summary

Positioning is a key weapon in the armoury of all marketers. Traditionally, it has been used by brand marketers, but now – after being neglected by them – it is used by direct marketers too. There are three basic types of positioning – product, psychological and real. These all involve a step-by-step, structured approach which starts and ends with your customers' perceptions of your product and company brands. This approach is not cheap, but its cost-effectiveness improves when you target tightly – hence the advantage of using it in direct marketing. Our three case studies showed how powerful positioning can be when used in this way.

13

making the right offer

- Your offer – the total proposition you make to your customers – is what your customers respond to.

- The offer includes not just the product, but also the price, terms and conditions, before and after sales service and promotional benefits.

- Every element of your offer must be designed to appeal to customers in your chosen target segment.

introduction

In direct marketing, the product or service is promoted through the offer.

> The **"offer"** is defined as "the total proposition made to the prospect". This includes the physical product and all the marketing mix elements, including prices, that go with it. For a direct marketing proposition to be effective, it must call for action by a certain date – ideally as soon as possible. The direct marketing contact is usually short – the telephone call is received, the letter read, the advertisement seen, for anything from a few seconds to a few minutes, so it must call for action to be effective, or it will be forgotten.

The central or *core* element in an offer (whether it has a direct offer or not) is the *customer satisfying benefit*.

To succeed, you need to acquire customers by your offers and keep them by satisfying them with a continuing stream of valued offers and by providing good service. The key principle here is to take broadly felt needs and satisfy them with a specific offer.

FAST TRACK

Successful companies consistently offer broadly-demanded benefits; unsuccessful ones often fail to do this.

Volvo's safe offer

Volvo car buyers get comfortable, safe transportation. Volvo has recognised that there is a safety segment that is large and accessible enough to be profitable. ○

EXAMPLE

However, customers do not simply buy these broad benefits – they buy them in a specific, tangible, form – the product. In our car example, they buy a specific manufacturer's product – a saloon, an estate-car, a coupe. These have recognizable physical features, of course, and the offer strategy must take full account of these.

Even services have a physical dimension, one which many service marketers use to good effect. Services are in some respects intangible. Many services cannot be felt, touch or seen eg money transmission. In this respect, bank marketers are at a disadvantage compared with their product marketer counterparts. But bankers do have a tangible offer (or tangible evidence of the intangible core service offer). They have the bank branch, the layout of the branch, the point of sale material in the branch, the bank staff, the cheque book, plastic cards and other paraphernalia – all of which have a strong physical presence. Many make frequent use of all of these physical assets, to remind customers even when they are not in the branch. For both physical product and service marketers, therefore, the second element in the offer strategy is the tangible evidence of the offer.

However, physical evidence of, say, an estate car or a money transmission service is not enough if it has to compete with somebody else's very similar tangible evidence. So you must differentiate the offer from the competition. This is where the *brand* comes in ie the essentially symbolic association that is formed between your company and product in the customer's mind. Literally it is a symbol, often a trademark. It may be a logo eg the prancing horse of Ferrari, the black horse of Lloyds Bank. Sometimes it is a strapline *and* a logo: "BMW – the ultimate driving machine" or "NatWest – the action bank". But ultimately it is, or should be, a fully integrated set of ideas about a company and its products that reduce to some memorable mental proposition. Mention IBM, BMW, AT&T, and around the world people will say "leading computer manufacturer", "leading car manufacturer", "leading telecommunications provider".

The different levels of the offer are summarized in Figure 13.1.

Fig 13.1

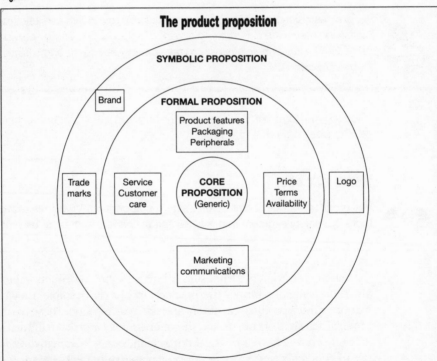

The core proposition is an abstract benefit, eg peace of mind, fear reduction, status.

The formal proposition turns the core proposition into functional benefits, eg lower price, stronger packaging, better credit terms.

The brand value converts the generic benefit and the functional attributes of the product into a specific and hopefully unique set of brand benefits, which might be condensed into a logo, strapline and/or trade mark.

To illustrate, Heineken's core proposition might be refreshment, it comes packaged in cans and bottles. Its strapline "It reaches the parts other beers can't" positions it uniquely in the minds of consumers.

*There is one final element – **customer service**. Whether you are supplying a product or a service, you must provide customer service. If your brand promises much, but your service delivery fails, your brand itself will be questioned by your customers.*

From service it is a short step to **customer care**, which is part of the **service delivery system** ie the means by which the complete range of customer service requirements is met. In customer acquisition and retention, customer care can be the crucial competitive differentiator.

choosing the right product for direct marketing

DON'T FORGET!

○ *Are your existing products right for direct marketing?*

○ *Is any product modification required?*

○ *Do you need new products?*

○ *How should you develop them?*

ARE YOUR EXISTING PRODUCTS RIGHT FOR DIRECT MARKETING?

Some products are not suited to some forms of direct marketing. For instance, few packaged consumer goods (eg grocery foods) are right for direct distribution, although it might make sense to send *samples* eg to known users of a competitive brand to encourage trial and repeat purchase. But direct marketing can be and is very successfully used to distribute coupons, customer recruitment questionnaires and information packs. Heinz and Procter & Gamble are the leading exponents of this way of using direct marketing.

IN THE REAL WORLD

Almost all financial service providers make intense use of direct marketing. For some, it's their only marketing channel (eg direct sales motor insurers). Obviously, the nature of the product influences the marketing channel. FMCG products are generally cheap, bulky, widely available and frequently purchased. Financial services are generally expensive, intangible, less widely available and less frequently purchased.

The most important determinants of which channels of communication and distribution are appropriate are what the customer needs and what channels they are prepared to use to receive messages from you, communicate with you and buy from you.

WHICH PRODUCTS ARE RIGHT FOR DIRECT MARKETING?

Products which:

- Appeal to niche markets.
- Are not normally available through other channels.
- Are poorly understood by retail staff.
- Need detailed explanation.
- Appeal to rational thought rather than emotions.
- Are novelties.
- Require selling in several stages.
- Are expensive.
- Are high margin.
- Are highly personal.
- Are infrequently purchased.
- Are business to business.

These are of course general rules – there are always exceptions. Most successful direct marketing products do fit into these categories.

IS ANY PRODUCT MODIFICATION REQUIRED?

Often, **some** product modification is required. For instance if the mail is used to distribute the product, then it will need to conform to postal regulations and might need to fit weight/price bands. Changes might need to be made to other mix elements. Price, for instance, is likely to be reduced to make the offer more attractive. Promotional offers might be added. Service levels might need to be improved eg faster delivery.

Quality improvements aimed at increasing, say, the functional performance of the product gives you the opportunity to use response-lifting words such as "new", "improved", "better" etc.

Feature improvements aimed at adding new features may improve your product's versatility, safety or convenience. Again, these changes give the copy-writer the chance to lift response.

Style improvements aimed at increasing the aesthetic appeal of the product can create a sense of product uniqueness and give rise to fresh visual treatments of the subject in promotional material.

ARE NEW PRODUCTS REQUIRED?

All marketers need "new" products if only because old products eventually die a natural death. New products are always needed. The key issues facing the direct marketer are:

- When will the need arise?
- What will be the source for new product ideas?
- How should their potential be evaluated?
- How should their potential be tested?
- Which test results indicate that roll-out is desirable?
- What effect will new products have on existing products?

pricing the direct marketing offer

You have more scope to be creative in direct marketing pricing strategy than for channels where you have, say, a national price. You have more scope to *reduce* prices and to *raise* them, because price levels can be chosen for each campaign in line with its objectives and the customers targeted for that campaign.

WATCH OUT!

The central requirement here is to budget properly and test price. This will ensure that the profit objectives of your campaign will be met.

promotional offers

When most direct marketers talk about offers they usually talk about response and purchase incentives which may be short-term and are normally extrinsic to the brand ie they are not a permanent feature of the brand itself. They include:

- Basic offers.

- Free trial.

- Free gift offers, including mystery gifts – when you order, order now etc.

- Discount offers, including temporary ones.

- Easy terms – more time to pay, low cost credit, no or small deposit.

- Sales offers.

- Extra merchandise free, eg two for one

- End of stock offer.

- Sample offers.

- Time limit offers.

- Guarantee offers, including money-back.

- Build up the sale offers.

- Competition offers.

- Club and continuity offers.

Not one is an intrinsic element of the product. All can be made or withdrawn without affecting the basic product.

"**Sales promotions**" are offers which give additional incentives to buy the basic product. They are loosely referred to as offers, but it makes more sense to think of them as motivators, ie additional incentives to buy your product or service.

Consider how and why such techniques work. This requires a different classification of offers:

- Product.
- Money.
- Service.
- Time.

This classification suggests that prospects can be motivated by, for example:

- The basic product.
- More of the basic product.
- Money now.
- Money at a future date.
- Product-related service.
- Service now.
- Time saving.
- Time in the future.

The important point is to understand who is likely to be motivated in these different ways and why. Consider prize draw offers. These usually offer very large cash prizes to very few "lucky winners" (and smaller value merchandise prizes to a greater number of less lucky winners). Who is likely to be attracted to such an incentive? It is reasonable to assume that these schemes will attract those who:

- Covet the big prize.
- Believe that they have a reasonable chance of winning it.

By spreading the cash value of say £100,000 amongst 100,000 people by giving them £1 off their initial purchase, however, you can attract a very different prospect, one who is intrinsically interested in the product and also needs a small incentive to switch brands.

distribution channels in direct marketing

Direct marketing is not synonymous with direct distribution although many products that are marketed directly are distributed directly. You can contact the customer in one way and get the product or service to them in another. For example, you can mail them with an offer, which they can collect in a retail store.

Marks & Spencer

EXAMPLE

Marks & Spencer regularly invites its charge card customers to special shopping evenings where customers can shop and at the same time enjoy a glass of wine, some snacks and a variety of live music. Such events add value at point of sale and constitute an integral part of the total proposition, ie the offer. Special sales preview days for "privileged" customers are another example. ○

For this reason, it is important to see distribution channels, particularly retail channels, as part of the offer strategy. Your service delivery system adds value by making products available when and where customers want them. The inducements described above may be far more effective incentives than lower prices, easier payment terms or product offers such as 20% more for the same price.

the offer strategy

WATCH OUT!

In recent years classical marketers have increasingly become aware of the dangers of short-term tactical promotions. They can erode brand loyalty through damage to brand values and only succeed in bringing forward tomorrow's sale to today, with no overall increase in purchase or consumption. Moreover, since everybody else is also promoting using similar techniques, short-term promotions have no long-term impact on brand share and are viewed instead as the price to be paid to stay in the market – a defensive rather than offensive tool.

FAST TRACK

You should integrate the best classical marketing incentives into your marketing strategy at the planning and creative stages and view them as brand-enhancing, rather than brand-eroding, incentives for your customers to purchase and keep purchasing your brand.

You should see the offer as the **total proposition** rather than as an individual element, and seek ways of developing integrated offer strategies. The creative stage in the development of a campaign is an appropriate point to do this. The ideas offered in this chapter provide the framework for such an approach.

An offer won't work unless you've sorted out your strategy!

● Is your product right for the market you have in mind?
● Will direct marketing work in the marketing strategy?
● What modification or changes need to be made?
● Are your customer care policies strong enough to support a direct marketing campaign?
● What effect will it have on your existing channels of distribution?

EXAMPLE

Suppose that a company markets high quality porcelain china collectables, mainly figurines. Its market is BC women aged 30-55. Media to be used are middle-market press and direct mail. Response is one stage coupon/telephone response with flexible payment methods. Fulfilment is direct by post within 28 days of receipt of the order. Previously response had been achieved with a premium offer of a pocket history of the great porcelain manufacturers. A new approach is sought. Consider these questions:

▶

1. What/where is the generic offer ie the core benefit or service?

To answer this, some research is needed. Suppose that research indicates three basic motives for purchase of china collectables: aesthetic value, investment value and status value. Suppose, too, that the figurines are purchased for aesthetic reasons. They beautify the home and are a pleasure to look at. They are not bought for investment reasons and customers do not regard them as showing indications of social status. So the generic offer is the **aesthetic value** of the physical product. Incentives to respond are best related to this primary purchase motivation. **Price** is likely to be less important than a promotional incentive which adds aesthetic value to the offer. Place incentives can be viewed in terms of media ie where the offer is seen and in terms of channels of distribution ie where and how the **offer** is made available – in this case in the home through postal distribution.

2. What physical evidence does the prospect need?

Clearly physical evidence is crucial. The prospect must be able to see the quality and aesthetic appeal of the offer. Dimensions, proportions, design, colour, detail – all these need to be clear. Above all, the advertisements must add value to the offer, featuring the products' aesthetic characteristics. Ideally, the prospect should be able to see, handle and even keep the product before purchasing. Should the response incentive therefore be, say 28 days free trial or simply the name and address of the nearest retail stockist (if this applies)? What about a premium offer, say, a miniature replica with each order? Or would a product-related premium work better, say a full-colour print of the figurine in equally tasteful design?

3. How will branding affect the offer?

China collectables tend either to be branded with a manufacturer's brand name eg Wedgwood, or with the marketer's brand name eg Compton & Woodhouse – or both. Which should be given most prominence? Which branding device is likely to work best, name or logo? Such questions reflect creative concerns, and are an important part of the offer strategy. But we also need to think about pricing considerations. If price is not an incentive, what about payment terms? If free trial is the incentive, then it will need to be supported by a "send no money now" offer. When will the customer be invoiced – on dispatch or receipt of the item? These are important policy considerations which are heavily influenced by branding decisions – the offer strategy must support the branding, not conflict with it.

Place considerations centre on media. Media make the product available either to specific market segments – direct mail does this particularly well – or to broader target markets, depending on media vehicles chosen. Will the media affect the message – particularly the brand values? How will brand values be affected?

4. How can the service delivery system be used to add value to the offer?

The service delivery system starts with the message "Have you made it easy for customers to reply?" and ends the first buying cycle with product fulfilment and customer care. Each point in the system is an opportunity to enhance the quality of the offer. Provision of alternative response vehicles, mail, telephone, even fax, alternative payment methods, alternative delivery points etc – all of these add value through the service delivery system. Opportunities to enhance the offer arise in the following areas:

○ Product inspection, availability and returns.

○ Payments methods, payments processing, refunds.

○ Premium availability and dispatch.

○ Efficient media planning, retail alternatives, postal delivery.

○ Faster delivery, better customer care, advice bureaux. ○

summary

This chapter started by saying that the best offer you can make to your customers is **to satisfy their needs**. To do this you must build your offer strategy from your product, which is at the heart of the offer, outwards towards the service delivery system. In this way, you arrive at the total proposition you wish to make. This in turn gives you the basis of your product positioning strategy.

We showed that this offer-building process incorporates potentially all the marketing mix elements. Indeed, your core benefit may be in one of these mix elements, eg swifter delivery (consider Next Directory: 48 hour delivery was a key feature of the product offer).

We showed that direct marketers have relied on extrinsic offers, often of a temporary nature. Such offers bear a close, if not identical, resemblance to the sales promotions run by conventional, classical marketers in FMCG markets – price promotions, premium incentives, competitions and so on.

14
hitting by mail

- Direct mail is the dominant direct marketing media in most of the world – except the US, where telephone dominates.

- Every element of your mailing – the outer envelope, the letter, the catalogue or brochure, the order form, the reply envelope and any other enclosures – plays its role in increasing response and sales, and should be planned to that effect.

- Direct mail is the most mature direct marketing medium, so in designing direct mail campaigns, we can draw on the experience of generations of past direct marketers.

- Project planning disciplines are needed to co-ordinate the design, production and mailing of a mailpiece.

introduction

"**Direct mail**" is defined as personally addressed communications sent through the postal service.

Direct mail has three main uses:

- *As a prime medium* – a self-contained vehicle for selling a product or service, promoting an event, etc.
- *With other media*, to support or follow up other activities.
- *As support to a channel* – before the sale (eg to provide leads) or after the sale (eg to follow up a sales call).

targeting

As with all direct marketing media, targeting is critical in direct mail. In a mail campaign, unlike with telephone marketing and some other media, the response cannot be instantly adjusted at the moment of interaction with the customer. It is no use finding out after the event whether the customer is the right one and whether the form of communication is right for that customer. Though the cost of each communication seems low, the costs of a large campaign are not. Hence the importance of testing.

WATCH OUT!

Misdirected mail-shots waste print and postage and alienate customers. A balance must therefore be struck between the suitability of a list and the cost of editing it. This is one reason why lists based on existing company data are usually the best.

In a direct mail campaign, you must be absolutely clear about what action your customer is expected to take as a result of receiving the communication. **You won't be there when the letter is opened to tell them what to do!** Your customers' motivation in taking the required step must also be understood. Don't forget that for your customer, **response equals effort** – the effort of cutting out, completing and posting, or picking up the telephone and dialling. Your mail pack design must take these issues into account.

DON'T FORGET!

Response equals budget too!

The likely response rate and the value of each response are critical in determining how much can be spent on the mail pack.

components of a mailing

THE LETTER

Consider the letter as part of a sales call:

● The outer envelope	*Knock on the door*
● The letter	*Sales pitch*
● The brochure	*Product or service demonstration*
● Samples and testimonials	*Reassurance providers*
● Order form and reply envelope	*The close*

WATCH OUT!

Just as you would never ask a sales-person simply to show his product without speaking, you should never send a brochure without a letter. However, some very successful campaigns have been without letters (or, for that matter, without brochures). There is of course no general rule except that what works, works, and this can only be discovered by testing!

Letters are deceptively simple. Because you write letters yourself, you might be tempted to approach direct mail letter writing casually. This would be a mistake. A letter has fewer ways of attracting and retaining your reader's attention than other media. But it has a good chance of being read, so effort invested in writing it brings rewards. All the rules for writing copy apply to letters. The key rules are:

1. Promise a benefit as early as possible in the letter, and then say more about it, and why it's so good and special, in your customers' language and relating it to the benefits they can expect to get from it.

2. Tell your customers exactly what they're going to get if they take up your offer and tell them what they'll miss if they don't.

3. Back up what you say with evidence, endorsements, testimonials and rational appeals.

4. Tell, tell and tell again – introduce the benefits you're offering, describe them and summarize them at the end.

5. Get the customer to act – now, and tell them what they'll miss if they don't.

These are "tried and tested" formulae, which direct marketers have used for years. However, don't confuse them with brash over-selling. The way to avoid this is found in Rule 1 – use the customers' language, not yours – hence the importance of research and concept testing.

THE BROCHURE

The brochure complements the letter. If the letter is your sales-person then the brochure is your product or service demonstration. Your brochure should demonstrate your product or service, and turn the letter into pictures. If possible, your product should be shown yielding the benefits claimed for it. Support your claims by a full and logical story, guarantees and testimonials.

the catalogue

The well-used catalogue indicates a solid relationship with your customer. It is a permanent representative in your customer's office or home, selling all the year round without additional costs of following up. It also supports other channels. It can help your sales-person to sell the full range of products and services without having to explain them all. To do this, your catalogue must be a direct response vehicle – more than a listing of product, features and prices. It must create the desire to buy and be as readable and productive as any other piece of marketing material. You can distribute your catalogue in various ways – by mail, at exhibitions, handed out by sales staff, at shop counters and so on.

order forms

Order forms may be part of a brochure, catalogue or letter, whether separate or detachable. The order form is your sales-person's close, but the sales-person is not there, so make it as easy as possible to complete. It should look valuable, be reply paid, with the customer's details already entered and with clear instructions on how to complete it. It could be a tollfree number with easy ordering instructions. This is increasingly used, as it gives you the opportunity to check customer details, confirm stock availability and delivery dates, and cross-sell.

WATCH OUT!

When using telephone order-takers try to avoid too many questions before the order is made. Customers ring to order, not to give numerous personal details which they consider irrelevant or which they believe you already have!

the envelope

The envelope encourages your customer to take the step of seeing whether there is useful information contained in it. This usually means overprinting and using paper of high quality appearance. Matching graphics on the envelope, letter and brochure can help make it stand out.

one piece mailers

One piece mailers are used to reduce costs or to provide ways of giving more material to your customer within a cost budget. They may attract a low response, but this can be made up for by the higher coverage obtained within a given budget.

EXAMPLE

One piece mailers are used by many holiday companies. For example, they send postcards at recognized booking times, reminding potential clients what a great time they had last year. ○

enclosures

Many enclosures have been tried, with great success. They include gifts, testimonials, imaginative ways of showing the product in use, samples, guides or other items of enduring value. As a general rule, the more pieces in a mail pack, the better – provided that they all reinforce the central offer.

EXAMPLE

The Consumers' Association found that an **eleven** piece pack gets the most response from cold files – ie of customers with no previous history of contact with them. In the US, up to **thirty two** pieces have been used with great success. Remember, the more pieces in the pack, the greater the chance that one will strike a chord with the prospect. ○

who uses direct mail?

The traditional heavy users of consumer direct mail are mail order-only companies, insurance companies, consumer credit companies, book clubs, charities and magazines. In recent years, they have been joined by credit card companies, retailers, airlines, government departments, political parties, motor manufacturers and dealers, and banks. In the business to business arena, most suppliers of goods and services now include direct mail as an essential element in their marketing mix.

The advantages of direct mail

- It is possible to target highly specifically.
- It is personal and confidential.
- It is more competitively secret.
- The message can be highly specific, enabling you to dovetail it very closely with messages put out through the less targeted media, such as television or the national press.
- Even in the lowest cost postage bracket, a lot of space is available in which to communicate.
- A variety of formats and materials can be used.
- There are many opportunities to introduce novelty (eg by different formats and types of enclosure).
- Mailings can be scheduled to arrive within a fairly well-defined period.
- Testing is relatively easy.
- The response vehicle can be defined so as to ensure that your customers know exactly what to do when they receive the mailing.
- Properly planned, it can be much more cost-effective per reply than most other media.

Direct mail has some specific weaknesses:

1. *It is not appropriate to all markets. For example, the mail of senior managers of large companies is usually intercepted by secretaries, and any mailings not considered relevant may be rejected.*

2. *It is not appropriate to all objectives. For some products, your customers may not trust direct mail, preferring to visit a retail outlet to gather information. In this case, it may be better to use direct mail to stimulate customers to visit particular retail outlets.*

3. *It cannot be used in isolation to build a brand.*

4. *Some customers are very sceptical of direct mail.*

You can make direct mail fail if you don't use it properly!

○ **Emphasize short-term response, rather than relationship building.** *Now that so many companies are committed to a database marketing approach, this approach is less common. But many companies still decide to "do a mailing" to bring in some leads. They rent a list, design and dispatch the mailing, and never work out whether the targeting was accurate. All the opportunities for learning and improving are thereby lost, as is the opportunity to build a customer database.*

○ **Use it tactically.** *Even if you have a good customer database, you may be tempted to use direct mail entirely tactically, just to generate leads. You may miss opportunities for building loyalty, developing a catalogue operation, selling additional products and services, cross-selling and researching your customers.*

○ **Don't integrate your contacts with the rest of your company's customer contact efforts.** *For example, letters may be going out at the same time that sales or service staff are due to call.*

○ **Choose your own messages**, *and don't worry about the other messages your company is sending out, or what branding you're trying to achieve. This is a great way to confuse customers.*

quality and the law

Given the risks to quality standards that might be incurred with such high volumes of mailing, the British Royal Mail works closely with direct mail users and agencies to ensure quality standards.

MAILSORT

To encourage the growth in direct mail, and to counter criticisms about the efficiency of its services (in particular unreliable delivery dates, which made it difficult for direct mailers to know when their mailings reached customers), the British Post Office introduced the Mailsort scheme in 1989. Mailsort was a new rebate scheme for bulk mailings.

THE DIRECT MAIL SERVICES STANDARDS BOARD LTD (DMSSB)

This was set up *"to help achieve and maintain the highest standards of practice and conduct in the provision of direct mail services and in the use of direct mail generally"*. It operates a Recognition Scheme. Recognized companies are closely scrutinised by the DMSSB. They also undertake to observe certain codes of practice and only to work for clients who do so. Recognized agencies must pay the appropriate levy to the Advertising Standards Board of Finance and, where relevant, to subscribe to the *Mailing Preference Service*. One of the problems this initiative faces is the rising number of in-house mailings, carried out directly by clients and not involving agencies.

The DMSSB's work also includes liaising with industry bodies, such as the regulatory bodies in the financial services industry. It also monitors agency samples, picking up problems such as unspecified delivery dates for cash with order offers, insufficient prize draw rules and breaches of the Sale of Goods Act. The DMSSB also monitors letterbox leaflet distributions. It works closely with the Advertising Standards Authority and Trading Standards Departments where appropriate. The DMSSB also publishes guidance notes – covering specific legislation and also giving general advice on the preparation of direct mail.

THE LAW

The British Code of Advertising Practice and the British Code of Sales Promotion Practice have been drawn up to protect consumers and suppliers. Provided that all suppliers observe these codes, consumers will not receive offers which break the law or mislead them and suppliers will not have to face unexpectedly high costs by being forced to comply with terms of an offer which were not properly worked out or by having to defend their actions in the courts.

WATCH OUT!

The main areas where problems occur are:

○ *Prize draws and competitions.*

○ *Misleading or exaggerated claims.*

○ *Guarantees.*

○ *Delivery times.*

○ *Appeals to fear.*

FINANCIAL SERVICES

Two Acts are particularly relevant to direct mail as used in marketing financial services. They are:

- The Consumer Credit Acts 1974 & 1980.
- The Financial Services Act 1986.

The key issues are:

- The interest rate charged on loans and credit cards must be correctly calculated as an APR.
- Past experience must be representative. Likely rates of return on investment must not be guessed at and if there is any reason to suppose that future rates of return will not be similar to past rates, this must be stated.
- Where appropriate, it must be stated that the value of an investment can go down as well as up.
- Graphical representations of increased (or decreased) value must not distort.
- The tax implications of any investment must be clearly stated.

THE DATA PROTECTION ACT

This was not set up solely to regulate direct mail, but it has significant implications. The Data Protection Registrar has already issued a number of rulings relating specifically to the use of personal data by the direct marketing industry.

The Act states specifically that personal data shall be:

1. **Obtained and processed fairly and lawfully**. This means that people who give data should know why they give it and should not be deceived into giving it.

2. **Data should be held for one or more specified purposes**. In other words, it is not legal to collect data without a specified purpose.

3. **It should only be disclosed for the purpose held**. For example, data collected for the purposes of checking creditworthiness should not be disclosed for the purpose of marketing products. So if the intention is to use it for both, the individual from whom it is being collected should be told so at the time of collection.

4. **The data should be adequate, relevant and not excessive**. In other words, if you collect data, you should be able to justify every element of it in terms of improving your ability to meet customer needs.

5. **The data should be accurate and updated**. It is not enough to collect it and continue to use it, even if it becomes outdated. You should ensure that you budget for updating – often very expensive.

6. **The data should be retained only as long as necessary for the stated purpose or purposes**. Provided you are using the data as a foundation for building a relationship with the customer, this should not pose a problem. But it would be illegal to collect the information, use it once and then keep it in case it could be sold.

7. **The data should be accessible to individuals at reasonable intervals and without undue delay or cost**. It must also be corrected or erased as appropriate. A charge for access to personal data has been fixed by the Registrar.

8. **The data should be appropriately secured against unauthorized access, alteration, disclosure or destruction and against accidental loss or destruction**. These are common sense provisions.

THE MAILING PREFERENCE SERVICE (MPS)

> The aim of the MPS is to *"promote with the general public the Direct Marketing Industry in the United Kingdom by providing facilities for the consumer to exercise a choice in regard to the receipt of direct mail"*. The emphasis is very much on encouraging the continued growth of direct mail by ensuring that customer alienation is minimized.

With the MPS, consumers may add their name to the register of those not wishing to receive unsolicited direct mail, free of charge. Many add their names in several different formats, according to the formats they are addressed by, so there are many duplicates on the list. The MPS is paid for by the subscribing companies, which include users, agencies, bureaux and list brokers.

To maintain quality standards, many bureaux and list brokers are insisting that clients lists going into deduplication are MPS-cleaned beforehand.

the brief for a direct mail campaign

This is not radically different from any other direct marketing brief. It should cover:

● Business objectives.
● Marketing objectives.
● Customers in the target market – who they are, how they behave, what they buy, how they are normally communicated with, what their needs are, how much they know about the product on offer and the company supplying it. This should include any market research that is available.
● What response is required, eg a complete sale, a lead.
● The features, benefits and USP of your product or service, and how these match customers' needs.
● The positioning and brand image of your product.
● The offer.
● What the rest of the market is doing – direct competitors, indirect competitors and suppliers of products and services that are in some way similar to the product in question, retailers etc.
● Your previous record with the product – sales, marketing campaigns and their results.
● What other marketing actions are planned for the product and for your other products.
● What might be learnt from the campaign.
● What should be tested.
● How responses will be handled

- The schedule.
- The budget.

formats

As mentioned earlier, one of the major advantages of direct mail is the variety of formats which can be used. The classic format is the following:

- The "outer" or, more fully, the "outer envelope", with the recipient's address and often overprinted with an additional message. However, overprinting can cause customers to think that the mailing is "just junk mail" to be thrown away. It must therefore be used judiciously.
- The letter itself, personalized if possible.
- A brochure, referred to in the letter.
- The order form.
- A flier (for some other product or service, or for an additional offer within the offer).
- An envelope for the reply (usually a business reply envelope – a BRE – or a Freepost envelope).

You could include non-competing companies' fliers to help cover the cost of the mailing, but beware of diluting impact. So test first!

FAST TRACK

making your mailing more effective

Ways of doing this include:

- Involvement devices – stamps, tokens, rub-offs, sealed envelopes, jigsaws, keys.
- Specialized devices which form an integral part of the print medium, eg attention grabbers, pop-ups, tip-ons, die cuts.
- Product samples (eg of furniture coverings or other fabrics).
- A second or "publisher's" letter.
- Closed face envelopes.
- Invitation formats – implying a special privilege.
- Simulated telegrams.
- Personalization – not just in the letter but on other items as well. Some printers can now personalize catalogues. One stationer's letter asks *"You have not bought toner cartridges for three months, are we too expensive? Turn to page 15 and take a further 25% off the sale price"*.
- Testimonials.
- Guarantees.
- Free trial and cancellation.
- Money-back offers.
- Reassurance about your reliability.

the creative

There is no formula for a *perfect* direct mail pack, but there are many "rules" which have helped make packs pull better. So, if you can't afford first line agencies or top creative consultancies, or if you use in-house resources, here are some guidelines.

the letter formula

IN THE REAL WORLD

Some of the best mailing pieces succeed because they are unusual. However, there is a degree of consensus about the kind of mailing that will usually work – provided that targeting has been accurate, timing is right and the offer is appropriate to the target market!

Calling to action

The aim of a letter is to get action.

- The envelope must make your customer open it.
- The letter must make your customer refer to the brochure.
- The brochure must make your customer find and fill in the order form or call you.

So your words must be powerful. But additional incentives may be required – discounts for early applications, free entry to prize draws and the like. Some argue that incentives should always be closely related to the offer being made, on the grounds that irrelevant incentives devalue the offer. However, irrelevant offers do pull responses. Even solar calculators had their day! As with all the points below, what form of words and what incentive works for the target market and product in question is best established by testing. To make sure that your copy pulls responses, it should repeatedly ask for and spur to action, with cut off dates, reasons to act and reminders of benefits at the point of asking.

A vital point is won if the offer is packaged to create a favourable first impression. What "favourable" means depends on the market and product. In some markets, an envelope which "screams" at the customer to be opened may be the right impression to create. In other markets, a favourable first impression may only be created by a businesslike letter.

FAST TRACK

Use market research to test ideas. Suggest a succession of ideas at one time. Then use those which have been favourably received one after the other, in a succession of mailings.

A call to action "out of the blue" often fails. You must lead your customer towards the call in a convincing way. Take your customer through the classic advertising cycle of attention, interest, desire, conviction and action.

Benefits

> **"Benefits"** are what your product or service does for the individual customer, by satisfying the customer's objectives.

For customers to understand that the product will meet their objectives, your copy must be written in their language. For example, if you are selling a washing machine, don't express the benefit of trouble-free and cost-efficient washing in terms of the pence per minute or likely need for service calls if these are not ideas to which customers relate their objectives of freedom from trouble and low cost.

WATCH OUT!

It is tempting to extol the features (the description of the product or service's technical characteristics) and advantages or functions of the product (what it does) rather than its benefits, particularly if not enough is known about customers (which makes it difficult to know their objectives and hence the benefits).

Consistency and quality

FAST TRACK

The tone, style and copy of the entire pack should be consistent with your company branding.

This is a matter of principle, the value of which is difficult to prove by testing. A very powerful creative execution which is entirely inconsistent with your company's branding might pull a very high response. But the question is – would too many such promotions lead to the value of your brand falling? Response might begin to fall. The vast majority of companies with strongly branded offerings insist on complete consistency with branding across all marketing communications media. Presumably this is not just due to a few smart marketing consultants!

The same point applies to consistency with product and target customer. "Cheap" creative can sell quality products, but testing is likely to show that "quality" creative would pull even better.

Using personal data

Increasing numbers of direct mail users are working with their own customer database. This creates the ability to incorporate personal details about the customer in the letter copy. For example, a letter might say:

"... When you bought your washing machine from us five years ago you returned us a questionnaire which indicated that you would be likely to replace

your machine after five years. Five years have now passed, so we would like to offer you a very special trade-in price for your old machine ..."

This might lead the customer to wonder how on earth you managed to remember what the questionnaire response was five years ago. The customer might also be slightly worried that information which he or she thought was used for market research has now been used to encourage replacement.

FAST TRACK

*A more subtle approach would be to use the data to target the customer in question, and make a trade-in offer, without actually reminding the customer about the data. The rule is that in the body of the letter, customer data should only be used where the recipient would expect you to have it. **This applies even if the customer gave you the information directly in the first place.***

The appeal

All direct mail packs appeal to the customer to respond in some way. There are various ways to make the appeal stronger – by appealing to logic – the rational appeal, to the emotions – eg guilt, humour, and so on. Whatever the basis of the appeal, it must involve your customer. It must talk personally to your customer, not impersonally. Where relevant, it should aim to solve your customer's problem.

Clarity and uniqueness

WATCH OUT!

It is easy for a copy-writer to get carried away with nice phrases which are bound to appeal to customers and fulsome praise of the product or service. However, the aim of your mail pack is to make an offer and get the customer to respond to it. Therefore, the offer should be clear at a glance. The proposition should be clear, precise and concise. One understandable, clear benefit should dominate along with a clear, memorable reason for buying.

Express the benefit of your offer uniquely. So many of the "magic words" of direct marketing have been used so often that they can no longer be relied upon to achieve the effect by themselves. These words include – **new, news, now, at last, announcing, introducing, for the first time, breakthrough, new kind of, first ever, how to, advice on, why, you, surprising, remarkable, save, improved, offer, bargain, opportunity, discount** and of course – **FREE!** The exclamation mark has also been overused!!!!!!!!!

One way to make maximum impact is for your communication to start with a unique benefit or offer, and say why it is important to the customer and why it is impossible to do without it. Of course, any claims to this effect should backed with examples and testimonials. Conviction should be built in by guarantees, testimonials, research figures, scientific or independent proof, sales figures, examples of experience of other people or other markets. Facts and figures should be specific.

The above notwithstanding, most direct marketers believe that all possible benefits should be mentioned in the copy. It gives the customer additional reasons to buy, even after the main benefit has been correctly emphasized. It also ensures that those not "captured" by the main benefit are captured by a subsidiary one. However good your targeting, you can't always be sure that every customer selected to receive the promotion will respond to the major benefit being promoted. Indeed, it is highly unlikely that they will all respond to your main benefits, as Figure 14.1 shows.

Fig 14.1

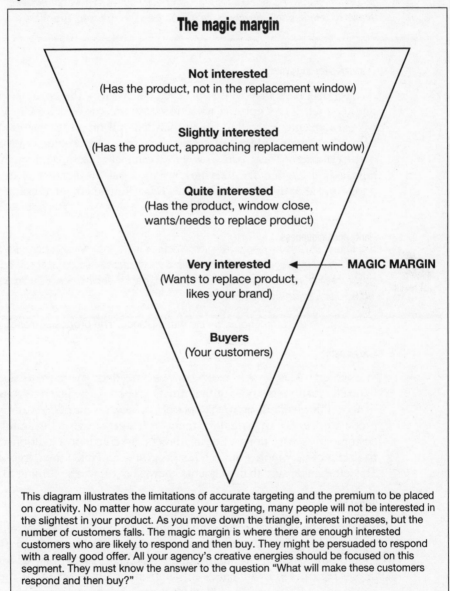

The magic margin

Not interested
(Has the product, not in the replacement window)

Slightly interested
(Has the product, approaching replacement window)

Quite interested
(Has the product, window close,
wants/needs to replace product)

Very interested ◄——— MAGIC MARGIN
(Wants to replace product,
likes your brand)

Buyers
(Your customers)

This diagram illustrates the limitations of accurate targeting and the premium to be placed on creativity. No matter how accurate your targeting, many people will not be interested in the slightest in your product. As you move down the triangle, interest increases, but the number of customers falls. The magic margin is where there are enough interested customers who are likely to respond and then buy. They might be persuaded to respond with a really good offer. All your agency's creative energies should be focused on this segment. They must know the answer to the question "What will make these customers respond and then buy?"

Honesty

Perhaps because a letter is printed and because it can be taken at its own pace, direct mail tends to be believed.

Transferability and synergy

A direct mail pack may consist of several elements – the envelope, the letter, a reply coupon, a brochure, a catalogue and so on. The pack itself may be part of a wider campaign, extending over published and broadcast media. It therefore helps if the creative idea used in the brochure can be extended over all elements of the campaign. This creative "synergy" can make a campaign much more powerful, as each element reminds the consumer of all the elements. Direct Line's red phone and Mercury Communications' Harry Enfield are good examples of this.

Copy length

The golden rule is – use as much copy as is needed. The more the letter is trying to qualify customers, the more information needs to be given to your customers to allow this qualification to take place. You don't want people to respond if the product or service isn't right for them. You'll get a high return rate and/or high customer dissatisfaction. A leading direct marketing consultant once wrote a 12 page letter to promote a speech he was giving, and filled the (large) auditorium. The letter made sure that recipients knew what they were coming to hear.

Copy style

Standard rules of good writing and technical layout should be followed. Sentences should be kept short. One paragraph should lead clearly on to the next. Long copy should be broken up by sub-headings. You can make copier easier and more interesting to read by indentations, handwriting, underlining, sub-headings and highlighting. All pictures should be captioned and the axes on all charts should be properly labelled. The copy should also flow logically. A test of logic can be run by

summarizing each paragraph as a sentence, and the letter as just one paragraph of connected sentences. If this works, then the letter has the right basis.

To make sure that the reader continues to read, use carrying phrases to continue the flow. These include: **but that isn't all, there is one more thing, now – here is the best part, here is all you have to do, more important than that, you'll also receive, so that is why, moreover**. Carrying tricks should also be used, such as questions at the paragraph end, pages ending halfway through a paragraph, or at a tantalizing point.

Your pictures or graphics should demonstrate the experiencing of benefits, or even better, make your customers feel they are already getting the benefits. They should be easy to absorb, without tricky effects. Show people, to engender interest. Of course, the pictures should reflect the copy and, if possible, tell a full and logical story.

Additional items

Apart from the brochure and order form that usually accompanies a letter, other items can be used to reinforce the message. These include testimonial facsimiles, gifts (eg pens, rulers), ways of showing the product in use, samples, and enduring information (eg "A quick guide to X", maps, calendars, telephone numbers).

managing a direct mail campaign

There are four main streams of work or processes which overlap:

1. Generating ideas for the format of the mailing (the offer and its creative expression), starting with the briefing of the agency or creative team.

2. Determining who should receive the mailing, and when (the targeting and timing), starting with the briefing of the list broker and/or the database manager.

3. Sending the letters via the mailing house and the Post Office. Preparation for this starts as soon as the general format, timing and volume of the mailing is determined.

4. Response handling and fulfilment – the completion of what you promised to your customers

However, because a direct mail campaign involves so many "pieces of paper", there are many campaign management points that need to be dealt with in detail.

LETTER STOCK

The weight and quality of paper must be determined. Weight is important because it affects the mailing cost (and also the quality). Lighter weights of paper tend to feel "flimsy" – an exception to this is that letters which arrive by air mail might be expected to be lighter. Also, the type of paper used (weight, kind of coating) affects what can be printed on it. However, today, the demands of the direct mail industry have stimulated a high degree of product innovation, and paper is available now to accomplish virtually any task. The only exception is that no-one has yet invented weightless high quality bond paper.

Any special paper requirements should be specified as soon as possible. These include any pre-printing, special sizes, gloss, embossing and the like. This is because these factors may affect the kind of machinery it can pass through at a later stage of processing. For example, embossing can cause problems with high speed laser printers. If continuous stationery is to be used for line printers, this should also be specified.

LETTER VOLUME

At the early stages of campaign development, it may not be clear exactly how many mail packs are going to be sent. This is because the systems and targeting side of the campaign run partly in parallel to the creative side. Thus, the target customer type may have been specified, but more work may be needed to establish how many of the target customer type are on your database. Or list development work may still be taking place, perhaps in consultation with list brokers or list vendors. So at an early stage, requirements may have to be specified in bands, eg between 30,000 and 40,000 packs. In some cases, there may be a target sales level. If you are very certain about expected response rates (perhaps because you have tested properly), then the mailing volume will be known. But if you are uncertain, a quick test may be necessary before roll-out volumes are finalized.

TESTING

In principle, direct marketing thrives on testing – in particular of target markets, offers and creative. These all affect the volume and character of a mailing. Provided you have planned your campaign properly, you should have time to order the print volumes required for the roll-out mailing.

STOCK LEVELS AND ORDERING

For the initial mailing and the fulfilment to take place smoothly, the sizes and locations of stocks of different elements of the mail pack should always be specified.

Different elements of the mail pack (eg the envelope, letter and brochure) may arrive from different suppliers at different times. Stocks for the initial mailing are likely to be held by a mailing house, stocks for fulfilment are likely to be held by the fulfilment house. The stocks required for the initial mailing depends upon the

volumes of outbound mailings required and the scheduling of the making-up of the mail pack. For fulfilment, the volumes of mailings required will depend upon the timing of the customer contacts which stimulate the response, eg television, radio or press advertising, a telemarketing campaign or an initial mailing. If high volumes are being moved very quickly, then the stock should all be ready before the start. But in some cases, a campaign could continue for up to a year, with response trickling in over the period. In such a case, a print volume optimizing calculation might be carried out. This involves working out what is the optimum batch size for printing and storage, taking into account print set-up costs, storage costs and finance costs. Also, response packs might be made up in small batches, particularly if there are many variations, because in this case the work might be manual.

Specify very clearly when suppliers are required to deliver, and to where, and when the stock will first be used. Also, as postal delivery schemes such as Mailsort give extended delivery times for lower prices, determine your campaign timing in the light of these opportunities, as long as they are consistent with meeting your marketing needs.

Print ordering should take into account the lead times of suppliers. Most direct marketing users operate with one or more printers with whom they have a continuing relationship. The user has an updated statement of supply lead times for different kinds of work. For really large and complex mailings requiring specialized printing and/or inserting machinery, the timing of the mailing itself may be determined by the availability of these machines, of which there might be only a few in the country.

LETTER COPY MANAGEMENT

A direct mail letter is very different in status from a brochure. A brochure – to the recipient – is usually very clearly advertising copy. But a letter is from a named individual, who can expect to receive many direct replies, ie through other than the suggested response route. These replies may be letters or telephone calls.

WATCH OUT!

The signatory of the letter therefore has a very strong interest in the copy, and may even insist on being allowed to draft part of it. Some direct marketing agencies do not like this, but it is unavoidable. Therefore, the input from the signatory should be obtained as soon as possible, and the signatory consulted at every stage of development of the letter. The same will apply to the head of any department mentioned in the letter – even if the mention is only in the letterhead.

All this means that you must be absolutely clear about who is writing, who is contributing to the letter and who will be the signatory. Finally, the type of letterhead to be used and the form in which the signature is to be supplied to the printer must also be specified (eg digitized).

PACK MANAGEMENT

FAST TRACK

The pack may consist of a number of elements. You must design them not just to relate to each other, but more simply, to fit together!

WATCH OUT!

You must avoid the situation where your mailing campaign reaches a late stage of development only for you to discover that your pack items do not fit into the chosen envelope.

This is why preparation of a pack dummy is needed as soon as decisions about pack contents have been taken. This also confirms that the pack will fit within the chosen weight band, to achieve target postal costs. Postal costs can account for up to 50% of the cost of a mailing, so it is obviously important to design the pack according to postal weight bands. If machine-enclosing is to be used, all folds and items need to be checked for this.

If your pack is complex, and particularly if it has a number of variations, every element of the pack should be coded. Each pack variation should also have a code. This not only makes print ordering and accounting easier, but also makes holding records easier. When performance statistics are reviewed, it can be extremely cumbersome to have to refer to every element and pack variation by name. Of course, every different response vehicle should be clearly coded, allowing response variations by pack type to be measured.

FAST TRACK

Pack management is a task in its own right, superimposed on managing the development and printing of the individual items. So clear responsibility for getting the pack right (in all its variations) must be allocated, and each variation is signed off appropriately. This includes any later variations which might be added.

Also, as the pack may involve many other people (eg mailing and fulfilment houses, sales staff, customer service staff), make sure that copies of the pack are available to these as early as possible. This avoids the obvious problems that can occur when someone involved in a campaign in any way does not have a copy of the pack to hand when their time to act comes. The worst example of this is where a customer calls in to a sales office to enquire about an offer contained in the pack and the person answering has not the faintest idea which pack the customer is referring to. Finally, to prevent confusion, have a clear procedure for disposing of old stock of the pack and its components.

ORDER FORMS

The order or response form is the most important part of the mailing. (The same applies to catalogues and other media, so what is said about these forms applies to all uses of order or response forms.)

In many cases, the form is detachable from the carrying medium. This applies even if it has to be cut out from a magazine – it may be left lying around until the customer decides to fill it in. So the form must be viewed as a medium in its own right. It must clearly state what the customer is asked to do, and what the customer will get in return for so doing. The reverse also applies – the medium carrying the form must make sense in the absence of the form. At the very least, the customer should be told how to obtain further copies of the form!

The form should be easy to complete, and easily understood when complete. Testing is always recommended – with the target type of consumer and not merely "someone in the office". Freepost is always a good idea for order forms. Faxed order forms are also becoming a popular form of ordering.

FAST TRACK

If you already know the customer's name and address and are using a direct medium to reach the customer (eg direct mail), print the customer's name and address on the form. This ensures that database cleaning takes place automatically if the customer's address is incorrect. It also saves the customer's time and ensures that there are no problems with legibility. If the customer has an account number, this should also be included on the form, as this reduces keying in time. You can also use personalized bar codes to ease order entry.

FAST TRACK

It is good practice to pay for your customer's reply. If the customer is ordering or is asking for more details, postage costs should be absorbable from the sale or expected sale.

ENVELOPES

In many cases, the envelope is just a standard size, weight and colour, with no overprinting. But because of increasing use of direct mail, companies strive to make their envelopes "stand out on the doormat or desk". Also, advanced printing and packing technologies permit the envelope to be an integral part of the mailing, in the form of a one piece mailing. At the other extreme is the simple transparent wrap with the mailing, allowing your customer to see at least some of the content of the mailing directly. This is used most frequently with directly mailed publications and catalogues.

However tempting it is to use all these modern variations, envelope choice should be made in the same way as with every element of the mailing, ie in accordance with the objectives of the mailing (and each piece within it) and the tone of the mailing. Thus, a charge card offer to high-flying businessmen would best be enclosed in a standard, high quality envelope, as with a piece of normal business correspondence. On the other hand, an offer of three free issues of a gardening magazine targeted at gardening enthusiasts should probably be overprinted with a strong message to this effect.

FAST TRACK

Unless the mailing is very low volume, the envelope should be machine-fillable and standard size, to minimize production and postal costs. Use of an address window depends on the kind of letter to be used. If it is to be personalized, a window is likely to be less off-putting than where the letter is addressed to "The Occupier". If a window is used, alignment of the address in the finished pack must be checked.

If a bulky promotional item is to be included, ensure that the mailing cannot be mistaken for, say, a dangerous object, and that the pack will be insertable into a normal letter box. The latter applies as much to business mailings, as many deliveries to smaller companies have to go through a letter box.

The envelope should normally have a return address, for undelivered mailings. For a high quality mailing, this should be printed in a conservative style and be given in a form which does not indicate that it is a mass mailing.

Choice of class of mailing depends on the tone to be established by the envelope, as a well-planned campaign should normally not need a hurried mailing. The kind of stamping used by discount mailing schemes such as Mailsort may be off-putting to the more knowledgeable consumer, but is unlikely to have an effect on most.

summary

Direct mail is a deceptively simple medium. In its simplest form – an envelope, letter and reply device – it looks as simple as writing a personal letter. However, it can be a very powerful message conveyer. To make it work, you need to follow the essential rules laid out in this chapter. You also need to comply with certain standards. So it's quite a technical business. For this reason, you need to plan your direct mail campaigns carefully, test them wherever possible, execute them with due control and precision, and evaluate them objectively when they are finished. This is not a job for the enthusiastic amateur. If you don't have the expertise in-house, don't hesitate to use an agency – there are plenty around, and they'll be only to happy to compete for your business.

We can't guarantee that if you follow all these guidelines that you'll have the best mailing campaign there ever was, but you will avoid the obvious errors made by so many of your predecessors! You'll also be ready to take on an even more complex area – telemarketing – the subject of our next chapter.

15

hitting through telemarketing

- Telemarketing is the fastest growing direct marketing medium, partly because information technology developments have made it so much easier.

- Telemarketing involves properly designed campaigns, usually working off your customer database and designed not just to get response but also to obtain more information as a basis for designing future campaigns.

- Don't confuse telemarketing with teleselling, which is mostly cold calling to an unqualified list.

- If you don't want the expense of setting up a telemarketing operation, you can use a bureau to do most of the work for you.

what is telemarketing?

> **"Telemarketing"** means using the telephone as a properly managed part of the marketing, sales and service mix. It differs from telephone selling, which is aimed at getting sales over the telephone. Teleselling is usually used as a stand-alone strategy rather than an integrated element of the marketing mix

In business to business marketing, telemarketing has been used for many years. In consumer marketing, teleselling is still common, but telemarketing is beginning to be adopted. At the other extreme from teleselling is full account management via the telephone, or "telemanagement". This is a more cost-effective way of managing customers than a field sales force.

Many businesses and consumers find teleselling a nuisance. Consumers have ready excuses to deal with poorly targeted calls. "*I've got one already*" or "*we had it done last year*" are the commonest. In business, such calls may be barred by secretaries, acting on their managers' instructions. Telemanagement is at the other extreme. The relationship with your customer is established, so your telemarketers won't be barred!

The difference between telemarketing and teleselling	
Telemarketing	*Telephone selling*
Controlled message	Individual communication
Uses structured scripts	Operator's own methods
Variety of objectives	Objective to sell product or service
All results collected and analyzed	Measurement haphazard – only sales
All parameters testable – list, offer, script, etc	Impossible to test elements
Possible to plan and integrate with all other media	Usually stand-alone, with some mail follow-up
Usually no commission paid	Commission paid, sometimes only commission

Telemarketing is a discipline in the fullest sense of the word. Highly trained staff use telecommunications equipment and networks to achieve your marketing objectives by carrying out a controlled dialogue with your customers, who need the benefits you provide. These staff are supported by systems which allow you to manage the workflow, measure it and follow through the outcome of the dialogue.

FAST TRACK

Telemarketing requires systematic management, measurement and control of every aspect of its operation. Without this, you could not know the relationship between the inputs and outputs of your telemarketing operation. This information is essential to achieve effectiveness. So, when you are considering the introduction of telemarketing, make sure that you are open to a re-evaluation of your entire process for managing your customers.

Telemarketing is growing quickly. Costs of contacting and managing customers by other means (eg the field sales force) are rising. More and more is being learnt about why and when customers are happy to do business over the telephone, and how to put this knowledge to work. Customers find the telephone a cost-effective way of learning about and buying your products and services.

STRENGTHS AND WEAKNESSES

Compared with other direct marketing media, telemarketing has the following strengths and weaknesses.

Strengths	Weaknesses
Immediacy: high impact, personal contact	**High unit cost per call:** but low cost per customer and per sale if well targeted
Two way medium: interactive, active qualification, information can be checked	**Risk of lack of commitment (verbal only):** needs good follow up
Flexible: variety of approaches, different scripts, answers, questions/objections	**Easily abused:** pressure sensitive, so requires careful control
Accurate and controllable: easy to target, result from each call, testable in low volumes	**Single dimension:** voice only, no pictures, no written commitment
Can optimize contact: selling or across ranges, setting up appointments, update list during call, market feedback	**Must be effectively integrated with other marketing strategies:** difficult to use in isolation

why customers may like telemarketing

Your customers find the telephone one of the best ways of conducting their relationship with you because:

- **It saves their time** – they do not have to handle the formality of a sales visit, or travel to see the product.
- **It allows them to feel they control the relationship** – they can tell you when it is convenient to call, and can call you when convenient to them. They can terminate the call when they want.
- **It gives them information when they need it** – they may find it frustrating to wait for information to come in the post or during a field sales visit. They can call you, and you can respond immediately or quite soon after.
- **It gives them a direct dialogue with your company** – this gives them confidence in the relationship.

TOLL FREE CALLING

An important element of telemarketing is the toll free number (800 in the US, 0800 in the UK). This allows you rather than your customer to pay for the call. Perhaps more importantly, it ensures that you are properly organized to take the call. In the UK, the 0800 service was launched in 1985, followed by the 0345 service, in which the consumer pays only for a local call.

Many prefer to use in-house telemarketing facilities rather than agencies. This is because a "live" call with customers shows that the caller is a true representative of your company, often with access to your information systems, and is able to check customer status, inventory position etc. Agencies have responded to this by offering "in-house" teams – effectively facility-managed telemarketing. Meanwhile, agencies are very popular for response handling (eg receiving calls asking for further specific information or a brochure) and market research.

FACSIMILE MARKETING

This is growing in popularity, although figures are difficult to obtain, because much of it is done in-house. It is often done in the evenings, at off-peak call rates.

key concepts in telemarketing

THE DIALOGUE PRINCIPLE

Telemarketing is best employed as an aspect of database marketing. A key principle of database marketing is the need for you to be in constant dialogue with your customers. This ensures that your customers' needs are being met and that the information on your database is kept fresh. In a dialogue, information flows both ways. Your telemarketer becomes committed to a dialogue with customers. This dialogue lasts as long as the customer remains your customer. It will consist of a series of "conversations", conducted over the telephone. Letters, brochures and other material confirm or add to what is said. A sales visit or visit to a showroom takes place where necessary.

FAST TRACK

The objective of telemarketing is to achieve a managed dialogue, consisting of a progressive series of conversations focused on your customers' needs. Each conversation is targeted to achieve specific sales cycle objectives – gathering information, presenting options and so on. Build this idea into your communications and sales planning, and develop measures of success which monitor the progressive deepening of the relationship with your telemanaged customers.

Conversations should have specific objectives in terms of conveying information and/or moving your customer forward one or more stages in the buying cycle. Some calls should be outbound, reflecting proactive management of the dialogue, but inbound calling is a key part of relationship-building. It is the way many customers want to access you.

IN THE REAL WORLD

To maintain the cost-effectiveness of the approach, calls should not be made at the convenience of the telemarketer. They are either scheduled to your customer's convenience, or programmed by support staff or systems, to maximize the effectiveness of the day's workflow.

THE NEED TO PLAN

Telemarketing requires detailed planning. Whether or not a precise script is used, each call must be under control and planned. Telemarketing differs from telephone selling in that every call is measured and the results analyzed. This enables the different elements of telemarketing to be measured and tested in the same way as with direct mail – the list, the script, the offer, the timing and so on. Telemarketing also needs to be tested in competition with other media, and also with different combinations of media in the contact strategy.

WATCH OUT!

The management of a telemarketing campaign must be very precise, including careful control of costs (eg operator time, list selection), through budgeting and planning of campaigns. Quality must be monitored particularly carefully. It is easy to target a telemarketing campaign to produce a specific number of appointments for the sales force, only to discover that the quality of appointments is very low.

Telemarketing must therefore be measured as part of the overall contact strategy, which is designed to yield more sales and profit, not just appointments. The customer database must therefore be set up to allow tracking of the effectiveness of every contact medium from beginning to end of the sales cycle.

functions performed

Telemarketing can perform any of these functions:

- Call reception.
- Enquiry handling.
- Enquiry qualification.
- Customer (market) research.
- Product research.
- List cleaning/enhancement.
- Complaint handling.
- Information dissemination.

- Order taking.
- Cross/up-selling.
- Lead generation.
- Servicing marginal accounts.
- Progress chasing.
- Account management/development.
- After-sales customer care.

telemarketing objectives

Telemarketing helps achieve many objectives. They include:

- **Call handling**: Answering customer calls on any matter, whether enquiries about products, requests for service, handling complaints or problems.
- **Moving towards a sale**: Lead generation, appointment creation, order taking, seeking or closing, selling up or cross-selling, converting non sales-related inbound or outbound calls into sales opportunities.
- **Cold calling**: Normally as part of a campaign or following up a mail-shot.
- **Building loyalty**: By meeting needs and by just listening and remaining in contact; by following up a mail-shot; by asking customers what they thought of X product, brochure etc.
- **Enquiry screening**: Obtaining information to confirm whether a customer is a prospect for a product, or how serious a particular problem is.
- **Customer and market research**: Gathering information to use in making business decisions. This includes screening of lists of customers or prospects to be used in particular marketing campaigns.

WATCH OUT!

If a market research agency is conducting this type of work they are unlikely to give you addresses as this is against the code of practice for market researchers. Many companies have found their customers only too willing to give information, provided the customer believes it is relevant to the relationship. So build a questionnaire into your script and hold the responses on your database.

- **Delivering customized advice**: By anticipating what your customers need to know, and briefing your telemarketers so that they can help.
- **Account management**: Improving the quality of account management, so certain groups of customers benefit from a better relationship with you. This may include finding new purchasers within existing accounts, preventing competitive inroads into customers, and reactivating lapsed customers.
- **New business**: Identifying and developing new customers and new markets, extending coverage of existing markets, or launching a new product or service.
- **Quality**: Improving the effectiveness, professionalism and economics of the sales force and other channels.

- **Customer care**: Improving customer service and satisfaction. Many customer care departments are using the telephone to speed up the complaint answering procedure. Stena Sealink has been using this method to great effect.

DON'T FORGET!

○ *Have you trained your telemarketing team sufficiently to close a sale?*

○ *Is it confident enough to cold call?*

○ *Will the cold call create strong lists to hold on your database?*

○ *Are you building loyalty with the most valuable clients or just the easiest to handle on the telephone?*

○ *Does the market research agency you are using have a direct marketing/telemarketing arm which will pass the contacts to you – provided they are collected under data protection rather than Market Research Society rules?*

○ *Is your telemarketing team up-to-date with all the products in your portfolio and will it be skilled enough to spot a cross-selling opportunity?*

○ *Will it identify new business opportunities?*

○ *Is your customer care/relations department using telemarketing yet? If not, is there a valid reason why not which you may not have considered?*

call handling centres

Use of telemarketing for inbound call handling is subject to none of the accusations often raised against telemarketing in its teleselling form. In this use, one or more telephone numbers are promoted as the best way to get information from the company (typically a large one). Two of the most publicized centres are General Electric's Answer Centre in the US and BT's Centre in Bristol (used for its own products and services and also for third party telemarketing). Such centres are often used by catalogue marketers, to handle incoming orders and enquiries. These centres are usually highly automated, with on-screen scripting, often on-line access to inventory systems to check availability and the ability to key in orders or book service calls on the spot. Such centres can be particularly effective for handling telephone responses to mass mailings or broadcast and published media campaigns. In the UK, many share offerings for privatized companies were handled in this way.

the technology of telemarketing

The progress of telemarketing has been facilitated by the development of telecommunications and computing technology. The systems and equipment used in telemarketing are of two main kinds: telecommunications-based and computer-based. The exact computer and telecommunication requirements will depend on the type of business and the nature of the company's existing systems that need to be linked to the telemarketing operation.

TELEPHONY

The telephony requirements are usually provided via an automatic call distributor (ACD) or through computer integrated telephony which can fully emulate all the features of ACD.

> An **ACD** is an independent unit which allows calls to be distributed between call receivers on a variety of programmed bases. It also allows the telemarketing manager to monitor each telemarketer's inbound and outbound telephone usage (since it provides call handling statistics).

ACD statistics help in monitoring telemarketers against their targets. ACD systems enable the telemarketing manager to listen to and record any conversation at any time. The telemarketers can also record their own conversations. They can then use these recordings to improve their technique.

The ACD directs calls automatically, for example:

● To distribute workloads evenly.
● To give valued customers preferential treatment.
● Directing particular calls to telemarketers with special expertise.
● Promoting personal relationships with customers.

All this requires either issuing different telephone numbers for different needs, or true digital telephone networks. The latter allow ACDs to identify the number of the inbound caller, so that the call can be routed to that customer's account manager, whose screen would then automatically display the customer's details. This is through a feature called "calling line identification". If several telephone numbers are used for the centre (eg for different products or different marketing campaigns), the "dialled number identification service" allows the ACD to determine which number was dialled and thence allocate the call to the relevant telemarketer(s).

Where a high volume of outbound calling is required, the "automatic dialling" feature can be used. This operates by automatically dialling the next customer number as soon as a telemarketer has finished the previous call. An advanced version of this is "predictive dialling". This dials many more calls than the telemarketer can handle, predicting that only some of them will be answered. Obviously, this makes sense in consumer marketing and not in business to business marketing. Only calls that are answered are distributed to telemarketers.

LINES

A telemarketing operation needs enough inbound capacity too. Here, you need to decide whether lines should be toll free. There is a strong argument for toll free, if you can afford it. A strong customer-oriented message is emitted if you allow the caller to call you at your expense. It also acts as a strong incentive for you to make the best use of the call (and of the customer's time waiting to be answered or being answered).

The number of inbound lines must be kept under review. Customer research and ACD traffic statistics indicate whether customers feel they have to wait often for a free line, and if so, how long for.

WATCH OUT!

COMPUTER-BASED SYSTEMS

There are a number of standard and "tailorable" computer systems that can be used to support a telemarketing operation.

The benefits of computer-based systems

- Provision of on-line scripts or call guides so that telemarketers are steered to cover all the required points in a structured way.
- Storing information about customers and dialogues with them. This takes place as the telemarketers are talking with customers and is especially effective if call guides are being used. The information can then be used either within the conversation, to trigger decisions about next steps in the sales cycle, or in a future conversation, to enable the telemarketer to "remember" customer details.
- A diarying tool for customer callbacks within a sales cycle.
- To prompt fulfilment, either by providing a feed to an automatic literature fulfilment process, or even directly to a product distribution system, which in turn can be attached to a stock control system.

RELATIONSHIP WITH THE MAIN DATABASE

Telemarketing works best when based on a comprehensive customer database. This should be borne in mind when choosing the system to support your operation. Some users of telemarketing support it via a central database, on which they hold their entire customer information set, thus integrating the approach to the market. They use this database to feed information to telemarketing systems, which in turn feed new information back to the central corporate database (see Figure 15.1).

Fig 15.1

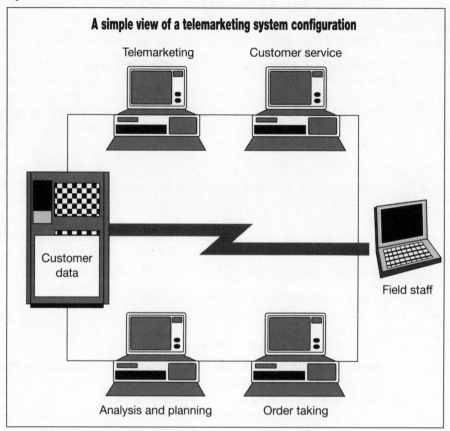

A simple view of a telemarketing system configuration

Telemarketing

Customer service

Customer
data

Field staff

Analysis and planning

Order taking

TELEMARKETING PACKAGES

These packages are sold under the generic title of *"Telemarketing Systems"* and run on anything from a personal computer to a mainframe. Some only perform telemarketing functions. Others offer a whole range of extra functions such as territory planning, direct mail and sales accounting. Almost all have some form of database management facility linking the different functions.

The four main areas covered by most computerized telemarketing systems are:

● Information management.
● Call management.
● Fulfilment.
● Performance analysis.

Information management

Current information about each customer, such as name, address, telephone number, is held on the system's database along with details of all previous contacts (eg name of operator, which literature was sent, quotations sent, purchases made) together with information gathered during the needs analysis carried out by the telemarketers. Each telemarketer can access records from their own list of designated customers by name or telephone number. Lists can also be put together using a variety of marketing criteria such as time of last contact, location or interest shown in a particular product.

Call management

The telemarketing system manages calls by the use of lists, such as an initial campaign list. Once the first call to each customer is made the system's diary facility takes over. This facility allows your telemarketers to set their own call back time, as well as providing an automatic scheduling facility for calls which are initially engaged or do not answer.

On most systems, calls are managed via interactive call guides. These start with a needs analysis to ensure that the required information is gathered from each customer in a structured and consistent manner. The facility to use call guides, scripts or prompts is offered on most telemarketing systems.

Telemarketers' screens prompt them what to say to customers. The system can be programmed with (if necessary) complex logic so that the telemarketer is steered to the relevant part of the guide depending on what the customer has said in reply. This process is called decision tree prompting. Telemarketers key in these replies from the customer directly onto the screen and a record is therefore kept for later use, either during that call, or in subsequent calls. Telemarketers also have access to other call guides, including those which are product-specific or for objection handling. They should be able to access any information on the system (customer information on the database, information from previous calls, information from this call).

FAST TRACK

The level of flexibility for call guide construction, length, decision tree branching and cross-referencing varies between systems. The more expensive systems offer more choice. Take the costs and benefits of greater flexibility into account in your purchasing decision.

Fulfilment

Personalized letters can be generated by some systems, either for local fulfilment or via a mailing house. Data for fulfilment can transmitted either over an electronic link or via a magnetic tape, directly to the fulfilment house so that they can send personalized letters and specific literature pieces directly to the customer.

Performance analysis

Telemarketing systems usually offer a large variety of reports which measure most aspects of performance and productivity. This ensures that telemarketing managers have the correct information at the right time to enable them to lead, motivate, train, coach, organize and plan the telemarketing team.

PERSONAL COMPUTER USAGE

As well as using the PCs as possible terminal emulators (linked to the telemarketing system), there are a number of applications which can be used in your operation:

● Processing pro-forma and customized letters to customers.
● Running spreadsheet analyses on past (and predicted) performance.
● Communicating with other parts of the organization via telex or electronic mail.
● Preparing standard (or tailored) quotations and contracts.
● General word processing applications.

productivity ratios

In telemarketing, the old management sayings *"You get what you inspect, not what you expect"* and *"If you can't measure it, you can't manage it"* apply with a vengeance. Telemarketing works with a number of targets and ratios. Here are some of the main ones for outbound telemarketing.

Dials

If telemarketers are not trying to speak to customers often enough, every hour, every day, every week and every month, few of the purposes of telemarketing can be achieved. So each telemarketer **must** be set a target number of dials per day.

Decision-maker contacts (DMCs)

A DMC is defined as making contact with the person who can make the decision to buy (not his or her secretary, spouse etc). A target is required for DMCs per period and the ratio between dials and DMCs. Achieving the target ratio of DMCs per day (or week) is important for two main reasons:

● It ensures that resources are geared correctly and effectively towards the level of customer coverage that is demanded by the telemarketers' role.
● Measuring the number of *decision-makers* contacted ensures that your telemarketers are getting through to the right person in the family or customer organization.

The level of these targets depends on target decision-makers' habits and telemarketers' skills. If the results fall below an acceptable level (less than one in five may make the job frustrating and selling rather expensive), the reasons for this must be established. These could include:

● **Market factors** – competitors having tied up the market, products not right, previous problems in relationships with the company. These are beyond the telemarketer's control and should have been investigated earlier.

WATCH OUT!
The telemarketer should not be the victim of poor marketing planning.

- **Telemarketer's attitude** – if there is a high level of "busy" tone or "not available" dial results for a particular telemarketer, there may be an attitude problem. If so, the telemarketer may be backing down at the customer's switchboard. Fear can lead a telemarketer to fake dial records. This can be checked by comparing the telemarketer's own notes to ACD records.

Decisions and contracts sent

Measuring the ratio of:

- DMCs to customer decisions (end of the sales cycle, for good or ill).
- DMCs to number of confirmed purchases

gives the information needed to drive:

- *Up* the number of calls that are active sales presentations or closes.
- *Down* the number of follow-up calls per sales cycle.

These measures show where telemarketers need coaching to close sales.

WATCH OUT!

New or tired telemarketers fear rejection. This leads them to avoid pushing customers to make a decision one way or the other. This makes each sale more expensive and can irritate customers – if a telemarketer won't take "No" for an answer.

Orders returned

To ensure customers are not being pushed into decisions on the phone, so that unwanted orders are sent out followed by unproductive chasing calls, you should measure the difference between orders and returns. This indicates the quality of the sale.

Detailed ratios

Various, more detailed ratios can be used to fine tune telemarketing, eg:

- Sales revenue per order.
- Sales revenue per customer.
- DMCs vs brochures/literature sent.
- Brochures/literature sent vs revenue received.
- Revenue per DMC.
- Number of orders per DMC.
- Product demonstrations per DMC.
- Revenue per product demonstration.

Many others can be used. Which ones are right depends upon the type of product sold and the type of customer. Your statistics should be measured for each telemarketer over longer and shorter time periods, to facilitate skills development and encourage personal endeavour.

ADDITIONAL TARGETS AND RATIOS FOR INBOUND TELEMARKETING

Many of the above ratios also apply to inbound telemarketing, except that DMCs as a target in their own right do not apply (the caller is presumed to be interested). Therefore all other ratios are per caller rather than per DMC. Other ratios include:

● Time to answer.
● Number of calls answered.
● Time taken to deal with each call satisfactorily.

The importance of a good call queuing system cannot be over-emphasized. This indicates to the telemarketing manager how many calls are on hold and tells the customer that the call will be answered shortly.

OTHER IMPORTANT MEASURES FOR INBOUND AND OUTBOUND TELEMARKETING

Two other main areas need specific attention.

Absolute performance, eg total sales

It is this, compared to the cost of the telemarketing operation, that determines its viability. It is also likely to be the basis for performance comparisons and their derivative – sales competitions.

Quality of customer dialogue

This is as important as absolute performance. However, it is more difficult to measure because it is qualitative. To measure this quality, your telemarketing manager must listen regularly to calls.

FAST TRACK

This is measured by listening to live calls, or by using a tape recorder so that the calls can be listened to later. In both cases your telemarketers should be informed at all times of exactly what is going on, and the reasons why it is going on. They should also be given clear quality criteria and shown how to improve quality. They should be encouraged to listen on their own to their tapes, particularly after a very difficult or successful call, to understand and learn from what happened. Note that laws on telephone privacy and equipment failures are two sources of problems for this approach.

FEEDBACK

To help improve the skills of your staff, and to motivate them, your sales management process should include:

● Setting performance targets (quantitative and qualitative).
● Measuring performance against these targets.
● Feeding back the results positively to that member of staff.

setting targets

Setting realistic targets can help ensure that your telemarketers meet their overall objectives. This allows achievement and relative progress to be measured. It also allows your telemarketers to see this progress and to be motivated accordingly. Quality must also be targeted. High quantitative targets may cause the quality of calls to drop. So targets should be based on experience. If you have just started using telemarketing, you should obtain advice about what performance levels are reasonable and have been achieved in similar industries using telemarketing for similar purposes.

Typical telemarketing target areas

- Number of dials.
- Number of DMCs.
- Number of hours at the workstation.
- Number of sales made (or other absolute measurement).
- Volume and value of sales made.
- Product mix sold.

IN THE REAL WORLD

Normal target setting rules apply. Targets should:

1. Be realistic.
2. Be reviewed regularly.
3. Reflect the company's strategic direction.

They should also be adjusted as telemarketing experience grows – ie increased. The learning curve is steep. Initial productivity is often low, as telemarketers and customers are learning. As customers get used to the approach, as your telemarketers gain more experience and as the relationship between the two deepens, productivity should rise steeply. A key productivity measurement is the "telemarketing phone hour", the number of hours telemarketers spend at their workstations dealing with customers over the telephone in any one day. The phone hour is not just how long the telemarketer spends actually talking on the phone. It includes time spent preparing for a call and time spent immediately after the call on matters related specifically to that call. It does not include lunch time, tea time, any breaks, meetings, training etc.

Factors affecting achievement

- Complexity of product/service being sold.
- Value of product/service being sold.
- Stage of evolution of telemarketing in your company.
- Level of awareness the customer has of your company and/or the product or service.

Variations in the above areas lead to different call structures – call guides are different and calls will last different lengths. These need to be built into each telemarketer's objectives. Their productivity is then tracked throughout each campaign and compared with their objectives for control and bonus purposes.

call guides

> The "**call guide**" in telemarketing is the equivalent of the copy in direct mail. It can be written in a completely scripted form, giving the telemarketer no choice of form of words, or it can be written as a series of prompts to explore topics.

In all cases, a prior stage to writing the call guide is setting out the "decision tree" or logic of the conversation. This states the sequence that the conversation is intended to take and also any branching that depends upon the answers given by your customer. Just as different forms of copy are tested in direct mail, so different decision trees and call guides can be tested. Call guides can be presented on paper, or they can be programmed into a computerized system. Most computerized telemarketing systems allow programming of customized call guides. The call guide allows telemarketers to navigate their way through the call. It gives prompts and support at every stage. This includes prompting on product benefits and prices. It also provides possible answers to tricky objections.

Benefits of the call guide for the manager

- Provides the telemarketer with a structured dialogue, ensuring that all possible points are covered.
- Eases the training process, as telemarketers use call guides to help them sell new products.
- Gives telemarketers confidence and professionalism quickly, so increasing the productivity of telemarketing.
- Permits standardization and adherence to specific marketing approaches without loss of techniques or skills. This in turn allows true testing with complete validity of results.

Benefits of the call guide for the telemarketer

- A chance to listen attentively to the customer without worrying about what to say next.
- Clear signs to the telemarketer of their exact position within a call, regardless of the number of seemingly similar calls made before that particular one. This applies even when a customer takes a different tack during a call. A telemarketer can be "side-tracked" by the customer (to mutual benefit) without losing the thread. This ensures the objective of the call is met.
- The opportunity to close more business as a result of a more thorough sales approach.

- The availability of detailed product information allowing them to answer many of the customer's questions there and then.
- The ability to enter answers to relevant questions speedily via the same screen as the call guide and store those answers automatically on the database for future use.

The most advanced computerized systems incorporate expertise, so your system can analyze the results of past conversations and learn from them which modules and links work best, ie what is the best path through a conversation for customers of particular kinds who give particular responses. However, whatever the sophistication of your approach to call guides, each call guide set should allow your telemarketers to:

- Identify and reach the decision maker.
- Accept detours the customer wants.
- Determine the decision-maker's needs and identify opportunities.
- Offer solutions.
- Handle questions and objections effectively.
- Keep the door open at the end of the call.

What to include in call guides

- The products on offer, their features advantages and benefits.
- Likely customer needs and how to identify them.
- How the products solve customers' problems and which solution is most appropriate to which problem.
- Likely competitive products and companies that will be encountered, and good arguments against them.

promoting the telephone number

With inbound telemarketing, you must ensure your customers know what number they are supposed to call. Most large companies can be contacted by any one of several numbers. But if your telemarketing operation is to work properly, the right number must be promoted. In a campaign where the first medium used is press or direct mail, this should raise no problem. The number can be strongly promoted – often on or near a mail coupon, where your customer will usually look for details of how to respond. With radio or television, the situation is slightly different.

WATCH OUT!

In television advertising, the telephone number is all too often added as a quick afterthought to a campaign which is not designed primarily to generate a direct response. In such cases, the response is usually very low. The advertisement does not lead up to the telephone number, thus maximizing its impact. It is very visibly an afterthought and attracts little attention.

Here are a few rules for the use of telephone numbers in television advertising:

- The number should be clearly visible on the screen for at least five or six seconds.
- The number must be spoken too, as part of the call to action. Since television advertisements are mostly watched in the evening, it is vital for the number to be available when the advertisement is shown and probably 24 hours. The call to action must stress "now" and "24 hours".
- The number must be highly visible. It must be at least one inch high and with a strong enough background colour to make it stand out (important if it is shown against anything other than a simple background).
- If the call is toll-free, the advertisement should emphasize this.
- The commercial should explain what will happen when the respondent calls (eg receive more information, enter a prize draw).

Of course, it goes without saying that the number should be a memorable one. With a toll free number, most consumers remember the toll free component (0800), so they only have to remember a six-figure number.

With radio, it can be even more difficult to ensure that the number is heard and then remembered. Many people have a stronger visual memory than an aural memory. The key here is repetition and grouping of numbers in a memorable way. For example 0171-213-1415 could be promoted as 017-12-13-14-15, even though this does not correspond to the exchange code grouping.

automated response and premium rate use

You can now make revenue directly from the telephone. By using a premium rate number, you can ask consumers to call in and receive a promotional message. The call is charged at a much higher rate than the normal rate and the advertiser receives a share of the call revenue. You should only use this where research shows that it will not prejudice your relationship with the customer. Many companies now have a block on their employees using these premium rate numbers, because of use of work telephones to call these numbers (often promoting dubious services!).

the Telephone Preference Service

This is the equivalent of the Mailing Preference Service. Sponsored by the Direct Marketing Association, it is a "do not telephone" file of people who have requested no telephone contact without prior consent. This service will eventually improve the image of outbound telemarketing, as unrestricted teleselling becomes harder.

summary

There is no doubt that telemarketing is one of the most powerful media you can use. With the costs of telephone time and systems and equipment in decline and database software so much better, you can now confidently plan to "telemanage your customers".

As we emphasized at the beginning of this chapter, powerful though telemarketing is, it can't convey every message. Telemarketing works best in combination with other media. We've already looked at direct mail. Now let's look at other media.

16

what else can you hit the customer with?

- The range of media you can use to contact customers is still growing, with new electronic media such as compact disks and the Internet just the latest examples.

- Your most successful campaigns will combine different media, using each medium to deliver those elements of the message to which they are most suited and for which they are most cost-effective.

it's not just mail or telephone!

You can use many other media in your direct marketing, such as:

- Broadcast and other electronic media, eg television – including teletext and viewdata, in all its distribution modes – land and satellite broadcast and cable, radio, facsimile.
- Publications – newspapers, magazines, journals, owned media such as newsletters you issue yourself, or issued by other companies but open to your use, eg newsletters for credit card holders or airline customers.
- Distributed media, eg door-to-door leaflets, catalogues, free newspapers.
- Display media – exhibitions, posters.
- The personal media – sales offices and sales forces.

You can combine these media too. At an exhibition, posters will be on display and your sales staff will be in attendance. These media can also be combined into a sequence of contacts (the **contact strategy**) in an **integrated media** campaign (see Chapter 22).

targetability – the disappearing difference

The key difference between mail and telephone, and most of the above media was that the former could be individually addressed and the latter not. Today, the difference is one of degree, not of kind.

FAST TRACK

Many of these media can be personally addressed or distributed so that they are restricted to particular types of customers. A catalogue can be sent to named customers, distributed house-to-house to areas of known average characteristics, as well as being given to anyone who wishes to take one. A magazine may have a subscription list of people with known characteristics (because of the details included on the subscription application), but it may also be available through retailers. Even broadcast media now have available private subscription groups (closed user groups), whether for videotext or cable and satellite TV. Exhibition attendees can be invited individually and their attendance logged on your database, so you can see how effective the exhibition has been in generating sales. So don't lose any opportunity to target individuals and record results on your database.

Most media – often working in conjunction with independent commercial agencies – have developed audience or readership measurement systems, enabling marketers to get a much more precise measurement of the audience they are reaching. This tendency has in some countries (including the UK) been reinforced by the rising cost of media advertising.

Many companies now regularly compare the pulling power of all media. This does not imply that the different media are always in competition. The best direct marketing campaigns usually combine different media. Each medium is asked to do a specific job. In some cases, the campaign is sequenced by media – with the first contact being by, say, published media, followed up by direct mail or telemarketing. In other cases, different media will be used to generate the first response. This is because different kinds of consumer respond better to different kinds of media. Some are more mail-responsive, others telephone-responsive and yet others are media-responsive.

**IN THE
REAL WORLD**

Irrespective of addressability and audience measurement, many companies have experimented with adding a response element to their existing advertising. Some of the issues involved in telephone response have already been discussed. Executed properly, a direct response element can dramatically increase the effectiveness of media advertising, and also help companies at the early stage of database building.

press

The volume and type of use of direct response varies greatly by type of published medium. The more targeted the circulation, the higher the proportion of advertising which aims for a direct response. Thus, magazines aimed at investors, managers of small companies, or companies in particular industries tend to have a higher proportion of direct response advertising than magazines aimed at enthusiasts of a particular sport or holiday magazines. In the latter case, the audience is less targeted, but also the products and services concerned are more likely to be available through retail outlets. In the former case, the aim is often to generate leads for a sales office.

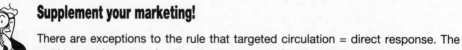

Supplement your marketing!

EXAMPLE

There are exceptions to the rule that targeted circulation = direct response. The weekly supplements of national newspapers (Sunday or weekday) have proved very successful in attracting direct response advertising and this advertising has proved effective. This is because in many ways these supplements are similar to magazines like the Readers' Digest. They are kept longer and referred to more often by more people. Well over half the advertising in some of these magazines carries coupons. Use of these media by direct marketers has made a great contribution to their financial success. This in turn has caused more and more publishers to enter this and related markets (eg women's magazines), contributing to media proliferation and audience fragmentation. ○

inserts

The biggest users of nationally distributed inserts are the specialist mail order companies (general merchandise, fashion, publishers), photographic laboratories, credit card companies and financial services companies (particularly insurance). Inserts combine many of the advantages of direct mail pieces with the advantages of press advertizing. This is an example of what is called **through the line** advertising.

FAST TRACK

The use of inserts is increasing quickly, *facilitated by more and more publishing companies including the insertion machinery required on high speed production runs. This machinery allows different combinations of inserts to be inserted. Use this facility to test different creative propositions. Also, where regional or local editions of a publication are produced, or production batches are allocated to different areas, inserting can be varied by region and area, even down to individual distribution depots or publication wholesalers. Less sophisticated insertion machinery can be used to insert leaflets in every copy of particular editions, eg for local papers. As a last resort, manual insertion can be used. So don't ignore inserts in your media mix, particularly for media with highly targeted circulations.*

IN THE REAL WORLD

Inserts can often be the only way of running a regional campaign with short lead times, as press lead times can be long.

You can also distribute coupon books. Known as free-standing inserts, these are already widely used by retail stores, banks, charities and consumer goods manufacturers. A free-standing insert takes its name from the idea that it is almost a publication in its own right, with coupons and possibly promotional articles from many suppliers grouped into one binding. This reduces the "confetti" problem so often experienced when the reader picks up the paper or magazine – leaflets fall out like confetti. An alternative approach here is to group inserts into envelopes, which can be produced by normal direct mail processes.

So, your ability to deliver leaflets to potential customers via inserts has increased rapidly in recent years. Although inserts are less targetable than direct mail, their delivery cost is a fraction of the cost of postal delivery. As testing raises no technical problems, you can easily find out which distribution mode is most cost-effective. If you need to increase your reach (the total number of individuals you talk to by any media), insertion in targeted media can be more cost-effective than renting lists and using direct mail.

THE ADVANTAGES OF INSERTS

- You can use different sizes and formats – different paper sizes and weights, ways of folding etc.
- Respondents can reply easily, eg tearing out coupon. Inserts can be perforated, but display advertisements can't.

- You can test copy and product variations easily and more cheaply than the cost of a split run advertisement.
- You get more space than with display advertising.
- You can advertise in media which traditionally do not advertise or greatly restrict the amount of advertising.
- Inserts are tactile. Even if they fall on the floor, they usually have to be picked up (except in the shop) – hence the saying, "*An ad in the hand is worth two in the mag*".

TIP-ONS

Inserts can be of three kinds, loose, bound-in or gummed on.

> **"Tip-ons"** are cards which are gummed onto the magazine advertisement to which they relate. They often consist of an entire coupon, in the form of a post-card. Because they are made of card, they allow the customer to respond without using an envelope.

They also stand out from the page, making it more likely that they will attract your customer's attention. However, tip-ons cost much more than a conventional leaflet or display advertisement, so their use should be carefully tested if possible. It is usually advisable to test the straight insert or display advertisement first, so that the tip-on can be tested for addition to volume or quality of response. Tip-ons can also be used to deliver small folded leaflets to customers. Some tip-ons are not response vehicles, but enduring information (eg useful telephone numbers, store location maps).

Even if the tip-on is the coupon, always include response methods on the advertisement itself, in case the tip-on is detached.

FAST TRACK

leaflet distribution and free newspapers

In many ways closely related to inserts, leaflet distribution has also increased greatly in targetability and cost-effectiveness in recent years. Leaflet distribution companies have worked closely with major providers of geographic data on social, economic and marketing characteristics of consumers to provide packages which allow you to target leaflets down to individual post-code areas or even smaller areas.

The rise of leaflet distribution has been closely associated with the rise of free local newspapers. In fact, leaflets which were once distributed separately are now often distributed as inserts in free newspapers. The existence of a local free newspaper distribution system has created a whole new approach to selective distribution of leaflets.

THE MAIN BENEFITS OF FREE NEWSPAPER DISTRIBUTION

- **Coverage and penetration.** Most households receive a free newspaper, and some several. In fact, free newspapers risk being a victim of their own success, in that overlapping coverage can be a problem, with some households receiving three or four newspapers a week.
- **Flexibility.** They are delivered weekly, so that the timing of distribution can be more or less exactly matched to client needs.
- **Targeting.** In addition to offering distribution according to post-code areas, some offer distribution by housing type. Because local areas are known well by the distributors, the right kind of housing can be selected.
- **Reliability.** Circulation is controlled and accounted for locally. Monitoring is carried out independently and therefore trusted by advertisers.
- **Credibility.** Free local newspapers are viewed by consumers as a highly credible source of information and leaflets included in them benefit from this status.
- **Service.** Because leaflets provide an important element of a free newspaper's income, the client service is good.
- **Cost-effectiveness.** Leafleting by free newspapers is cheap.

Of course, not all leaflet distribution is direct response. Much of it is used by retailers to stimulate visits to their local stores. They frequently include coupons and special offers.

coupons

Your coupons may not be redeemed against your product (malredemption). This is usually caused by poor targeting – too many people receiving the coupon who don't buy your product. Still, most coupon users view them as an essential part of their communications mix.

WATCH OUT!

Coupons have benefited considerably from the use of direct marketing and direct distribution techniques, which enable you to get coupons to exactly those customers who will use them properly, eg take up an invitation to try your product, or get a reward for loyalty or multiple purchasing. The combination of coupons into free standing inserts may reduce the accuracy of targeting, but makes an immense difference to the cost of coupon delivery.

Today, some coupons have personalized bar codes, so that it is clear precisely which consumer has redeemed them. This information is then used as the basis for targeting future promotions. If your product is sold through third party retailers, send your coupons direct to your customers, bar-code them and have them scanned when they are presented back to you by the retailers, to check who's taking them up.

FAST TRACK

designing press or magazine response advertising

Most of the rules of good copy writing apply to display advertising. However, there are some important differences.

The first aim of a direct response is to get the reader to stop and read before turning the page. If you don't make sure that your advertisement does this, your response rate is likely to be very low.

Your advertisement is doing the same job as a direct mail envelope or the first words of a telemarketing call. For this reason, arresting graphics or pictures, or extremely large and bold headings are often used. These may include challenging statements of the kind you would never include in a direct mail letter.

Your advertisement aims to get readers to respond, so your whole advertisement should lead to the response device. If a coupon is included, your copy should refer to it and lead the reader to it. Some advertisers prefer not to include coupons because they believe a coupon might damage the tone of the advertisement (eg for a very high quality car, domestic appliance or furniture). In this case, the address must be prominent and the information the reader needs to send or call in should be clearly stated. If telephone is the main response device, tell the reader what will happen when they call (eg get asked their address for sending an information pack).

SIZE AND PLACING OF YOUR ADVERTISEMENT

This is critical. There is evidence that response tends to increase roughly as the square root of the size of the advertisement. For example, doubling the size will only bring in 40% more response (the square root of 2 is 1.41). However, full page advertising must be powerful for it to stop the reader turning over the page, so many advertisers prefer to go for smaller sizes, so the advertisement is "present" while an article is being read. However, this can raise problems if the article is not appropriate (eg an article targeted at men beside an advertisement targeted at women).

Editorial policy may not permit pre-planning of advertisement placement (although editors are becoming more marketing-oriented, understanding that to keep advertising revenue flowing in, they must show some flexibility).

TIMING

For daily newspapers, daily variations in readership are important. For products aimed at the business to business market, insertion on Saturday is less likely to produce response. Avoiding holiday periods may also be appropriate. However, consumer products and services are often better advertised during holiday periods, when consumers have more time to consider taking up offers.

An additional issue is frequency of placement. Unlike with direct mail, you can get reduced prices for multiple insertions. Multiple insertions have an attrition rate – response can die off quite quickly. For a product or service which is advertised regularly, you should test "drip" advertising – frequent, regular and perhaps small advertisements – against "burst" advertising – infrequent multiple insertions in close succession. You should also test insertion in one medium versus insertion in several media (again on a drip versus burst basis).

IN THE REAL WORLD

If you run a direct mail campaign at the same time as an advertisement campaign, you can expect the response rate to be significantly higher.

television

For the direct marketer, the major advantages of television are:

- Nearly every home has one (and in some countries most homes have two or more).
- Many people spend many hours watching TV.

The disadvantages are:

- It is usually expensive to use as a direct response medium.
- There are sometimes problems in telling the consumer how to respond during the few seconds available (hence the use of toll free numbers).
- It can be difficult to find out exactly who in the family has been watching what.
- A high degree of audience fragmentation has been introduced by video recorders and satellite and cable channels. However, this has existed in the US for many years and there direct response is a much stronger element of TV advertising. Fragmentation is only a problem for advertisers who are not sophisticated enough to target accurately. The other side of the coin of fragmentation is better targeting.

FAST TRACK

The proliferation of TV media is causing many TV companies to work hard to attract direct response clients. Some offer payment by results (PI or per item schemes). Here, you pay a small amount for airtime and a royalty per item sold. This allows low budget advertisers to test the medium. Find out if this facility is one you can use.

Telephone numbers in commercials are becoming more common, and viewers are now getting more accustomed to phoning these numbers. A special case of this is the charity appeal, where consumers phone in and donate using their credit card number.) Premium rate calling can be used in the same way. Other examples of direct response include the viewer poll.

In the UK, one of the major barriers to direct response use of TV was the shortage of airtime. The near monopoly situation of the ITV companies drove up the price of airtime to astronomical levels. In the US, where airtime is much more freely available, much longer advertisements, demonstrating the product and giving testimonials and full details of special offers and how to order, can be mounted cost-effectively. A direct response advertisement on the TV in the US is scripted in a similar way to a direct mail letter, with the additional power of the moving image to make sales by calling for the order "face to face".

In many countries, direct response TV advertising is very successful. Examples include not just the US, but also France, Australia, and Hong Kong. DRTV, as it has come to be known, works differently from normal TV advertising. Normal rules of TV buying (coverage, frequency etc) are suspended in favour of profitability measures. The higher the profit, the more often the advertisement is shown.

IN THE REAL WORLD

In DRTV, no plans are made to gain specific audience ratings. Roll-out of a campaign is determined entirely by profitability. Advertisements are specially targeted to appear in low interest programmes, when consumers are likely to take more interest in the commercial than in the programme and when they are less likely to worry about missing part of the programme when they take time out to note the details or even make the telephone call. Programming is changed at very short notice, according to which items sell the best.

For similar reasons, DRTV is less likely to be successful during the "busy" hours of the day and week, and more likely to succeed in the late evening, early morning and weekends (the "bored" hours). For cost reasons, commercials tend to be shown in off-peak viewing hours. They are much longer too – ranging between one or two minutes. This will include several repeats of the phone number. Of course, it goes without saying that DRTV requires 24 hour inbound telemarketing facilities.

The high cost of UK airtime has also created a barrier for charities, who are major users of other direct marketing media. Even though charities are now allowed to appeal directly via the TV, initial results have been discouraging, with revenue way below the costs of advertising. However, there is some evidence that TV works well as an awareness raiser when accompanied by a direct response campaign for raising money. This is much more in line with the traditional role of TV advertising in a direct environment.

Where subscription is required, the ability to access the list of subscribers by different media can be a strong asset (provided that collection of the data has been carried out in accordance with local legislation eg the Data Protection Act).

Another reason for charities' lack of success is that in direct response work, charities often make a very strong appeal to the emotions. These may be quite distressing to some recipients (eg pictures of starving children and mistreated animals), but they work. In the UK, charities are not allowed to use such images on TV. In countries where they are (eg Australia), TV response advertising has proved more effective.

SHOPPING CHANNELS

These channels, such as QVC, consist entirely of editorial which sells. The presenter discusses the product, often with a group of prospects or customers. Programming is changed to maximize revenue per second. Programming is up to 24 hours a day and coverage continental. The best products for this approach are ones which might be of use to many types of people, but where it is difficult to segment in ways that other media could use for targeting, eg teeth whitener!

teletext, electronic mail and the Internet – watch this space

Electronic media are exciting. From the rather primitive Viewdata approach, using spare capacity on broadcast TV signals, via the more complex but still one way telephone-based systems designed for business purposes, and the French Minitel system, which was the world's first large scale system for interfacing between consumers and businesses, the situation has changed to one in which we can expect individuals to set up their own relationships with companies, receiving complex images and text, placing orders, and so on. The increasing storage and speed of personal computers has been the enabling factor.

FAST TRACK

For any mass market direct marketing campaign, consider including electronic mail as one (albeit initially small) element – unless of course your product is targeted at customers at the forefront of technology, in which case it might be the main campaign.

catalogues

Catalogues are one of the oldest direct marketing media, in both consumer and business to business marketing. The most conspicuous catalogue marketers are traditional mail order suppliers. They all benefit from considerable economies of scale in purchasing and stockholding, so the number of major players has fallen steadily over the years. In business to business marketing, virtually any supplier of a wide range of products has a catalogue – in particular suppliers of frequently-ordered lower-value items (eg components, office supplies, consumables).

However, there have been many new entrants. Some are niche marketers eg fashion. High street retailers are using mail order operations to supplement their store sales. When combined with store credit cards, these operations have proved a powerful and profitable way of retaining and increasing customer loyalty. As retailers have become increasingly specialized and focused on specific target markets, so mail order suppliers have responded with more specialized catalogues (**specialogues**) aimed at particular market segments and carrying smaller merchandise ranges. Some have tried (successfully in the case of the Next Directory) to break out from traditional markets to supply consumers who did not traditionally buy mail order.

Catalogues are "the perpetual mail-shot" or the "ever-attendant sales person", because they are there all the time, asking your customer to place an order. You can combine other media with the catalogue, to achieve maximum effectiveness. In business to business, telemarketing is often used to prospect for customers for the catalogue and then to stimulate catalogue holders to buy more. Mail-shots are used to generate orders, particularly for special offers. Inbound telephone is used to take orders.

FAST TRACK

Your main aim should be to place your catalogue where it is most likely to generate orders. Even the best designed catalogue, in the hands of the person who will shelve it or use it to develop ideas about what to buy from other companies or shops, is useless.

Because catalogues are expensive to produce, experienced catalogue operators test the effect of extending their market very carefully before distributing catalogues to a new segment. In consumer markets, applicants for catalogues may be screened carefully before being sent a catalogue, while catalogues which have generated no orders may occasionally be requested back by the supplier.

Consumer catalogue marketers are therefore past masters of segmenting markets according to propensity to buy, sizes and types of orders placed, credit worthiness and payment habits. They keep very detailed records of customer habits, and develop "scoring systems" to enable them to predict the likelihood of payment defaults, high merchandise return ratios, or low ordering, based on an individual's location and personal characteristics. Many of the techniques of the wider direct marketing industry have their origins in the practices of catalogue marketers.

In consumer markets, the propensity to buy from catalogues varies considerably between different economic groupings and between countries. For example, Germans are more than twice as likely to be catalogue shoppers than UK consumers. Within the UK, less well off consumers are much more likely to be catalogue buyers.

The major advantages of a catalogue are:

- It is more stable and less volatile than many other direct response promotional formats. Once a catalogue is well-established and seasonal and other patterns of buying are understood, response rates tend to be much more predictable than direct mail one-off offers or cash with order, press or broadcast advertising. One reason for this is the spread of merchandise – there is a much greater chance of meeting one or other customer need.

- A catalogue is also less vulnerable to competitive activity – once your customer is used to ordering from one catalogue, they are less likely to switch to another. Also, sales are unaffected by circulation shortfalls in print media.
- The cost-effectiveness of the operation improves in line with the growth in your customer file. If recruitment of customers can be predicted, then sales can. Although new customers may be less likely to order, their order rate should still be predictable. Also, the more experience a customer has (provided the experience is satisfactory), the higher that customer's order rate is likely to be.
- A catalogue has a longer life than most other direct response media and therefore encourages repeat purchase. Catalogues are treated like magazines or – even better – as reference books.
- Catalogues are a useful testing ground for new products and concepts. Catalogue space is not free, but it is not as costly as a dedicated mail-shot. A catalogue has high fixed costs, but low marginal costs. The cost of including one more product is low. Of course, every product should bear its full cost of inclusion over its life cycle. A corollary of this is that your catalogue can be used to promote a range of items, none of which could be cost-effectively promoted individually.
- Catalogues can be treated like published media, with scope for inserts, articles and the like. This can make your customer keep the catalogue even longer and refer to it more often. In this respect, your catalogue can be treated as a customer service, containing all the information a customer needs to do business with you and use your products and services.
- Because catalogues have a relatively stable customer base which is responsive to promotions, seasonal workloads can be smoothed out by the use of well tried incentives to order early and order extra.
- Customers are encouraged to consolidate orders and therefore to order ahead.

DESIGNING YOUR CATALOGUE

Once the catalogue is in the hands of the right buyer, then it can start its work. Its success in this is determined by merchandise range and presentation. The main conflict, which exists in virtually all distribution channels, is the conflict between breadth, merchandise, range and focus.

WATCH OUT!

In a catalogue, this conflict emerges in the decision about how many products to feature on each page. Too many will prevent the creative staff (graphic and copy) drawing attention to every item, too few and the turnover per page will not be high enough. The same applies to the overall size of the catalogue. The best and most successful catalogues are usually a compromise between these two pressures. There is no simple recipe.

The best advice is that every part of each page, every page, every section, the catalogue itself and the wrapper, enclosed letter, other enclosures and order form, should all be treated like a direct mail-shot – but economically, because there is far less space per product. If your customers are interested enough, they will buy from a straight listing of products, but this will deter customers who are not interested or who are unfamiliar with the merchandise. Direct mail experience indicates that long copy is required to capture interest and properly qualify the customer. In catalogue marketing, the unqualified customer who orders is the customer who returns the merchandise. However, the copy can be less "aggressive" than in a direct mail piece or a media advertisement. This is because the reader's attention is already secured and the reader is expecting to be given useful information about the product in your photograph.

FAST TRACK

The catalogue is the carrier of your brand and must therefore convey this brand on every page. This should guide the layout, the copy and the photography.

The best selling pages in a catalogue are nearly always the back cover, page three, page two, followed by early right hand pages through to the middle of the book. This is where the big sellers are likely to be and where the profitable items should be. The best items should also be given more space, as the return is likely to be proportionate to the space used. There are diminishing returns, of course.

Photographs must highlight the main selling points of the product, eg looks or usefulness. However, they should not exaggerate the product's size or attractiveness – a sure way to get high return rates. Crowding a photograph with many others makes it less likely that your customer will appreciate what the product really looks like.

Traditional catalogues used to group products within product categories rather than according to customer needs. Today, increasing numbers of catalogues are grouped according to related ideas eg products that could be used on holiday, products for home entertainment, furniture for particular kinds of room instead of types of furniture. This is how some (but not all) customers think about products. Of course, both kinds of catalogue may be needed, to cater for different buying styles.

There is a lot of evidence available on what print is most readable. Because a catalogue has so much print in it, good practice would suggest that the print style used be researched and tested for readability. This includes the size of type of print, the background colour, breadth and length of paragraphs.

THE CATALOGUE PRODUCT

Very few products cannot be sold via a catalogue, but whether your product can be sold profitably in a catalogue is another matter:

● Is it the kind of product that target customers are likely to want to buy from a catalogue?

- Does it have a price that customers will want to buy it at?
- Can it be properly presented in a catalogue (copy, pictures etc.)?
- Is it orderable by mail? If it has to be completely tailored, then ordering by mail would be too complex.
- Is it shippable, without great likelihood of damage?
- Does it have the right image for the catalogue?

If your product has a price advantage, it should be strongly emphasized, or it will be lost in the welter of price and product information.

exhibitions

Exhibitions are a hybrid medium. Some exhibitions are like broadcast media advertising. The aim is merely to put products on show to a large number of customers and excite their interest. Many national consumer exhibitions are of this kind. There may be a direct marketing component. You can ask consumers showing interest to give their name and address to stand staff. These can then be distributed to local dealers for follow-up, or customers may receive a mail-shot to sustain their interest and trigger a visit to an outlet where they can buy.

Increasingly, especially in business to business, exhibitions are used as an integral part of the contact strategy. Prospective or existing customers are targeted through your database or rented lists. They are invited to the exhibition and perhaps asked to confirm their attendance. An appointment with stand staff may even be booked. After the exhibition, depending on the success of the visit, there may be a follow-up contact (sales force, telephone or mail).

WHEN TO USE EXHIBITIONS

- Sales calls are expensive and you want to get many customers visiting you rather than your visiting them.
- You want to attract new customers and the exhibition has proven quality of attendance. In this respect, the exhibition functions like a rented list.
- Complex concepts are being demonstrated, so instead of individual demonstrations having to be mounted all over the country, many customers can see the demonstration in one location.

sales seminars and other company-sponsored special events

These include the following:

- The straightforward sales seminar, where a concept is described and perhaps audio-visual techniques used to demonstrate it in action.
- The physical demonstration of the product – often held in your sales office or at the factory.
- Awareness and training events, where your aim is to educate customers so that they can appreciate the value of your company offering. This is the "soft sell" approach.

- Entertainment, eg visits to sporting and cultural events. Here, your aim is to reward your customer for loyalty and to further cement the relationship.

All these have much in common with exhibitions from a direct marketing viewpoint. The difference is that, being sponsored by you, all those attending must be invited by you. To ensure the right quality of attendee, direct marketing is the medium most commonly used to market such events. In some cases, this direct marketing takes the form of personal invitations from your management and sales staff.

WATCH OUT! *Because the event is taking place by itself, without other attractions to support it, make sure you design it to retain your customers' interest for the duration. There is little point in identifying high quality prospects for a product and then demotivating them by an event which is not absorbing, useful and/or entertaining.*

the sales force

Most sales managers would not be happy to call the sales force a direct medium. However, a sales force satisfies (or can satisfy) all the criteria for being a direct medium, in that:

- It is directly addressable.
- The costs and results of each contact can be measured.
- Tests can be carried out on the frequency, depth and type of contact.

In many respects, the sales force is like telemarketing, because contacts are made directly by human beings. For your sales force to work as a direct medium, you need the strong control over activity rates that characterizes telemarketing. So some types of sales force cannot be considered direct marketing teams, eg a major account sales force, selling complex and large technical products, where several calls are required to carry out diagnostic and negotiating work before a sale is made, and much preparatory work is required between calls. At the other extreme, for sales staff selling relatively simple products and calling on large numbers of customers every day, carrying out a quick check on requirements before closing the sale, direct marketing disciplines can be very valuable. In fact, these kinds of sales force are increasingly working in harness with other direct marketing media, specifically direct mail and telemarketing.

sales promotion

Sales promotion covers ways of giving people reasons to react in the desired way towards a product or service that go beyond the basic benefits of the product or service. Sales promotion focuses on triggering the action, on motivating the prospect to take the critical step of responding. The simplest example of sales promotion in direct marketing is the premium – the gift received by customers who respond or order. However, there are many other ways of motivating customers to buy using sales promotion. Many of them are associated with close-dates. The aim of most direct marketing campaigns is to sell or get response within a defined period. So customers must be motivated to act as soon as possible and certainly within the campaign period. The speed of response is important, because the impact of most campaigns fades with time.

Other examples of sales promotion techniques which can be used with direct marketing include:

- Free samples of the product (although related to the product benefit, it does not change it in any way).
- Offers of more of the product for a given price.
- Joint promotions – eg discounts off other products.
- Coupons and cash refund offers.
- Trading stamps and additional credit card or similar promotional points.
- Loyalty point schemes.
- Sweepstake/lotteries (subject to the law).
- Free trial or demonstration.

posters

Posters are not normally a good response medium. This is because when people see them, they are in no position to respond. However, as radio advertising has shown, car telephones can provide a valuable response channel even for the most mobile customers! Certain kinds of poster do afford some prospect of response – in particular static transport advertising (eg in rail stations and other places where people have to wait). However, in general, if posters are used with direct marketing, it is as back up to the campaign, to reinforce awareness or branding.

public relations

Public relations aims to improve communication and understanding between your company and those you need to influence. In marketing campaigns, this need is focused on:

- Media relations – where the aim is to create a positive climate towards your company by influencing the influencers, ie those who talk to the market through the media. This can be particularly valuable during a major direct marketing campaign.
- Customer relations – direct liaison with your customers in contexts other than immediate sales or service. This is particularly important with large customers in business to business markets. Strengthened relations at a time when a major direct marketing campaign is launched can considerably increase the response rate and also minimize any problems caused by poor targeting or

errors on the database. Conversely, if customers are selected for a campaign and your database does not hold details on those experiencing customer service problems, you risk targeting customers who are not only unlikely to buy, but who also may be further alienated by being targeted when their relationship with you is weak.

summary

This chapter has demonstrated the immense variety of media that you can use in direct marketing. However, this very variety can be direct marketing's own enemy if these different media are not planned and managed properly – the subject of the next few chapters.

17

hitting through creativity

- Creativity plays a vital role in direct marketing, by providing the images, symbols and phrases which make your brand recognized whichever medium you decide to use to contact customers.

- Creativity is required not just in how you show your messages, but also in what message you want to convey.

- Good briefing is the key to obtaining relevant, cost-effective and timely creativity.

introduction

Put two creative people together and three different views of creativity will emerge! Direct marketers often disagree about the meaning of "creative" and about the role of creativity in direct marketing. Some see little or no place for it, because tried and trusted methods work. Others argue that times have changed, society has moved on, what used to work now works less successfully, so new ideas and creative approaches are required.

These new ideas come mainly from the younger generation of direct marketers. Many of them have had experience "above" as well as "below" the line. They talk about integrating the two traditions, about working across or through the imaginary line. This requires a different way of thinking, they argue, in particular a focus on long-term brand values rather than short-term sales. It requires creative ideas which shape, sustain and develop those values. Such ideas differ from those which underpin traditional (and very successful) direct-response advertising. However, making sense of these opposing points of view depends on the interpretation of "creative".

understanding creativity

> **"Creative"** is often applied to ideas which are original or stimulate the imagination. In direct marketing, it's best to define creative as "ideas that work to achieve their objectives".

However, originality of ideas often means reworking a familiar idea in an unfamiliar way or context. For instance, the French mineral water Perrier has consistently played about with the *sound* of the French word *eau* (water) in its advertising, creating pun after pun by placing *eau* in familiar English words which normally create the 'O' sound with that single letter, eg "poetry in m*eau*tion". Other examples which play on language include classics like "Beans Means Heinz" and Zanussi's "appliance of science" strapline. Silk Cut and Benson and Hedges advertisements rework familiar objects and contexts in visually unfamiliar ways – to great effect. However, ideas which are *too* original will be hard for consumers to understand, so they usually won't react to them with the required behaviour.

WATCH OUT! *Your aim is to stimulate the **consumer's imagination,** not the creator's. Beware of ideas that appeal to their creators but leave their targets cold.*

It may help you to think of creativity as the process which produces the *relevant unexpected*, ie the juxtaposition of familiar and unfamiliar images in a way which has relevance to the customer. Not too much direct response advertising fits *this* definition! Too much of it looks too familiar to create any sense of excitement by arousing the imagination.

FAMILIARITY AND CREATIVITY DO MIX!

Creative ideas must be relevant, but they don't need to be unexpected. Customers loyal to your product, brand or advertising will be comforted by **familiar messages** and even seek them out. They like to find them in **familiar places**. Knowing **where** to look for them is a comfort and an aid. Still, your advertisement must stand out on the page and differentiate itself from competition, especially for customers who don't know you or your product. Faithful customers will spot the familiar name as readily as they spot their own in the telephone directory.

*Creativity and targeting go together. A familiar message works with regular customers – if it is relevant. Some degree of surprise may be required if the target audience are prospects. So make sure your message is **relevant**.*

FAST TRACK

creativity and action

Relevance to target customers is a key idea in creativity, whether your message is expected or unexpected. However, your message must also be **seen, understood** and **acted upon**. These are the key stages in "**hierarchy of effects**" models of the communication process.

> "**Hierarchy of effects**" models of communication analyze the consumer's reaction to a marketing communication in terms of successive stages, usually starting with attention or awareness and ending with purchase. The most widely used is AIDCA – Attention, Interest, Desire, Conviction, Action.

AIDCA suggests that consumers need to see and have beliefs about your product before buying it. Communication influences these "receiver effects" as in Figure 17.1. This suggests that seeing, believing and buying are a function of:

● Your customer's perception of the **source** of the message, particularly the credibility of the source (both you and the medium you use).
● How your **message** affects your customer.
● How the **media** you use shape the message (through their different physical characteristics, for example).
● The nature of your customer's world.

Fig 17.1

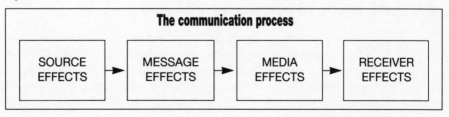

The communication process

SOURCE EFFECTS → MESSAGE EFFECTS → MEDIA EFFECTS → RECEIVER EFFECTS

Creativity should not be judged by message design alone. Creative ideas must *work*, ie obtain the result you want – change or reinforcement of behaviour eg purchase, brand-switching, increased frequency of purchase etc.

how can you create creativity?

There is lots of research on why some individuals out-perform others in creativity, but little conclusive evidence that one set of factors matters more than another.

FAST TRACK

The ability to associate does seem to make a difference, ie the ability to think laterally rather than vertically by combining related ideas (eg a chair that warms you), adding unrelated features (eg speaking video recorder), taking away problem features (eg bulk), creating associations with unrelated products or benefits (eg a credit card and charity), making things simpler (eg buying motor insurance over the telephone), substituting (eg the "eau" Perrier campaign), switching (eg the Health Council's pregnant man poster). So you can use techniques aimed to stimulate association. Lateral thinking is just one of many techniques used to help groups produce new ideas. Brain storming and synectics are other techniques. You can complement these group approaches by helping individuals improve their creativity by using techniques to get away from the constraints imposed by their current thought patterns.

Whatever techniques you use to produce creative ideas, creativity is above all about ideas that work. Direct marketing is essentially about making a sale. Combining the two leads to creative ideas that work to make a sale (or generate a lead that will produce a sale). Whether your ideas are visual, original, clever or aesthetically pleasing, they must achieve your objective.

WATCH OUT!

*Don't allow all your thought to go into offers and response devices, rather than the longer term objective of building your brand. You will allow a creative vacuum to emerge between awareness and action and your direct marketing will become less effective. The key stage in AIDCA is conviction ie, building your customer's **beliefs** about your brand. Once they are established, the desired action is likely to follow.*

direct marketing vs advertising creativity

Your media advertising usually aims to create awareness and brand images. Your direct marketing communications usually aim to make a sale. Your direct marketing can build on foundations laid by image advertising. However, much direct marketing is unsupported by image advertising. It does the whole job – creating awareness, interest, desire, conviction and action, all in one piece. However, because the key requirement is to make a sale, it tends to be action-oriented at the expense of brand values.

The beliefs you should be interested in are customers' estimates that if they do what you want them to (buy, reply etc), they will derive benefit from doing so. For example, "If I send off for a Bullworker, it will arrive in 28 days and within six weeks I will feel as fit as a champion boxer".

Aim to form beliefs – they are essential for any form of marketing communication to succeed. Use ideas to build lasting beliefs about your brand. Don't just use offer strategies to raise response levels.

FAST TRACK

Your success in creating belief depends on:

- Being single minded about the kind of belief you are trying to form.
- How often and how strongly you reinforce them.

Consistent *creative themes should run through all your campaign elements, in whichever medium each appears. Your campaign will then be "seamless" – consumers will understand that whichever communication they receive, through whatever medium, it carries the same underlying message. The whole will be greater than the sum of the parts.*

FAST TRACK

There are few examples of such a consistent approach in direct marketing. This is because clients tend not to think this way, while agencies tend to take the client's approach. But the "big idea" that characterizes most successful advertising campaigns – the mental bridge between the product's features and the consumer's perception of the product's benefits – is a target for every direct marketing campaign.

The little red telephone

EXAMPLE

The success of Direct Line's red telephone campaign, in a market where brand loyalty is low, price competition fierce and brand switching is very frequent, is a goal for every direct marketer to aim at. In direct response television advertising, the telephone is a highly flexible branding device. It can appear in every medium. It can change its shape, size and speed of movement to identify with different types of cars and therefore with different target groups. It can be used to suggest that the company is more dynamic, bigger or cheaper than its competitors. It is also used to improve response, of course. Moreover, as the company moved into other types of personal insurance, eg house contents, the red telephone was used to stimulate home-related images, by changing its shape to that of a house, for instance. The red telephone is a simple idea. Carried through all advertising and adapting to circumstances, this simple little branding device plays a strategic role in the communications programme. The effect is powerful because there is a big creative idea behind the little red telephone. ○

developing the creative strategy

There are seven basic steps in developing a creative communications strategy:

1. Identify and understand your customer.
2. Know your product's strengths and weaknesses.
3. Assess your competition.
4. Position your product.
5. Develop the customer benefits.
6. Communicate the message.
7. Build a dialogue with your customers

FAST TRACK *Don't insist on taking these steps in strict order. Do it **interactively**. Try starting with step seven in order to proceed to step one. Lead generation programmes first establish a dialogue (step seven) in order to identify the prospect/customer (step one).*

UNDERSTANDING THE CUSTOMER

Use all your knowledge of market segmentation techniques to understand who customers are, what they think and perceive, how to reach them, through which media, and how they buy. A key role is played by information and emotion. How much information do they need? What kind of message are they likely to respond to? How persuasive does the message need to be?

KNOWING THE PRODUCT'S STRENGTHS AND WEAKNESSES

Your product's strengths will build its Unique Selling Proposition, but some strengths are more important than others. A car may be high on comfort, speed, economy and safety, but it would not make sense to give all these strengths equal weight in the message. You need to concentrate upon key strengths to achieve clear product differentiation. For Volvo, it is safety, for Ferrari it is motor racing heritage.

FAST TRACK *Don't forget your weaknesses. Try to eliminate them from the message or turn them into a strength. In Bill Bernbach's advertisements for the Volkswagen Beetle, the copy said "noisy", "ugly" and "slow". It sold millions of Beetles!*

ASSESSING YOUR COMPETITION

Competitive analysis is central to positioning strategy. You need to decide whether you should make references to competition in your message. In the UK, clear guidelines forbid "knocking copy" – but justifiable competitive comparisons are permitted.

POSITIONING YOUR PRODUCT

Everything in your communication strategy should support your positioning strategy. This consistency should run through all your media and message components for a sustained period.

DEVELOPING CONSUMER BENEFITS

Consumers want to hear about benefits – immediately. Hence the maxim "get the main benefit in the headline". This idea has stimulated much of the best copy, including many "How to …" headlines, such as:

- How to improve your memory.
- How to burn off body fat hour by hour.
- How to make your second million.
- How to double your power to learn.
- How to make a fortune in mail order.
- How to win friends and influence people.
- How to get more for your money at …

The hardest task is to turn the product feature into a genuine benefit – in short "sell the sizzle, not the steak". A technique which identifies genuine benefits, not features, is called FAB analysis: Features, Advantages, Benefits.

How to do a FAB analysis

- List the features – what your product or service consists of etc.
- Express these as advantages – what the features mean it can do or what can be done with it.
- Convert the advantages into benefits – how the customer's needs are satisfied by these advantages, expressed in your customer's language.

For instance, a washing machine has a built-in spinner (feature). This means it takes up less room in the kitchen (advantage). This means that there is now room for the dog's eating bowl (benefit). Notice the phrase **"which means"**. In searching for the benefit, keep asking yourself "which means?" until you get to something the customer would say about how your product or service helps them meet their objectives.

Most products have several features and therefore several benefits. The way a given feature benefits each customer depends upon that customer's needs, so one feature can produce a variety of different benefits. The benefit of the above washing machine to a non dog-owner may be that there is also room for a dishwasher! A feature may produce many benefits, only the most important of which should be stressed in the advertising.

FAST TRACK

You can only find out which are the most important benefits by research. Ask customers which benefits matter most. You can also develop different types of copy, highlighting different types of benefit. You can see from response rates which benefit appeals to which type of customer.

COMMUNICATING THE MESSAGE

This refers to what your words and pictures should say and show and to how they should be combined. This raises several important direct response issues:

Length of copy

It used to be argued that long copy out-pulled short copy, that long headlines could often beat short ones. David Ogilvy is fond of reminding audiences of his famous headline "At 60 miles an hour, the loudest noise in the new Rolls Royce Silver Shadow is the ticking of the electric clock". Nowadays, direct response ads tend to work well with shorter copy and briefer headlines. If in doubt, test!

Number of pieces

How many pieces? Again, a general rule is the more the better. Each piece is a selling opportunity – the more selling opportunities the better.

Personalization

This is generally considered a good idea, because it is flattering to be mentioned by name. However, it is important to get the name right, and not to overdo it. More importantly personalization should mean relevant, personal details, not necessarily repetition of your customer's name. With laser printing you can personalize many details in one pass through the printer. For example, insurance mailings often feature age, renewal date, maturity value, surrender value and so on.

Mood and tone

This can be crucial to response, but the mood you create depends on the target. Established customers like to be treated gently, but prospects may need a harder sell. Some customers need to be cajoled, pushed and even threatened. Others need to be given an incentive to respond.

BUILDING THE DIALOGUE

Communication means interaction: a two-way process. A dialogue is the simplest form of communication. Therefore, it should start as soon as possible. Headlines which pose questions immediately involve the prospect as do all involvement devices, eg "yes/no" envelopes. Reply coupons which say "Yes, I do wish to receive my introductory copy of X", also use the dialogue-building technique.

the seven ws of the creative brief

- Who? (the source of the message)
- What? (the message)
- Whom? (the target audience)
- When? (timing)
- Where? (media)
- Why? (reasons for consumer purchase)

- **With what effect?** (desired objectives)

You should then translate these seven Ws into a structured communications brief, with the following sections:

- **A clear statement of your communications objective** – like all objectives, your communications objective(s) should be **SMART: specific, measurable, achievable, realistic and timed**. Media advertisers usually express objectives in terms of awareness, recall and attitudes. Direct marketers usually focus on response rates and cost-effectiveness. This concentrates the mind on how the communication strategy is to work.
- **Your product** – its key characteristics (physical *and* emotional).
- **Your target market** – size, location, behaviour etc.
- **Previous advertising performance in the market** – campaign results (response rates, etc).
- **Competitive activity** – who are your main competitors and how have they performed? How are they positioned? Are they different/better?
- **Media** – which media do you want to use – direct mail, press, telephone, television, inserts etc.
- **Main thought** – the major consumer benefit.
- **Support for the main thought** – any argument or evidence to corroborate the main thought, including testimonials.
- **Subsidiary thoughts** – additional reasons for buying your product, including offers.
- **Tone of voice** – hard or soft sell?
- **Mandatory inclusions** – logo, telephone numbers, etc.
- **Restrictions** – codes of practice, data protection issues etc.
- **Timings** – when your campaign will start and end, and when individual communications should be sent.

summary

This chapter began with an examination of the word "creative". The best interpretation is "ideas that work to achieve their objectives". These ideas are more likely to work if they are relevant to the target audience. Beyond being relevant they must be communicated effectively. This depends not just on the brilliance of the idea, but also on effective marketing and communications programmes.

Ideas must work either to make a sale or to produce behaviour that leads to a sale. Often direct marketing communications work without the support of image advertising and this means that creative ideas must sustain the whole process in the conviction or belief stage. Without a strong conviction that the product will satisfy your consumer's need, you won't get the right response. Ideally a big idea should be sought and executed throughout the campaign. This big idea could also be a branding device.

Effective direct marketing creative strategy depends on a carefully written creative brief. This brief should provide all the relevant market background data, isolate the main thought and provide convincing rational and emotional support for the main thought.

18

the hard work in hitting – production and fulfilment

- A good direct marketing plan, backed up by well-designed campaigns, is no use unless you get it to market through production and fulfilment.

- This involves a series of activities, ranging from graphic design and typesetting, through to printing, stock management and dispatch.

- Mailings can and often do go wrong because failures in planning, briefing or communication are translated into material which is poorly designed, badly printed, sent out at the wrong time or to the wrong people.

production

"**Production**" is the process by which print material is produced ready for outbound mailing and fulfilment. Once, when direct marketing was completely dominated by direct mail, the term "production" accurately described the production process for all direct marketing. Now, with telemarketing increasing in importance as a direct marketing medium, the term production should be qualified by adding the word "print" before it.

FAST TRACK

Direct marketers need expertise in print production. Production costs account for a large proportion of total direct mail costs. In this chapter, we outline some of the main production tasks, but we avoid details of particular production techniques, as they change rapidly. If you are new in direct marketing, find out more about production by asking to spend time "on the floor" with your print suppliers.

THE START – ARTWORK

The first step in production is preparing copy and illustrations. This usually involves using specialist graphic art agencies and studios. They know what is possible using the latest techniques and what different approaches will cost, so they can design taking into account any constraints on feasibility and costs.

WATCH OUT!

Buying artwork is not easy. Whether a piece of artwork meets the brief is a matter of professional judgement (except for obvious cases of sub-standard work). You can minimize problems by ensuring that the brief for artwork is comprehensive, covering all requirements from the effect the print is meant to have on customers through to cost constraints.

The situation is complicated by the fact that there are fashions in artwork. For example, one year, pastel shades are in fashion, the next year bright shades, one year, fuzzy shapes, the next year sharp edges.

GRAPHICS

All pictures are either line graphics or halftone. Line graphics are composed of black and white only, with no intermediate tones. This includes drawings, plans, charts and cartoons. Halftones are used to reproduce original photographs or multi-coloured artwork. In most printing processes, ink of only one density is possible, so shades are simulated by changing the number of dots per inch of the colour to be shaded. For multicoloured images, the original is separated into primary colour images which combine to produce the final image.

TYPESETTING

There are also fashions in typography. Every typeface has a different effect. Legibility is of course critical, though it is surprising how much type is not very legible. This may be, for example, because type which is designed to emphasize a few characters or words has been used for an entire piece. Similarly, type meant for body text may be ineffective when used to headline.

FAST TRACK

As with pictorial designs, you will do best by adopting a clear style which endures over time. A clear communication style becomes recognized by your customers and supports branding.

WATCH OUT!

If your company has an existing typeface used in all communication, check if it is acceptable to deviate from the style.

Most typesetting is now computerized, although some type (eg large headlines) is still set by hand. This does not mean that typesetting is an unskilled job. Software has removed some of the unskilled work, but the skills required to produce a really excellent piece of work are still required. Image manipulation techniques allow images to be rotated, sized, reversed, overlaid with effects and repositioned. Manual assembly of page elements is now much less widespread. Publishing software enables composition and lay-out to be carried out more quickly, so the finished material can be checked with clients more quickly. Laser and ink-jet printers allow signatures, text and formats to be stored, allowing every communication to be customized and large numbers of variations to be created around basic themes.

FAST TRACK

Digitized images can be stored and transmitted, making libraries of print images easier to manage and reducing communication problems between artwork and printing organizations. Many of these techniques can be used to speed up the proofing process. This enables you to respond more quickly to market needs. Complete these processes before the artwork is finally agreed to avoid a last minute hitch.

MAKE-UP

Once all the original elements of the job to be reproduced have been converted to printable images, they are assembled into the correct position and fixed. The complete job is then sent for plate-making. A variety of processes have been developed to go straight from artwork to plate.

PRINTING PROCESSES

Nearly all printing processes convert the required design into a printing image carrier. This has an image area which will receive and transfer ink to the material being printed. The exception to this is laser printing, where toner is transferred from an electrostatically charged drum to the paper. Printers often refer to the printing image carrier as a plate or cylinder. Here are a few of the techniques used at this stage.

● In **letterpress**, the image area is physically higher than the non-image area. A roller carrying ink is rolled across the surface and the ink directly transferred to the material being printed.

● **Flexography** is similar to this, except that the ink is less viscous.

● In **gravure**, the image area is lower than the non-image area. The carrier is flooded with ink, which is then removed from the non-image area by a blade.

● In a **screen** process, the image area is open and allows ink to pass through. The non-image area is closed.

● In **lithography**, the difference between the image and non-image areas is based on the fact that ink and water do not easily mix. Materials which are ink-receptive are used for the image area, while water-receptive materials are used for the non-image area.

● **Offset** printers use an intermediate roller between the plate and the printing roller.

fulfilment

Fulfilment represents the practical completion of the direct marketing cycle.

WATCH OUT! *The best planned campaign, with the cleverest offer, the most brilliant creative and the most professional targeting and timing will come to nothing unless it is handled well at this stage.*

In theory, fulfilment starts when a customer first responds to a campaign, ie after the first contact between your customer and you. The **first contact** may be via direct mail, outbound telemarketing, a television or press advertisement, a leaflet, or any other medium. The customer then responds – whether by telephone, mail or even a call into a showroom. The handling of this first response – whether by processing coupons, receiving telephone calls or directing customers to the right counter or display, is called **response handling**. The next step is that you give the customer something – a brochure, a catalogue, or the product itself. This latter step is **fulfilment**.

TIMING

From a management point of view, dealing with fulfilment differs very little from managing delivery in the two direct media which dominate initial contacts – mail and telephone. The main difference is **timing**. An initial mailing can be scheduled to take place within a defined period, taking advantage of postal rebates and allowing workers and machinery to be optimally scheduled. Handling a mail or a telephone response (processing coupons or receiving a call, sending a pack in return and in some cases making a telephone call) takes place when the customer decides to respond. With campaigns that are repeats in markets you know well, timing of response can be predicted fairly well. However, in new markets, or with new products, prediction is harder.

VOLUMES

The other major difference is in **volumes** – outbound mail and telephone campaigns usually involve larger numbers of customers than the responses. However, when your first customer contact is a media advertisement, response is likely to be high volume and involve collecting a lot of basic data about the respondent.

FAST TRACK

Many handling houses cover both initial mailings and fulfilment. This has the advantage that you only need to brief one company, which does not have to find out from you or another supplier about outbound volumes and timings. If you think this sounds a small point, you should understand that half of the problems that occur in campaigns are caused by poor communication between client and supplier, or between suppliers. So consider the advantages of one stop shopping!

FULFILMENT TASKS

As we have already covered management of inbound telemarketing, we focus in this chapter on handling of direct mail.

The main steps in fulfilment

1. **Providing a communication point** – somewhere where customers can phone or write to make contact.

2. **Recording the response** – by creating or updating the database. Errors here can cause packs to be sent to the wrong address and wrong packs to be sent to customers.

3. **Processing the order** – anything from an acknowledgement letter, through to a brochure, to a complex pack of several inserts, and of course a product.

4. **Warehousing literature and/or goods** – receiving deliveries, warehousing, picking, packing and dispatching. Delays here, particularly in dispatching, can create lots of customer queries. You won't be happy with your suppliers, because of the damage to your image.

5. **Inventory control** – so both you and the handling house know precisely how much is in stock at any time, and when re-ordering should take place. Lack of control here can also lead to high levels of pilferage and other forms of stock wastage.

6. **Financial control** – this includes reconciling customer payments (credit card and cash) with dispatches and returns, invoicing and credit control. Errors here can lead to campaigns failing to meet financial targets. They can also lead to financial problems for the handling house, which may be debited with any errors.

7. **Returns handling** – receipt, quality check, repacking and/or rewarehousing or disposal.

8. **Customer query handling** – failure to handle your customers' queries properly and promptly can lead to high levels of dissatisfaction, cancellation of orders and damage to your image.

9. **Reporting and forecasting response** shipment and returns data – errors here can cause stock to run out or surpluses of stock to be created. They may also cause campaigns to go on for too long or too little (if the aim is to bring in a target absolute number of responses).

*Unless all these steps are fully catered from the outset of the campaign, you may end up with a **high profile mistake** communicated to all your customers!*

WATCH OUT!

FULFILMENT STEPS

How these capabilities are put to work can best be seen by following through the fulfilment process. This is described below. It may not be exactly like this in all handling houses, but it will be more or less the same.

The brief

You brief your handling house, specifying exactly what is to be done when. Brief them as early as possible. Consider sending it in draft form, before final numbers are specified. You may still be doing some work on targeting and response rate forecasting. A draft brief gives your handling house time to respond and point out problems or opportunities.

The response

In response to the brief (and where necessary, having finalized the brief from the draft version), your handling house issues a quote, usually on a per item basis, with a fixed charge to cover overheads and set-up costs. It is also good practice for the handling house to add to their quote their understanding of the project plan, ie when items will be arriving from print suppliers, who is responsible for producing what, when action is likely to be required.

Preparation

If the quote is accepted, the handling house makes preparations to run its part of the campaign. Likely response levels are forecast and work schedules devised to cope with them. Machine and warehousing capacity is allocated. Postal and telecommunication arrangements are made (including Freepost and toll-free numbers). Temporary staff are recruited and permanent workers allocated.

Implementation

The campaign starts and responses come in. Mailbags are received, opened, sorted (by client or promotion – hence the importance of properly coded and clearly labelled envelopes), envelopes are arranged for feeding into opening machines. Order forms are checked for completeness. Applications and orders are checked against order forms. Payments are checked for validity (eg cheque signatures, dates, wording and amounts). Items to be queried with customers are batched up for inspection, while responses that pass these checks are batched up for data entry. In the telephone room, calls are answered and details entered in for processing. Inventory is checked. Numbers are reported to ensure that stocks will be sufficient. Payments are sorted, verified, totalled, reconciled and banked in the client account daily. Payments for stock-out items are held pending availability of stock.

Details of orders are entered onto the computer. This includes not only information about the order and the customer's name and address, but also other information about customers that may have been collected by questionnaire. Stock is allocated to individual customers (this may have taken place on-line with inbound telemarketing). Where relevant, existing information about customers is accessed, eg past payment records, to check whether the order can be processed or whether it should be queried.

Using the order information, consolidated picking lists are created for mail-order companies. Where the fulfilment is in the form of more information, in a pack which is built from several items, each selected to match the customer's need, data is created for transmission to the relevant inserting and labelling machinery.

Stock is released from storage (valuable items may require supervisory signatures). Picking machinery may be used. Items are packed and held pending dispatch, via post or a distribution company.

THE MANAGEMENT OF HANDLING

You need to be confident that the handling house you choose is able to perform the required tasks, at the right time, within the agreed budget. For this reason, you may wish to develop a close relationship with just a few handling houses (perhaps only one). This enables you to develop in-depth knowledge of your handling house's capabilities. It also allows the two of you to align systems and procedures. For example, your campaign briefing process must give the handling house the right instructions early enough for it to prepare to handle the campaign (secure additional staff, schedule machinery and storage, etc).

Handling houses tend to be process driven and may not perform a fundamental duty if you have forgotten to put it on the brief. Work with them and encourage them to be proactive in identifying omissions and opportunities.

WATCH OUT!

HANDLING CAPABILITIES

From the point of view of the handling house, meeting your requirements depends upon a wide range of factors, of which some are listed below. If you are considering carrying out your own fulfilment, you should consider whether you have these capacities and whether you are prepared to dedicate resources to such activities. Remember that an independent handling house achieves great economies of scale by handling fulfilment for many clients. Expensive machinery, staff and space are not left idle for long periods.

Size

The house must be of the right size for your job. If the job is very large, the house must have the right storage facilities, staff and equipment to handle your job, or at least be able to demonstrate its ability to subcontract some of the work reliably. Conversely, if your job is small, the large handling house must have the right processes for handling smaller jobs. Size also affects whether the handling house can cope with the inevitable late deliveries, overloads and rush jobs.

Condition of premises and equipment

The premises and equipment must be clean and well-maintained to ensure that there are no problems with deterioration of stock or damage to material while it is being processed by the equipment. The premises should also be secure and fire-safe.

People

Firstly, there must be enough staff to handle the job. They must be of the right specializations and know the type of work and their processes well. Too high a staff turnover, particularly among management, may mean lack of familiarity with procedures and consequent errors. Proper personnel management procedures need to be in place, for recruiting and managing them. This includes payment, training and motivation systems and quality procedures. Supervision should be careful and professional, with regular checks being carried out where appropriate. Staff should be well looked after, with staff welfare facilities and appropriate benefits. Clients have many problems with handling houses that are due to poor personnel management and very low pay levels. Avoid such companies by finding out who they are from other users.

Account management

The relationship between you and the handling house depends critically on the quality of account management. This depends partly on the house's processes, partly on the quality of the account manager – the person responsible for managing all relationships between your company and the house. The best way of checking this is to ask to see completed process documentation, management systems and reference clients. Note that if the house has high staff turnover, account management quality is likely to be low and you won't be able to rely on your account manager knowing how you like to work and what your processes and systems are.

Processes and systems

The handling house must have clear processes and systems for handling all jobs, from quotation, through to agreement to a schedule, to signing off work as it goes through different stages. Computer reports should be routinely available on where any project stands and the numbers of items/customers processed when the fulfilment goes live. These processes and systems should fulfil all customer requirements in the quality sense of the word. Ask for a list of current clients.

Client conflict

You need to decide whether it matters to you if the house is also handling competitors' campaigns. The risk is that they will find out what you are planning to do. Even if "Chinese Walls" are claimed to exist, discovering plans can happen by chance (eg the competitive client is in the warehouse and spots some of your merchandise). So think about any possible client conflict.

Performance

Make sure your handling house has a good track record of delivery of projects on time, to high quality standards, on budget.

THE EQUIPMENT

Fulfilment is the factory of direct marketing – it requires a lot of equipment. The equipment used in handling is listed below. Only the largest handling houses have all of this, although the majority of houses would have most items.

Computing equipment

- Data capture equipment, enabling data about responses to be captured and transferred to storage. These include terminals for keying in data from coupons or from telephone calls, and scanning equipment (bar-code and optical character readers) for capturing coded, written and typed data. As the technology becomes more robust, voice recognition equipment will become common, particularly for processing orders from catalogues.
- The computer itself (processor, storage, software etc) for processing the information keyed in and matching it (where appropriate) to pre-existing customer records. Desk-top publishing software may be used on some micro-computers to compose copy and layout.
- Networking equipment and software, for transferring data around the handling house and between the handling house and your computer. In some cases, particularly in business-to-business markets, but increasingly in consumer markets with the arrival of electronic mail, there may be data links with customers' computers and telephones, allowing them to order direct without writing or speaking to anyone at the handling house.
- Data-output machinery. This includes printers of all kinds (impact, ink-jet and lasers). Laser printers range from small correspondence printers, printers for desk-top publishing and high speed laser printers for personalizing mass

correspondence. Other technology used here includes plastic card embossers with magnetic stripe encoding, and bar coding printers.

Print machinery

This ranges from small office offset equipment to full four-colour machinery.

Telemarketing systems

These are used for inbound telephone fulfilment and can range from a single answering machine to a 1000-line fully automated system, including digitized voice-response.

Materials storage and handling equipment

On major campaigns, hundreds of thousands and sometimes millions of items need to be sent out to customers. All this material needs to be stored securely (so that it does not deteriorate and can be handled by machines without problems) and accessibly (so that it can be located quickly and transferred to where it is going to be processed, packed and dispatched). Proper storage and materials moving equipment is therefore required.

Addressing and labelling equipment

This includes electronic and mechanical addressing and labelling systems, eg ink-jet systems (for printing directly onto envelopes) and automatic labelling machines that accept names and addresses in computer printout format (up to four across), then guillotine to label size and affix to envelopes. For very low volume mailings, it may still be necessary to type individual labels. Cheshire machines are used for high volume labelling.

Finishing, packing and wrapping equipment

Machines are required to finish the print items and fold and insert them. Equipment is also needed to shrink wrap, band and strap items together. These must be able to handle many different sizes and weights. Finishing equipment includes bursters, trimmers and collators.

Weighing and calibrating equipment

This includes electronic and mechanical scales for all purposes, measuring weights from fractions of a gram up to a fully loaded pallet. Also required are electronic counting machines.

Print design equipment

Some handling houses are involved in producing some elements of the mail pack. Those that are need a studio, dark-room and design equipment.

summary

In this chapter, we have covered the bare bones of production and fulfilment. It should give you the clear idea that these are areas where quality is critical, as the best designed campaign can fail if it is not implemented properly. You should select suppliers of these services with the same care as your other suppliers. It does not pay to cut corners. Big houses may be more expensive, but they are usually better managed and pay a lot of attention to quality. However, word-of-mouth recommendation – from a number of clients – is the ultimate test.

Of course, it's no use demanding high standards of campaign management if yours are not up to scratch. In our next chapter, we show you what high standard campaign management looks like.

19

managing the hit

- The planning cycle for campaigns covers planning, development, implementation, measurement and evaluation.

- The better the planning the higher quality the implementation, and the better the results.

- The key areas to plan are targeting, timing, the offer, creative and media/list selection.

- The brief is the key to the process, as it contains instructions on what is wanted, from whom, by when, and how results are to be measured.

- Project planning and resource management disciplines are required to manage direct marketing in large organizations.

introduction

A quality, high volume, properly managed campaign requires between three and four months to plan and get ready for launch. In very large companies, using databases covering millions of customers, a lot of database analysis and planning may be required, followed by simulation of campaigns. Complex contact strategies may need to be designed and tested. In such cases, the lead time may be six months or more. Faster campaigns have been run, with good results, but the norm for most companies is between three and six months. Trying to mount a campaign at too short notice almost invariably leads to quality problems.

the campaign process

The process of developing and implementing each campaign should run through the following sequence:

1. Planning – deciding how marketing objectives are to be met, through one or more campaigns, with specific objectives, target markets, promoting specific products and services, at particular times.

2. Development – when the details of each campaign are determined.

3. Implementation – when each campaign is run.

4. Evaluation – when the results of each campaign are analyzed.

CAMPAIGN PLANNING

Ideally, your marketing plan should give clear overall objectives, strategies and targets. These now need to be translated into direct marketing actions. The first step is to summarize intentions in the form of a campaign brief. Many companies use planning formats to draft and finalize their briefs. The brief describes what the target market is, when it is to be hit, with what offer and product, and how, what objectives are to be met and as part of what strategies. Figure 19.1 gives an example of a briefing format.

You refine and add to this brief as the time for initiation of more detailed work on each campaign approaches. By preparing the brief early and by circulating it to all parties involved (within your business and amongst agencies), clashes, data problems and resource bottlenecks are minimized and co-operation maximized. So drawing up the brief early and, where necessary, getting agreement to it by the various parties involved (eg product or brand managers, sales managers, advertising managers) should be undertaken as soon as possible.

Fig 19.1

Example of briefing format

Campaign definition and accountabilities

Campaign name..Code...

Originator..Date of issue ....

Description of requirement ....

Planned launch date ....Planned close date ....

Measurement criteria ....

Campaign manager.........................Internal clients..

Suppliers

Company	Contact name	Objective/role of company on campaign
1.....................	....	....
2.....................	....	....
3.....................	....	....

Others on circulation list for all campaign documentation (keep to minimum)

....

Campaign coverage

Test or roll-out .... Objective of test ....

If test, roll-out strategy...

Country/region involvement

Country/region/branch	Type of involvement
1...	....
2...	....

Objectives and strategy

Objectives of marketing strategy of which campaign forms part

1. ....

2. ....

Main elements of overall marketing strategy

1. ....

2. ....

▶

Fig 19.1 (continued)

Promotional objectives

1. ....

2. ....

Required consistency with other campaigns and activities

1. ....

2. ....

Desired customer response

1. ....

2. ....

Proposition – key issue/offer from prospect's point of view

....

Previous promotional activity targeted at the same audience

....

Products/services/programmes to be promoted/offered   Code

....

Target markets (customer types)

1. ....

2. ....

Relevant customer perceptions

....

Direct competition

Company   Product   Comment (eg comparison with your offer)

....

....

DON'T FORGET!

Does your brief:

○ *Help organize thinking?*

○ *Give top-line guidance to implementers?*

○ *Communicate the campaign within your company and to your suppliers?*

○ *Act as the supporting document for more detailed forms covering different aspects of the campaign?*

CAMPAIGN DEVELOPMENT

This is when all your campaign details (targeting, lists, timing, offer, creative etc) are determined, using agencies where appropriate. Here, your main concern is to get all the details of the campaign right. This will ensure it runs smoothly once it is launched.

FAST TRACK

Making sure all suppliers are working well, to a common plan and communicating progress, is a critical task in this period. This includes any internal suppliers, eg in-house print, telemarketing. So build a team with them. Brief them together, and encourage them to work together.

CAMPAIGN IMPLEMENTATION

Your campaign actually runs. Here, your main concern is to ensure that campaign logistics are running smoothly (eg mailings going out on time, responses being handled properly) and that interim results are analyzed to see whether any campaign details need modifying. This stage may be controlled through your customer database system and possibly managed through your management information system.

CAMPAIGN EVALUATION

After the campaign has run, it is critical to find out what worked and what did not. Here, the prime activity is analysis of response rates by different categories (media, market segment, timing of response). However, checking that the statistics were correctly measured is also important, to prevent false conclusions.

Now let's look at these stages in more detail.

campaign planning

SETTING CAMPAIGN OBJECTIVES

Your first step in relating the campaign process to the marketing plan is to determine which marketing plan objectives can be achieved through direct marketing. Here are some likely objectives and the campaign strategies that might help achieve them.

Gaining more business from existing customers by:
- Identifying, from purchasing data, whether there are gaps in your product and service range/variants, and creating relevant products and services, and promoting them.
- Promoting existing products and services to customers on your database.
- Creating new relationships with existing customers, tying them more closely to you and increasing customer loyalty.
- Developing loyalty programmes, which allow customers to develop a closer relationship with you.
- Identifying your customers' requirements for levels of service, developing and promoting the required level of service, and following up afterwards to ensure that good service is remembered and poor service compensated for, to

achieve higher levels of customer satisfaction and loyalty.

● Identifying competitive threats to particular customers, developing stronger incentives for these customers and promoting them heavily.

Increasing your customer base by:

● Developing profiles of existing valuable customers, applying these profiles to selected external lists and promoting relevant products to customers so identified, and offering relevant relationships.

● Re-awakening past customers, by identifying them, determining their needs, developing and promoting offers which meet these needs.

Reducing promotional costs by:

● Examining current methods of communicating with customers and seeking to achieve the same effect through direct communication.

Positioning and branding:

● Every direct marketing campaign should support the creation of positioning and branding (master and sub-brands) with all customers. You should maintain strict standards in relation to the types of offer promoted and their creative presentation.

Your objectives form a critical part of the brief to the agencies involved in a campaign. Specify them clearly and in quantified form, and check that your agency understands them. If testing forms part of the campaign, or perhaps the whole campaign, the test objectives should be specified clearly.

FAST TRACK

One rule must always be observed – **keep campaign objectives simple and specific**. If you aim to recruit good new customers, all your campaign objectives should relate to this. The meaning of "good new customer" should be specified and the target number of them you want as well. Too complex objectives lead to weak campaigns.

JUSTIFYING THE CAMPAIGN

In your planning documentation, justify the campaign in terms of the main marketing objectives it supports (eg the need to increase sales of a particular product, or to capitalize on a growth trend). The statement should be as specific as possible, particularly in terms of:

● The type of customer involved.
● The attitudes and behaviour you are trying to influence.
● The influence of timing of customer behaviour on timing of campaign (eg when they are most likely to buy).

This provides the key to campaign co-ordination, as well as to setting clear, quantifiable campaign objectives.

RELATIONSHIP OBJECTIVES

You may want to create a relationship with your customers that transcends individual campaigns, just as a sales-person develops a relationship with his or her customers that transcends the individual sale. You must therefore have some measure of the progress of the relationship – for example, the number of customers of a specified value or greater that you have recruited onto your database through the campaigns.

Various themes can be developed during a relationship. Here is an example of development of a theme.

Stage 1	Recruit a set of customers (new or existing) into a new relationship.
Stage 2	Promote to them an offer which is relevant to the relationship.
Stage 3	Promote second and further offers to them (up-selling, cross-selling).
Stage 4	Develop further offers based upon a study of those with the greatest take-up (more cross-selling).
Stage 5	Enrol customers in member get member programmes.
Stage 6	Develop offers which group products together.

The development of a relationship can be over a short period (say six months) or over several years. In practice, very long-term relationships should be composed of a series of short, feasible steps, paid for all along the way by the take-up of offers. For example, to achieve your marketing objectives, you may need to:

- Increase usage by existing users.
- Get existing customers who don't use your product to start using it.
- Make conquest sales from those who do not use your product but use competitive products.
- Attract totally new customers.

These tasks are arranged in order of difficulty. These strategies can be expressed in terms of the classic product-market matrix shown in Figure 19.2. Earliest results are likely to come from existing customers (they have already demonstrated that they need the product). The slowest results will come from totally new customers. It may be possible to attract a few totally new customers as your sequence of campaigns begins, but achieving significant numbers (and getting them to stay with you) is likely to involve a more concerted effort.

CAMPAIGN OBJECTIVES AND MEASUREMENT

Direct marketing requires quantified objectives. These should come from the quantified objectives of your marketing plan. If these are not quantified (at all or in enough detail), you must still quantify your direct marketing objectives. Include in your campaign plan details of how performance against objectives will be measured, eg through responses, actual sales or research measurements. Your quantification should include:

- Target levels of achievement.
- Dates by which the achievement is to be reached.
- For longer-term campaigns or a sequence of campaigns, where you may wish to change objectives along the way, interim measures to show whether you are achieving targets, and dates for taking these measures.

Fig 19.2

The classic product-market matrix

		Markets	
		Existing	New
Products	Existing	Market penetration	Product development
	New	Market development	Diversification

campaign development

"**Campaign development**" is the heartland of direct marketing. It covers targeting and timing, combined into contact strategies using particular media, the offer and the creative.

Targeting

Your targeting should be as specific as possible. With a clear statement of your marketing objectives and strategies, you should be able to identify the customer types who form the target market for the campaign. Good targeting is a creative process, split into two separate and very different issues:

- Who the campaign is aimed at.
- How to find them and gain access to them.

Creativity is required in answering the "who" question, to determine the different customer types who fit into the target market definition. You use your knowledge of customers to build a picture of the different types of person who form your target market. For example, the target market for a very high contribution executive pension plan might include directors of very profitable small businesses, directors of big companies and so on. Your customer database should give you the ability to turn each of these definitions into different selections. Then different, relevant promotional actions can be developed for each customer type.

If your database has been built over several years of promotions, you can use another kind of creativity – the statistical. A variety of statistical techniques are available to help identify clusters of customers who are similar in one or more ways (eg usage of particular products, location, interests). The higher the quality of your data, the more you can rely on this approach for creative targeting. Also, you will have fewer problems in finding and gaining access to identified groups.

The *number* of customers in your campaign target market should be determined by your quantified campaign objectives. You may be targeting *all* customers in a particular geographical market who fit a particular definition. Quantified sales objectives will also lead through expected response and sales rates to a target number to be contacted. If response or final sales rates are difficult to forecast, then test them. If you have a proper marketing and campaign planning framework, you'll be able to build in time to test.

Timing

Timing can be split into two elements:

- **Macro-timing** – when the campaign should be run. It takes into account other campaigns you might be running and your target customers' needs.
- **Micro-timing** – when each element of your campaign's contact strategy should be run. It takes into account the timing of other elements of the campaign and what is known about the likely receptiveness of customers at different periods.

Macro-timing is determined by your marketing plan. It should lead to a co-ordinated series of campaigns. Obviously, a key part of the justification for any campaign is why it should run at the proposed time. A specific issue is frequency of mailing to good customers. You should control this, but also test it across different products. Evidence from many sectors shows that there is almost no limit to the number of times a loyal customer can be mailed. However, one condition applies to this. Every mailing must be good quality, relevant and consistent with other mailings. The same applies to telephone calls, particularly in industrial markets. No calls must be idle. They must all be of benefit to both you and your customer. If you have no policy on frequency, develop one and keep it under review in the light of experience. Testing and customer research are required to monitor response and attitudes under different mailing frequencies. If you are selling many products and each sale requires more than one contact (eg an initial letter followed by a mail pack, which produces the order), the risk of over-contacting is even greater. Optimum frequency should be established by testing (for response) combined with research (to ensure no customer alienation).

Micro-timing should be based on your in-depth knowledge of customers' receptiveness to different types of communication and how different media work together. Information on this will come largely from past campaigns and from agencies, if they have experience in similar markets.

The offer

The offer is not just a description of the product. It combines one or more propositions with incentive(s) to try the proposition. More than one proposition may be promoted in a campaign. The areas to explore for propositions include:

- Product characteristics – performance, quality of service, reliability, variety of functions.
- Market factors – types of customer, market share, exclusivity.
- Ways of using the product – to save time, to make more profit, to treat.
- Surprising facts about the product, users or usage (ie used by celebrities).
- Price characteristics – value for money, money-back guarantee, discounts.
- Image – top quality, good value, friendly, reliable.
- Needs-satisfying – physical, status etc.
- Company – nationality, energy, direction, customer-orientation.
- Drawbacks of non-use – what the customer loses or misses by not buying.
- Competitive comparison – product, company.
- Newsworthiness – recent changes, anniversaries, topical events, new facilities.

WATCH OUT!

*All these propositions will be **weak** unless your customers are given a reason to respond and a date to respond by. This applies at any stage of any promotional action during the contact strategy. Use sales promotion disciplines to check that your customer is being motivated all the way.*

There are many ways of generating response through the offer. For a high quality response, the offer should be related to the product or service. For example, a free solar calculator may give a high response, but the end result may not be good. However, if your targeting is very accurate (ie those receiving the promotion are the right ones and in the market now!), it may be sensible to "artificially" push up the response by a non-related offer. The offer that is most relevant to the product is normally value-added to the product itself or more of the product (eg two for one), with the "call to action" being a limit on the period of availability of the offer.

To be really sure which offer is the best, test. If there is no time to test, examine the results of past offers for similar campaigns (similar products, media and target markets). Some customers are mail-responsive, others telephone-responsive. Certain kinds of customers respond to certain kinds of offer, others to other kinds of offer.

Creative

In all forms of marketing communication, the creative element – the expression of the campaign in words (printed, broadcast or telemarketing scripts) and pictures – is always the most obvious and attracts the most interest from management.

WATCH OUT!

Poor creative is a major contributory factor to delayed campaigns and last minute rushes. Worse, the scope for confusing customers through the form in which offers are put is also great. Creative usually goes wrong because of poor briefing, lack of standards applied to each medium (eg copy style, typeface), lack of understanding of the target customer and poor communication between client and agency (eg no version control).

Consistency in creative standards is essential. This means much more than standards on the portrayal of the corporate logo. You should have clear standards on the layout of print, the look of pictures, the tone of copy and so on. This need not impose a grey uniformity on your campaigns. But if your aim is to develop a long-term relationship between the customer and your whole company (as represented by your master brand), then the master brand must come through every presentation for it to be reinforced. Each sub-brand must have a clear relationship with the master brand. Rules for relating the two in every medium must be stated.

Where problems arise with the creative

- Imprecise or too generalized a description of the target market.
- Inadequate specification of how the buying process takes place.
- Lack of clarity on desired tone, proposition, and branding.
- Inclusion of too many objectives for the medium being used.
- Not putting every item of creative through the proper approvals process.
- Inconsistency of message and tone with the particular medium being used.

Different media can sustain different degrees of complexity of message. For example, in a mailing several pieces can be included, with different objectives. Provided they are clearly from you and have something in common, there should be no problems. This is because customers tend to look at each enclosure, which may have separate messages. But each enclosure should be single-minded. The portfolio approach is therefore allowable. The same does not apply to television or radio, where the same approach would cause customer confusion.

PROMOTIONAL ACTIONS

The promotional actions used for any campaign should be as simple as possible and based on what the company *knows* works for customers in the target market. Any really new approach should be tested. For each promotional step specify:

- The objectives – what should happen to customers who are the target of the campaign, eg be informed or persuaded, give information, identify themselves as being in the target market, ie hand-raising, buy a product.
- How customers should respond, eg fill in a questionnaire and send it, buy a product and give proof of purchase.
- How the promotional action will achieve this, eg description of mail pack or advertisement, in particular the response device if any.
- How many customers are expected to respond in different ways.

Keep the number of promotional steps to a minimum. However, you may need more than one step. For example, if you want to recruit new customers, you may want to use media advertising or external lists with a straightforward letter and small leaflet to identify prospects, followed up with a more expensive mail pack to those who have confirmed that they are in the target market. This might achieve a more effective contact (in terms of final results versus costs) than sending an expensive pack to the external list.

SELECTIONS

Once your campaign has been drafted out, in terms of target segments and promotional actions, there may be too many segments. This can lead to high promotional costs and poor results. So segments should be prioritized and combined where possible to reduce the complexity of the campaign. Through testing or experience with past campaigns, you should be able to identify rates of trade-off between response rates (and sales rates) and campaign coverage. Too high a response rate, and too much contribution per promotional contact, may mean that the campaign is too small. If the opposite occurs, the campaign may be too big.

SIZING THE SELECTION

The process for determining campaign size should go as follows:

Segment

Break down your target market into target segments

Costs and benefits

Identify the likely cost and benefits of promoting to each target segment. Distinguish fixed costs from variable costs, and also the effect of more precise targeting and targeted offer design on your response rates. If the benefit to you cannot be stated in profit terms but the promotion is essential for strategic reasons, an "alternative cost" measure can be used. This measures what it would have cost to promote to the customer using the next best method. The implication here is that the difference is being saved.

Lists

If your target market is not well represented on your database, consult with your database administration or list brokers about which lists should be used. Consult your agency about which advertising media to use.

Database analysis

If large numbers of your target market are on the database, experiment with selections until:

- Several target segments have been identified as not overlapping and differing significantly in the kind of offer that can be made to them.
- A simple selection criterion will suffice, because more complex selection criteria do not give target segments of sufficient size for cost- effective promotion.

Selections

Define the segments for final selection purposes.

Measurement

Specify all the criteria by which success of the campaign will be measured.

LIST USAGE

In choosing a list, follow these basic rules:

- Your own database will give better results than external lists.
- The best external lists will have customers that resemble your existing customers and have many of your existing customers on them.
- A responders' list pulls better than non-responders (eg compiled), and a list of customers with proven histories of buying from a medium (mail, telephone, off the page) pulls best of all for that medium.

Mail order lists

Mail order purchase lists include fashion, gardening, household, book/record clubs, magazine subscriptions, holidays, investment/insurance, gifts and self-improvement. If a list is not available, try inserts in a publication that reaches your target. Choose a publication which defines a strong affinity (eg a members' publication).

Responder lists

Lists of responders but not purchasers (enquirers who didn't buy, controlled circulation publication requests, exhibition attendees, life-style databases compiled from returned questionnaires) are usually less responsive but often offer a better ability to target.

Compiled lists

Compiled lists (investors, professionals, electoral roll, etc) are less responsive. They are often compiled as part of a data-gathering exercise rather than to find good prospects. In business to business marketing, job title may be better than the name, due to high staff turnover. Shareholder lists are valuable in the UK, because of privatizations.

Deciding on lists

To make a decision about lists, you need data on the source and type of offer from which the list was derived. The source may be a mail promotion, insert, media, readership/membership (controlled/paid), compilations (source, how built). A list broker's working knowledge of the list may be needed, not just the profile. This means knowing what works and what does not. You will need to know the following about a list:

- Frequency (how often list members buy/respond), recency (when they last did so), amount (how much they bought) and category (what type of product they bought) of purchase.

- Date of expiry, if the list is subscription expiries (this shows they have at least bought at some time in the past).
- Who the most recent purchasers are ("hot-line").
- How often the list is mailed – the best are usually mailed most often, because they work and because list members like receiving and responding.
- When and where it was sourced, and when it was last cleaned.

WATCH OUT!

Although externally provided data may be very valuable, if you have a customer database, be selective about what information you buy. Always test the usefulness of additional data, whether it is new names and addresses, or additional information on customers you already have on file. Deduplicate and carry out spot checks for poor spelling and data in the wrong fields. A mailing addressed to Mr Deep-Sea Diver instead of Mr Brown may be funny but not for all customers. It does nothing for your credibility and your brand!

Most lists are rental only, with a high degree of security. Lists will also have seeds on them (usually members of staff from the owners or their agencies) to ensure that you do not misuse the list. You may be asked for samples of mailings by list owners. Plan your list usage well in time, to ensure the right coverage and quality for the right price. Allow time for the various data processing operations needed before you can use a list.

Allow time for testing each list. To test a list, the volume needs to be large enough to test it against other sources of data, to check that the variance in the result is due to the list. The recommended size of a list test cell is 5–10 thousand for a first time test, 25-50 thousand to validate. If the list is too small, a sample of the list should not be tested – test the whole list.

campaign implementation

IN-HOUSE WORK

In direct marketing, much of the work in delivering campaigns is done in-house. This can surprise companies which are used to communicating with their customers mostly through media advertising (television, radio, press etc). Large users of direct marketing have to manage relationships between many people. They include:

- Specialist direct marketers.
- Internal "customers" (eg product and brand managers, sales management, store operations management).
- Systems staff (for the customer and other databases).
- A wide network of suppliers (direct marketing agencies, print production, telemarketing agencies, mailing and fulfilment houses etc).

The "norms" of managing direct marketing have their roots in the practices of traditional mail order suppliers. These include publishers, general catalogue operators and speciality suppliers (eg collectables). Most of them have well developed management procedures for planning and implementing direct marketing campaigns. The same procedures should underlie direct marketing management in companies which have "real operations" (retail stores, factories, sales forces and branches). But managing direct marketing in such companies poses very different problems. These include problems of ensuring that the many people involved in direct marketing work together and produce quality campaigns and implement them in a quality manner.

If you are or aim to be a serious direct marketing user, try to be methodical about the planning and execution of campaigns, to ensure high quality.

WATCH OUT!

Lack of quality leads to:

○ *Lost market share.*

○ *High costs of late response to competitive challenge.*

○ *Too high expenditures to achieve a given effect.*

Causes of quality problems

- Late, incomplete briefing by "internal clients", eg product managers. This results in hurried campaign development cycles, poor targeting, rushed printing, unclear instructions and the inevitable consequences of poor material or the wrong material being sent to customers, or responses being handled badly.
- Too aggressive objectives relating to size of database. This leads to high volumes of low quality customer data being brought onto the database. This in turn leads to high mis-targeting and returns rates, and high costs of database maintenance relative to financial returns.
- Lack of analysis of past results. This leads to poor targeting and wrong media choice.
- Lack of communication with those at the "coal-face" (eg field sales staff, branch workers). This leads to systems being developed which are cumbersome and difficult to use. It also leads to applications being developed in the wrong order (eg direct mail instead of telemarketing). This is because unless those who work at the coal face do their bit in "closing the sales loop", even the best laid campaign plans will not be realized. For example, a mail shot which produces a 20% response rate is no use if sales-people are too busy to follow up the leads, or do not understand what they are supposed to do with them.

The solution to these problems lies in using industrial project management disciplines.

PROJECT MANAGEMENT

Direct marketing usually involves running many campaigns a year. Each of these campaigns is a project. The problem with managing these projects is that each is different. To manage this kind of work, project management techniques are required. These are designed to progress complex projects through teams of people working on them. These processes include the following.

The project file

You need a comprehensive project file for each campaign. It includes the relevant marketing plan details, forms for briefing all suppliers, the project timetable, sign-off authorities, criteria and codes for selections, descriptions and codes for all promotional material, forecast returns and actual results. A master copy of this file should be held by your campaign manager and duplicates with all parties involved.

Project planning software

This is used to schedule the tasks required to deliver campaigns and reschedule them where slips occur. It is also used to identify bottlenecks. It also produces status reports and enables us to identify accountabilities for failures. However, you can do this manually through using a simple spreadsheet template. This allows you to sort tasks according to their type, accountability, budget etc. See Figure 19.3 for a simple spreadsheet template.

Targeting and scheduling processes

You need processes for targeting and scheduling campaigns. These reduce clashes and increase the effectiveness of targeting. The processes range from consensus to directive. The consensus approach may be through a team of all interested parties. The directive approach may be through a database directorate having authority to determine campaign sequencing. In both cases, your in-depth understanding of the database and past campaign results should be deployed in determining which campaigns go forward.

Communication

You need structured processes for communicating campaign status to all parties involved. In their most advanced form, these processes are computerized. In some cases, an extract from the campaign database is sent by electronic mail. In more advanced companies, all those involved in a campaign have direct access to relevant parts of a computerized campaign project file. Local area network software has progressed dramatically in the last few years. It is easy to adapt workflow packages to the needs of direct marketing project management.

Training

Your staff must receive the training they need to develop the skills their position requires. Typically, a specialist group of database/direct marketers, acting as both a consultant and a technical expert with authority to decide, needs training in:

- Basic "consultative skills" – listening, communicating, influencing, interactive skills (meetings), contracting (fixing agreements).
- How to put together projects that will meet customer needs, and manage the projects.

Fig 19.3

A simple campaign project plan spreadsheet template

P = planned, R = revised plan =done

Task name	No.	Resource	Budget	1	2	3	4	5	6	7	8	9	10	11	12	13	14	15	16	17	18	19	20	21	Comment
																	Week number								
Define target markets	1.01																								
Analyze database	1.02				P																				
Brief research	1.03																								
Research customer needs	1.04				P	P																			
Workshop	1.05						P																		
Quantify objectives	1.06						P																		
Define plan	1.07						P	P																	
Define contact strategy	1.08							P	P																
Brief print	1.09								P																
Brief script	1.10								P																
Select test list	2.01								P																
Prepare test mailing	2.02								P	P															
Prepare test telemarketing script	2.03								P	P															
Send test mailing	2.04										P	P	P	P											
Follow-up calls	2.05										P	P	P	P											
Follow-up sales visits	2.06											P	P	P	P										
Compile results	2.07														P	P									
Evaluate	2.08															P									
Finalize list	3.01																P								
Modify mailing	3.01																P								
Modify script	3.02																P								
Send mailing	3.03																		P	P					
Follow-up calls	3.04																		P	P	P				
Follow-up sales visits	3.05																			P	P	P			
Compile results	3.06																							P	
Evaluate	3.07																							P	

THE MANAGEMENT PROCESS FOR PROGRESSING A CAMPAIGN

Today, many direct marketers have to design and deliver campaigns without any management process. Some are given as guidance a list of "stages of campaign development" (see Figure 19.4). This was fine in the days when direct marketing consisted of the odd tactical campaign. Today, when direct marketing has become central to the strategic marketing of many companies, it is not good enough. Your process should specify clearly:

1. The steps involved in developing and delivering a campaign, and who is responsible for them.

2. A specification of the data and communication requirements required to support the flow of work, and who is responsible for providing and communicating the information.

Fig 19.4

Stages of campaign development

Brefing/planning
Campaign confirmed
Agency brief
Proposition agreed
Concept agreed
Contact strategy agreed
Media brief produced
Confirm media plan
Receive media details
Issue media details to suppliers
Systems team briefed by direct marketers
Systems programme produced
Internal lists ordered
Lists produced
External lists ordered
External lists delivered
Go/no go
Check campaign logistics
Brief internal staff HQ regions/branches
Campaign live
Campaign ends
Evaluate results

Advertising
Creative agreed
Copy approved
Artwork approved
Copy dispatched
Advertisements appear

Mail
Creative agreed
Approved pack dummy
Lists ordered
Final copy approved
Mailing/fulfilment houses briefed
Print production schedule issued
Approved artwork
Artwork ready for print
Laser proof approved
Sign off live pack
First mailing
First fulfilment

Inbound telemarketing
Brief telemarketing agency/group
Scripts agreed for testing
Operator briefing
Systems test
Scripts revised after testing
Scripts live

Outbound telemarketing
Brief telemarketing agency/group
Scripts agreed for testing
Operator briefing
Systems test
Scripts revised after testing
Scripts live

Cross-campaign planning and co-ordination

Unless all your marketing communication is based on direct marketing, you need to co-ordinate direct marketing with other marketing communications. Campaign planning and co-ordination is not theoretically complex. It is just a question of making sure that campaigns deliver messages whose content and timing is co-ordinated and which contribute to the development of the company's brand(s). This means co-ordinating every aspect of campaign development.

Co-ordinating targeting, contact strategies – media and timing

Co-ordination within direct marketing is mainly a question of selections (or lists) and timing their use. In companies whose main marketing channel is direct, such as mail, and which have good customer databases, co-ordinating selections is the key activity. It is so important that some companies treat access to the database as the key marketing decision. Brand managers and sales managers are required to submit their briefs to the database manager. The database manager's job is then to determine who are the best prospects for the campaign in question and when they should be addressed. In deciding, targeting, timing and offers of other campaigns are taken into account, as well as strategic priorities and degree of selectivity of campaigns.

IN THE REAL WORLD

In some companies, the database manager suggests which campaigns should be run and what contact strategies they should use. From being a gatekeeper of the database, the database manager becomes the initiator of campaign ideas. This is because, through analysis of the database, the campaigns that should be run can be identified. The database manager plays the customer-advocate, with customers speaking through the database on the basis of what campaigns they have responded to and what campaigns are missing.

Offer co-ordination

If your company needs direct marketing to push several products at the same time, co-ordinating can be difficult. Direct marketers live with the constant possibility of clashes in timing. However, the earlier the warning about the need to promote a particular product, the more time you get to develop ways of presenting products through offers – hence the importance of the link with the marketing plan and of communications with senior marketing management.

If products differ greatly in their nature and target market, co-ordination is not a problem. But if products are similar, with overlapping target markets, ways of positioning products relative to each other must be developed. You need time to test how far target markets actually do overlap, so that non-overlapping segments can be identified and promoted to differently.

Offer co-ordination demands a deep understanding of target markets and product benefits. The secret of offer co-ordination lies in early briefing on product benefits, clear and early-stated views on target markets, and early warning of campaign timings. So make sure this happens with you, by insisting on the need for process.

Organizing co-ordination

Many companies organize co-ordination by committee. Briefs are collated and submitted to a campaign co-ordination committee. This meets regularly to review all briefs and slot them in. In other companies, a planning department receives all briefs and allocates them a budget and timing slot. Whatever approach is used, the most important achievement is getting briefs submitted well in time. The output of the planning process must be properly communicated, so that the whole team knows what it must do when.

Campaign statuses

Because it takes time to decide if and when a campaign should run, a campaign can have different statuses, from being a gleam in the eye of a product manager, to finished. Here are the kinds of statuses your process needs:

- **Provisional** – you have identified the campaign as needing consideration, but have not yet submitted it for formal consideration by the campaign co-ordination process. Normally, a deadline for such consideration should be set. The campaign proposal should contain an outline brief, timing and suggested budget.
- **Submitted** – you have submitted the campaign for consideration through the campaign co-ordination process, with the brief and timing firmed up. Again, a deadline for approval or otherwise should be set.
- **Approved** – the campaign has been approved by your campaign co-ordination process, with timings for development, launch and close agreed.
- **Budgeted** – although an outline budget should be considered when a campaign is at earlier stages, final budgeting should not take place until quotes are received from suppliers. There is no point in your getting detailed quotes before the campaign is approved, because this wastes suppliers' time and may slow down other projects. Your outline budget should be based on experience with earlier campaigns. An outline budget also stops you wasting suppliers' time if the requirement turns out to be infeasible within the outline budget.
- **Under development** – you have started serious work on the campaign, your suppliers have been briefed and money is being spent!
- **Live** – the campaign has hit the market.
- **Completed** – the campaign is completed. No further actions in the market will be taken.
- **Closed** – the results of the campaign have been analyzed and properly documented.

The above statuses are "operational" statuses. They describe where your project stands in its normal process of development. However, things do not always run so smoothly. Campaigns may be cancelled, deferred or even absorbed into other campaigns. So four further statuses are needed, as follows:

- **Current** – the campaign is at one of the above statuses and progressing normally.
- **Cancelled** – your campaign will not go ahead. This may be determined at any stage until the campaign is live. Records of the work done for the campaign should be kept, as they may be needed later.
- **Deferred** – the campaign is deferred until later. No new timing has been specified and it will require resubmission through the co-ordination process.
- **Absorbed** – the campaign has been absorbed into another campaign (perhaps after a delay)

WATCH OUT!

The above four statuses are "management statuses". Changing a management status has important resource implications and may have legal or contractual implications with suppliers. For example, cancelling a campaign may create a risk of breach of contract with suppliers.

If these statuses are used, then it becomes much easier to manage campaign co-ordination and resource allocation processes. The whole team, including suppliers, will know at any one time what campaigns are being considered, planned, worked upon and finished.

STAFFING

One neglected aspect of direct marketing management is recognition of the different roles that need to be carried out to ensure that campaigns are delivered properly. Some have already been discussed implicitly – the campaign manager, the manager responsible for co-ordination. However, there are other roles that management must fulfil:

- **Initiation or origination** – coming up with the ideas for campaigns.
- **Workload control** – ensuring that the resources of the team – including suppliers – are adequate to meet the demands upon them and that work is scheduled so as to optimize use of these resources.
- **Campaign administration** – ensuring that all campaigns are well documented and communicated and that everyone in the team meets their deadlines.
- **Delivery** – actually doing the job of bringing the campaign to market.
- **Sponsoring** – providing the funds.
- **Being the internal customer** – the person benefiting from the campaign, typically a product, service or sales manager.

In some companies, these roles are combined in the direct marketing manager. But in large companies doing lots of direct marketing, the roles are often split. The most under-rated of all these functions is campaign administration. Although quite a junior person can fulfil this role, good campaign administrators are worth their weight in gold.

All the foregoing may seem a little top-heavy for the small company. However, there is no reason to suppose that the small user of direct marketing will face any fewer problems in managing direct marketing than the larger user. Indeed, the small user may have one person doing *all* the marketing. With a few adjustments, all the foregoing can be used to manage any kind of marketing campaign – whether an advertising campaign, a sales force campaign, a product launch or a sales promotion.

MANAGING RESOURCES

A large marketing department also requires a production process. This views the department as a sort of jobbing workshop, through which campaign work progresses. Each "job" requires certain resources to progress it, and each resource is required for a certain amount of time. If all campaigns are organized using the kind of status descriptions used above, then it should be relatively simple to organize production planning. The key question is how much each campaign takes of the different resources available. These might include direct marketing managers, print specialists, database and systems people, media planners and so on.

The production planning process reviews forward workload with these aims:

- To check that the workload required of each resource is feasible.
- Where the workload of any individual or department is temporarily too high, to arrange for the redeployment of resource or the hiring of external resource on a temporary basis.
- Where the workload of any resource is permanently too high, to arrange permanent redeployment or increased resource.
- Where budgetary constraints prevent resource readjustment, to recommend that work be deferred or ended.

The planning horizon depends on the average period from the time a campaign is identified is likely to run, to the time it goes live – its gestation period. The planning period should be at least double the gestation period.

INFORMATION REQUIREMENTS

To plan properly, all planning information should be collated periodically, typically every few weeks. The following information is required:

- The status of all projects under gestation or live.
- The likely loadings of all these projects on different members of staff and agencies.
- Likely bottlenecks

FAST TRACK

Some companies have computerized the whole process of campaign management, using local area network technology to ensure that each member of staff involved in the campaign can access information about the status of their own and other work. When your systems requirements are next under consideration, put forward this area as a possible candidate for investment.

summary

All that we have described above is no more than common sense. The problem is that most direct marketers find it hard to make the time for good management. However, times are changing and the value of quality is being understood more widely. Quality also depends partly on testing campaigns, to make sure they're right for the market. A critical aspect of good direct marketing management is making time for testing. Let's see what you have to do to test campaigns properly – in our next chapter.

20

testing the hit

- Every aspect of a campaign can be tested.

- Testing costs money, so focus your testing on the most important and costly aspects of a campaign – targeting, media selection and the offer.

- To understand the results of tests, you need to know a little basic statistics.

what is testing, and why should you test?

The key to direct marketing success is to discover what works and to repeat it. Testing helps you discover what works, and what doesn't, to repeat successes and avoid costly failures. There are two main kinds of test:

- On a sample of the target market, before full roll-out, eg to test whether targeting and media are right.
- Within a full campaign, eg customers receive different offers or packs, and you discover which works best.

FAST TRACK

Try to combine both kinds of test – test before your full campaign and during it. You may not have time for the first, so at least do the second, so you know what will work best next time.

specifying testing

In nearly every campaign, you should have scope for testing. You can test:

- Media – which to use to contact your customers.
- Lists – whether your own or external.
- Offers – the core offer and also the promotional offers that motivate customers to buy – now!
- Contact strategy – the sequence of promotional steps that make up your campaign (for example, does mail followed by telemarketing work better than straight telemarketing?).
- Creative – how each offer is expressed.
- Pack composition – how many offers, how they are enclosed etc.

In all your campaign briefs, you should specify clearly what should be tested, and what you are trying to learn by testing (sometimes more than just "which pulls best?" eg what sales targets you should set for future campaigns, your hypotheses about particular segments).

the objective of testing

The starting point for all testing is to identify what questions you want answered.

- Do older people respond better than younger people?
- Do richer people respond better than poorer people?
- Do people who have seen and remembered a television advertisement respond better than people who haven't?
- Is product X a better basis for an offer than product Y?
- Does the level of education of customers affect their response?

*Don't test without hypotheses that you **need** to have checked. Testing can be expensive. Variations in copy cost money. Including a group of people in the test to see whether they will respond costs money if they turn out to be low responders. So justify your need in terms of:*

○ *Your marketing objectives in respect of the target market.*

○ *The likely benefits of testing, set against the costs.*

Define your test needs in measurable ways. For example:

○ *Define in quantifiable ways the terms you use ("level of education", "younger", "poorer").*

○ *Ensure that data that support the quantifying criteria you use will be available (eg because it is already on the database or because it will be gathered as part of the campaign, perhaps through a questionnaire).*

Definitions and quantifiability are central to testing. If you haven't got an agreed definition of a factor to be measured, or if it can't be quantified in practice, you can't test whether it is important.

A question expressed in a form you can test is called a *hypothesis*. Thus, a computer company might want to test the hypothesis that at least 5% of its existing customers who ordered more than £3,000 of supplies from it in the previous 12 months would take up an offer of one box of computer paper free with every 10 boxes if ordered before a given date.

the aim of statistics – to generalize

Once you have agreed what needs to be tested, the next question is how to test it. The simple answer is – try it out on different groups. So how should you choose the groups?

The main use of statistics is to show what the characteristics of a population (customers in a particular target market) are. The population might be a past or present population, or a future population. For the latter, the description is a forecast. In direct marketing, your aim is to use the characteristics of past and present populations to predict the character of future populations. The future may only be 10 weeks away. For example, you may want to forecast the response of all consumers of a certain type to a given offer. The definition of past, present and future populations stays the same – except for time. But as time passes, the world changes. Competitors may launch spoiling campaigns if the test has been noticed by them. They may launch new products. The government may raise or lower taxes. In the more distant future, the composition of the population changes. So never forget that testing is a predictive activity.

The "centris paribus" problem applies particularly to the use of media advertising in direct marketing. There may be great variations in the level of attention achieved by your advertisement or insert and in the effectiveness of the circulation you achieve. Certain days of the week might produce better responses.

In consumer markets, list composition changes constantly – if for no other reason than the fact that people move house – about 8-12% a year, depending on the state of the housing market. Also, some types of people (eg the young, students) move much more often than others. If a list owner has very good tracking of members of the list, and if you can assume that the fact of moving makes no difference to the behaviour of the movers, then you might be happy with using that list for some time, because a single test result showed that it was better than another. However, this may be unwise, particularly if when the list was tested, another list produced nearly as good a response rate. There is a strong argument here for retesting at least annually.

narrowing down what is to be tested

You can't test every option. You can use research and judgement to narrow down the range of options to be tested. Your judgement should be based on your experience of what has worked with which types of customer and product in the past. If details of your past campaign results are computerized or available in an accessible form, you should be able to analyze them and narrow down possibilities early on in the process of campaign development. If you're new to direct marketing, choose an agency with a lot of experience in your market sector, as you'll need to rely on their experience.

sampling and inference

Testing is used to generalize from past and present to the future, and from part of your target market to your whole target market.

> This process of generalization is called "**statistical inference**". The term "**inference**" is used for good reason – you can never "prove" that a future response rate will be x% – you can only infer it. In other words, you can only say that it is **likely** to happen, not that it is **certain**, ie test results are **probabilistic**. The smaller the sample you're testing on, the less certain you can be that your inference is correct.

Even if you could analyze your entire target market, forecasting its future response rate would still be an inference, because other things might have changed. But if your target market is composed of thousands of customers or more, analyzing your whole target market is likely to be expensive and time-consuming, so you need to test on samples.

CONFIDENCE INTERVALS

Because tests are probabilistic, you need a separate estimate of the likelihood that your test prediction will be fulfilled. Here, we use the idea of the "**confidence interval**". For example, suppose your campaign produced a 5% response rate for a particular pack sent to a sample of your customers, you can't say that this will be the exact response if you repeat the campaign for your whole market. You might be able to say that there is a 95% chance that the response rate for the pack would be between 4% and 6% when sent to the whole population. Put another way, there might be a 5% chance that response will be outside the 4-6% band.

Use of this kind of language raises problems. Many marketers' knowledge of statistics is confined to the simple analysis and presentation of tables. In testing, slightly more advanced statistical concepts are used. The problem is that although statistics has a strong foundation in common sense, as soon as numbers and technical statistical terms start to be used, the eyes of many managers glaze over. They ask for the table or the graph.

FAST TRACK

*It is **your** job to make statistics intelligible to management – and of course the job of this book to help.*

The language of statistics is drawn from sampling theory, which deals with how to choose samples from populations and then predict the characteristics of the population from the characteristics of the sample.

EXAMPLE

Suppose a retail store wants to test the take-up of a unit-linked investment product by its 1.5 million storecard holders. The product has been designed by analyzing competitive offerings and identifying which have been most successful and what extra features could be built in. So the detailed specifications of the product are not being tested, but the way in which it is presented to the target market is. Three ways of presenting it are designed and a test is set up to discover:

1. Whether the product would succeed if marketed to the entire card-holder base.

2. If not, whether there are groups within the customer base to whom the product could be marketed cost-effectively.

3. Which version of the offer draws the greatest response (or "pulls the best").

Let's focus on the first objective. If 20 samples of 1000 are drawn from the population truly randomly (so that everyone has an equal chance of being included), they should have more or less the same characteristics, but they will not be identical. This is because even if each sample is chosen truly randomly, it cannot be guaranteed that each sample will have exactly the same composition. This also applies to their likelihood of responding to the promotion. So, when tested, these 20 samples might give these response rates (rounded to the nearest 0.1%):

○ Six samples gave 2.0%   ○ Two samples gave 1.8%

○ Five samples gave 1.9%   ○ Two samples gave 2.2%

○ Five samples gave 2.1%

Fig 20.1

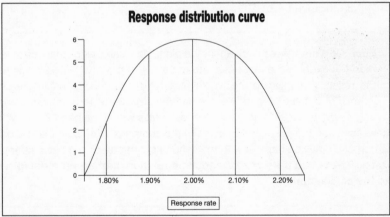

These are depicted in Figure 20.1. Suppose then that a prediction had to be made as to what the result would be if the offer was made to the whole target market. The simple response is to say 2%. But there is obviously a good chance that it might not be 2%. After all, in 70% (ie 14) of the samples, the response was not 2%, but greater or less). Perhaps it would be better to say that there is an 80% chance of the response rate falling between 1.9% and 2.1%? This would be a much fairer summary of the situation. Would it be possible to say that there is a 100% chance (certainty) that the result will be between 1.8% and 2.2%? Unfortunately, the answer is no. The 21st sample (which was not drawn) might have produced a very low or a very high response rate, destroying the neat generalization.

▶

► This raises another point. When the expected response rate is as low as 2%, it would be quite easy to draw a sample which contained very few or even no responders. With a sample size of 1000, this only means missing 10 or 20 people out. So the smaller the expected proportion, the larger the sample needs to be to ensure that it is representative. If a response rate of 50% was expected, then it would be quite hard to draw a sample with no respondents or even one with a proportion as low as 25%. ○

Obviously, the more samples that are drawn, the more accurate your prediction. But more samples cost more money, which statistics can save. Statistical theory can show what the range of likely outcomes in the total population might be, based on one sample. The larger the sample, of course, then the more accurate the prediction. But the prediction should always be a range, with a probability attached to it, as above. As the example also showed, the broader the range, the greater the probability. The range used in a prediction is called a **confidence interval**, since it indicates the range that the predictor is confident about. The probability that the response lies within the range is called the **confidence level**. The four key statistical measures are closely related, namely:

● Expected response.
● Size of sample.
● Significance level (the probability that the estimated range of responses is accurate).
● Confidence interval (the upper and lower limits of the estimate for a given significance level).

Suppose a market research agency is planning a campaign to launch a new market report. It expects the response rate to be 4%. If it wants to be 95% sure whether the result, if applied to the whole target market, will fall within the confidence interval of between 3 and 5%, the sample size needs to be much larger than if it only wants to be 90% sure that the result falls within the band 2-6%. What size is chosen depends upon the costs and benefits of the campaign. For example, if break-even is 1.5%, the company may be happier with the second set of criteria, and so be happier with a smaller test cell. **Note that the size of the total population, perhaps surprisingly, does not enter into the calculation.** ○

The confidence interval can also be expressed as the error level you are prepared to tolerate. In the above example, the company might be able to afford an error rate of 2.5%, the difference between the expected response rate (4%) and the break-even response rate (1.5%).

The formula for determining the size of a test sample is:
$$\frac{C^2 \times R\,(100 - R)}{E^2}$$
where
E = The percentage error from the response rate that you are prepared to tolerate.

R = Expected response rate.

C = A constant determined by the required significance level. For example, for 95% confidence, it would be 1.96. 95% is the level most direct marketers work to. The constant is higher for higher significance levels. The constant comes from a **distribution table** (see below), which shows the likelihood of outcomes.

The same formula is used to find the effect of changes in the tolerable error rate when you change the size of the test sample.

distributions

Distributions are a vital asset to statisticians. They are used to generate tables, which allow you to look up what one of the above statistical measures is, given the other three. As four dimensional tables are quite complicated, they are simplified by using grouped sample sizes (eg 500-999) and by using two or three levels of significance (eg 95%, 97.5% and 99%). These tables can be bought separately and are also included in statistics text books. They are based on the known properties of the distribution of random events. The commonest distribution curve used for this is the **normal distribution**.

FAST TRACK

Always aim for an accurate prediction. Too low a roll-out response may mean financial losses. Too high a response may mean that your fulfilment house runs out of stock – not good for your customer service image. However, provided that once the roll-out campaign is launched, close track is kept of responses to see whether they are exceeding the prediction, and provided that new stocks can be obtained quickly, you may just want to predict what your lowest likely response rate will be.

In the retail example above, 90% of the samples produced a response of 1.9% or above. In the market research example, if break-even was 3%, the company might want to be 99% sure that the campaign would exceed this level. This is called a "one-tail" test, because it concentrates on one tail of the distribution curve, ie the proportion of the distribution to the right of 3%.

testing differences

In direct marketing, you often need to use several samples, perhaps to test different creative expressions, different offers and different selections. Each sample is usually called a "**test cell**". It will often be necessary to test whether the response in one cell differs significantly from that in another. For example, two samples might have response rates of 1.2% and 1.8%, with 95% confidence intervals of 0.9% to 1.5% and 1.5% to 2.1%. You might want to know whether it is likely that these samples came from the same population. In this case, specific statistical tests are available for the difference between two sampling proportions.

sampling methods

All statistical inference relies on **truly random** samples (the distribution curves are based on this assumption). Samples that are biased in any way give a poor basis for prediction, but, in the interests of economy and speed, compromises are sometimes made, but these can be risky. In theory, the only way to produce a truly random sample is to number all the population and pick the sample using a random number table. This is feasible with small samples or where the list or database is computerized. Most computers have random sampling routines.

The most familiar method used is the **one in n** sample. This means picking every nth (eg 4th or 5th) name. However, if the names are in any order (eg alphabetical) and the length of the list is not known accurately, then this approach can omit names from the end of the list if the sample size is given and the proportion to be sampled is over-estimated. This could lead to the omission of many people whose names come at the end of the alphabet, or if male and female names alternate, then choosing an even number will lead to a horrendous gender bias.

"**Quota sampling**" is a cost-cutting technique. Here, sampling takes place (often on a haphazard basis) until the quota is reached. A good example of this would be stuffing a leaflet in the first 500 packs sent out, or handing out 500 leaflets to shoppers in a town centre. In theory, quota samples are not truly representative because they are not randomly drawn.

"**Stratified sampling**" is used where prior information is available about the population. Random samples are chosen within defined groups. This is done to make sure key groups are represented in the sample. Strictly speaking, generalizing from these samples should be based upon information about the distribution of the stratifying characteristics in the overall population.

---

test matrices

In order to test what factor is producing the response, you must try to hold as many factors equal as possible between test cells. For example, if there are two test cells, each with different offers and different list selection criteria, it will not be possible to say whether any difference in response rate is due to the offer or the selection. If the response rate is the same, it will still be impossible to say whether the result was achieved by the offer or the targeting, or some combination of the two. So if two offers and two target markets need to be tested, then each pack should be offered to each target market, as in this diagram:

	List M	List N
Offer P	Test cell A	Test cell B
Offer Q	Test cell C	Test cell D

A more economic solution might seem to be this:

	List M	List N
Offer P	Test cell A	Test cell B
Offer Q	Test cell C	Not test cell

This assumes that the result of Offer Q on List N can be inferred by the difference between the two offers on List M. This may not be correct, as Offer Q may work relatively better on List N than on List M.

When the test is carried out, it might yield these response rates.

	List M	List N
Offer P	2.2%	2.5%
Offer Q	2.8%	2.9%

These should be subjected to two statistical tests:

● Are any of these rates significantly different from zero, given sample size?
● Are the rates significantly different from each other?

> The term "**significantly different**" means that the results cannot be explained by random sampling errors and that it is unlikely the two cells' response rates are the same, ie it is likely that the difference was caused by your actions (targeting, offer etc).

split runs

"**Split run**" is a term used to describe sampling when different inserts are used for a given published medium. With modern inserting machinery, it is possible to alternate packs to achieve a one in n effect for the whole circulation of a paper. The old way of doing it was to physically split the run and insert one pack in one run and a second pack in another run.

the control group

In many tests, one cell is designated as a control group, to which you don't promote. For example, an airline club card marketing department might send to members of a control group only normal club mailings and no special offers. This would allow identification of the overall effect of mailings on flight volumes. Or a credit card company might try a variant on its standard membership solicitation mailing. The control cell would be the standard mailing. In other cases, the control cell may be chosen as the one believed to be the best option. In this case, tabular presentation may be of differences relative to the control cell. To ensure that the control cell produces high levels of statistical validity, a larger sample may be allocated to it.

response rates vs sales rates

Most of this chapter is phrased in terms of response rates, which measure success in terms of the proportion of customers making a first response. This is a good (but not the only) measure of the success of the initial communication. However, in the end, you are interested in sales. **Every test that can be performed with response rates can also be performed with sales rates**. However, the contact strategy that leads to sales may require higher and higher levels of human intervention as the sale nears its completion. This applies particularly to complex industrial products. For example, the sales performance of a lead generating campaign may be higher in one market segment than another. This may be because the sales force specializing in the first segment was better trained or more highly motivated. This would be visible in the better sales closing ratio (ratio of sales to leads). Would this higher closing ratio necessarily be attributable entirely to better selling, or could the offer design have appealed more to that segment, for example? On this information, there is no way of knowing.

TESTING COMPLEX CONTACT STRATEGIES

The simplest form of testing – of response rates to a mailing – has been carried out for decades, almost ever since mail order was invented. More complex testing of multi-stage contact strategies is a newer activity. It has become more common as direct marketing has become involved in achieving a wider range of tasks and working with a greater variety of marketing channels (eg retail, sales force). Tests involving these channels usually take a long time to set up. This is because you need to:

● Brief and motivate sales staff.
● Distribute materials to a large number of sales points.
● Set up systems and procedures for distributing leads to a large number of offices.

Some of these tests could more accurately be described as pilots. Because the costs involved in using different contact strategies vary, simple comparisons of sales rates are not usually appropriate.

EXAMPLE

Suppose a company in the business to business market wants to compare these three contact strategies:

1. Direct mail followed by a personal sales call only to those customers indicating a definite desire to order.

2. Telemarketing followed by a personal sales call only to those customers indicating a definite desire to order.

3. Cold sales force calling

(Note the simplifying assumption that there is no drop-out from those customers asking for or agreeing to a sales call in strategies 1 and 2.)

The overall cost per initial contact will rise from the first to the third, but the effectiveness

---

of initial contact will also rise. This would be measured by the chance of moving to the next stage of the sale. Therefore the revenue per initial contact will be much higher. So the only comparison that makes sense will be some measure based on profitability (revenue from the sale less the total cost of the contact strategy). Statistical tests can still be applied to such figures, although it can be argued that many of the assumptions underlying these tests will not be valid. It might be better just to use management judgement. Suppose the figures for the three strategies were as follows:

	List 1	List 2	List 3
Number of contacts	1500	400	100
Sales rate (%)	2	5	10
Number of sales	30	20	10
Revenue per sale (£)	500	750	1200
Total revenue (£)	15000	15000	12000
Cost per initial contact (£)	1	5	60
Total initial contact cost (£)	1500	2000	6000
Cost per follow-up contact (£)	60	60	0
Cost of follow-up contact (£)	1800	1200	0
Total contact cost	3300	3200	6000
Total contribution (£)	11700	11800	6000

This shows that strategies 1 and 2 are clearly the most cost-effective, with little difference between them. The test shows that the direct sales call by itself is very ineffective. However, if the objective is to cover the market thoroughly (perhaps to fend off competitive attack), the direct sales call might be used for companies which are known not to be responsive to direct mail or telemarketing approaches. Their characteristics could be discovered by analyzing the results of the tests of strategies 1 and 2. ○

FAST TRACK

Even in a direct mail test, the same approach should also be used. This is because in many direct mail tests, there is not a fixed sum that the customer is paying. So use profit as your preferred measure of success.

One list may draw a much better response than another, in terms of numbers of respondents, but a much lower revenue per respondent. This is only for the first sale. If the mailing is being used to recruit new customers, the estimated life-time value of customers should really be used to assess which list is the best.

EXAMPLE

A book club company selling non-fiction "household" books (do it yourself, beauty, health etc) is investigating the market for romantic fiction, following its receipt of a research report indicating that about 20% of its customers also read romantic fiction. This figure would yield a reasonable business return, but not enough to justify investment in new titles. To justify entering this market, it needs to recruit

▶

many more new customers. It is considering which lists to rent for this purpose. A demographic analysis of readers of romantic fiction (from the research) suggested that the prime readership group for the product would be women – late teenagers to mid 40s. It decides to trial three lists which list brokers have recommended as containing a high proportion of mail-responsive people in this group. In the test, an identical pack is sent to 10,000 members of each list. The test gives the following results:

	List 1	List 2	List 3
Number mailed	10000	10000	10000
Response rate (%)	3.0	2.0	3.1
Number of respondents	300	200	310
Average value of first order (£)	7.5	12.9	6.9
Total value of first orders (£)	22	2580	2139
Cost per pack, including postage (£)	0.3	0.3	0.3
Total cost of mailing	3000	3000	3000
Loss against first response (£)	750	420	861

On response rate, List 3 looks best, but not on revenue, where List 2 pulls best. However, all hangs on second and later orders, where the situation might be reversed. Also, management might want to use the lower band of the confidence interval rather than the test response rate, to identify the risk. ○

advanced statistics

In many companies where direct marketing has been in use for some time, more advanced methods of interpreting test and campaign results are used. These methods are applied particularly to segmenting within databases and lists, to find out which members are most likely to respond or to buy, or how much they are likely to spend. There are many methods for doing this. One of the most commonly used is regression, in which the aim is to predict the likelihood of someone responding/spending by deriving an equation. In the above example, the equation to predict the amount likely to be spent by someone on List 1 might be:
Spend = 0.2 (a constant) + 0.3 x (a measure of age) + 0.2 x (number of children) + 0.5 x (number of years of education after 16).

This equation could then be used to select from the list next time in order to achieve a higher response rate. Of course, in practice regression equations are more complex and you need to pay very careful attention to the significance of each coefficient (the numbers in front of each variable) and the overall success of the equation in explaining the variation in spend levels (technically known as the R-squared).

USING STATISTICS

Interpretation of tests is not easy. If you are not a statistician, you might interpret test results incorrectly. So if you suspect you don't understand what's going on, refer to a good statistics text book for this purpose, or even better, to a statistician.

summary

Direct marketing's key characteristic is measurability. With some media, such as direct mail, you can measure very accurately the response to your campaigns. However, you often need to predict response, to improve your planning and reduce risk. This chapter has reviewed briefly some of the techniques you can use. These techniques derive from statistical probability theory and the properties of the normal distribution. When we have a test result for a sample market, we can estimate with specified degrees of confidence the likely range of response rate outcomes when the same campaign is run for the whole market. This is because we know whether our test result was significant. We also examined test designs, including the design of test matrices. We then noted that more advanced statistical techniques, such as regression analysis, are available for predicting responses and analyzing how they differ by market segment, using a range of explanatory variables. Good testing, properly interpreted, is the key to financial success in direct marketing, the subject of our next chapter.

21

making profit from the hit

- Profit comes from getting a good response and from turning high quality responses into profitable sales.

- Very high volumes of responses may be poor quality, be expensive to manage, and lead to few sales.

- Getting the right quality of response depends upon your learning from past campaigns, and testing your current campaigns.

- You should have standard campaign budgeting procedures, to allow you to control the many categories of cost in direct marketing.

introduction

The only real justification for direct marketing is results. For a profit-motivated organization, the result should be immediate profit or events which lead to profit (eg good sales leads). For a non-profit organization, the result should be cost-effective contacts. Of course, you may want to combine these with other objectives (customer care, quality, attitude change). But the prime justification is normally monetary.

planned and actual results

Direct marketing financial figures are presented in many ways, for example:

1. A budget showing the anticipated results of a single campaign.

2. A performance statement showing what happened with a campaign.

3. An analysis of the value of customers recruited by a particular campaign.

4. A database evaluation, showing the value of your customer base, often analyzed by value and loyalty (as shown in Figure 21.1).

5. A direct marketing budget, showing expenditure required for direct marketing and the overall results likely.

6. A direct marketing performance report, showing expenditure on direct marketing and the overall results.

Fig. 21.1

Example of customer base value

		Loyals	Balanced	Switchers	Total
High usage	Number	120k	300k	350k	770k
	LTV	£90m	£90m	£70m	£250m
Medium usage	Number	200k	250k	120k	570k
	LTV	£60m	£50m	£12m	£122m
Low usage	Number	300k	220k	120k	640k
	LTV	£30m	£11m	£6m	£47m
Total	Number	620k	770k	590k	1980k
	LTV	£180m	£151m	£88m	£419m

In this example, the focus is on the different lifetime values (LTV) of loyal customers, switchers and an intermediate group who occasionally switch, the "balanced" customers. They are split between different value categories. Whatever dimension you segment by on the horizontal axis, it always makes sense to try to identify what the characteristics of different value users are.

Short-term justification and campaign evaluation is usually by methods 1 and 2. You may split this into **front-end response** (how many responded with an order) and **back-end performance** (how many actually bought, net of returns and bad debt). For longer-term evaluation, back-end performance may include methods 3 and 4. You can easily drive up front-end performance by not selecting according to credit-worthiness or by giving a valuable premium for response. But back-end performance could be very weak, creating big losses. Longer-term evaluation of a single campaign is usually by method 3. Periodical evaluation of the effect of several campaigns or of the entire contribution of direct marketing to your success is usually via methods 4, 5 and 6. Method 6 is used for the longest-term evaluation.

general budgeting

The contribution of direct marketing to your marketing budget may not be identified separately, particularly if many campaigns use several media. However, direct marketing activities may still need budgets as part of the normal corporate budgeting cycle. Budgeting usually follows a sequence like this:

1. Budgets prepared as part of corporate plan.

2. Implementation of plans and control of expenditure according to budgets.

3. Performance measured and evaluated against budgets.

4. Variances between planned and actual expenditure and revenue statistics identified.

5. Corrective actions taken.

6. Feedback to next period's planning process.

You may have budget hierarchies. Your marketing budget may be part of your overall corporate budget, while there may be a separate direct marketing section in your marketing budget. Campaign budgets will be part of the marketing and/or direct marketing budget.

realistic budgeting

Budgets are used to:

1. Communicate and motivate.

2. Allocate resources and accountabilities.

3. Control and co-ordinate activities.

4. Report results and provide feedback on performance.

How to make sure your budgeting process works

● Different budget holders must co-operate and communicate with each other.
● The objectives which are set for individuals via the budget must be consistent

with your company's overall objectives and with the individual's job goals.

- The feedback developed by the budgetary process must be constructive (ie indicate where and how improvement is required), not just punitive.
- Targets set by the budget must be feasible and mutually consistent.
- The budget process must be designed to be usable in practice, ie not over-complex, and be a normal part of the working process of each department. For example, it must be used to provide internal control as well as to report the performance of the department "upwards". It must be used to provide "what-if" and other planning analyses.
- Reports and statements of performance must be produced in time for them to be acted upon.
- The process must be accurate, so that people are confident in it.
- The information must be of the right level of detail to be useful (ie more general the higher up the organization, more detailed the lower down). To save time and create focus, a common technique used is exception reporting. This singles out variances from budgets of more than a specified amount for management attention.
- The budgetary process must be able to cope with new types of activity (eg with different timescales, resources).

campaign budgeting

A budget is a structured plan for the financial aspects of a campaign. It does not summarize other aspects of a campaign. These are covered by the brief and subsequent marketing documentation. The budget should be structured – meaning that it follows a standard format. This ensures that budgeting is done properly, that the figures can be interpreted correctly and that comparisons with other campaigns can be carried out easily. It also makes it much easier to compare the budget with results. The following are elements likely to be included in a direct marketing budget.

Media

- ✓ Press/journal space
- ✓ TV time
- ✓ Radio time

Agency

- ✓ Design
- ✓ Copy

Agency (ctd.)

- ✓ Artwork
- ✓ Filming/recording (for TV/radio)
- ✓ Consultancy/management

Mail production and dispatch

- ✓ Initial envelope
- ✓ Return envelope
- ✓ Brochure/leaflet, letter

*Mail production
and dispatch (ctd.)*

- ✓ Sample
- ✓ Lasering (set-up and production)
- ✓ Handling and dispatch
- ✓ Postage
- ✓ Premiums
- ✓ Customer service correspondence

Telemarketing

- ✓ Script design and testing
- ✓ Set-up
- ✓ Agency costs (if calling subcontracted)
- ✓ Direct and indirect calling cost (if in-house)
- ✓ Telecoms costs
- ✓ Customer service calls

Fulfilment

- ✓ Opening mail
- ✓ Order sorting
- ✓ Inbound telephone
- ✓ Outbound telephone (for coupon check)
- ✓ Data capture
- ✓ Credit check
- ✓ Labelling

*Fulfilment
(ctd.)*

- ✓ Picking, packing and dispatch
- ✓ Return postage

Product

- ✓ Fixed costs
- ✓ Per unit costs
- ✓ Returns refurbishing costs
- ✓ Inventory holding costs (storage, deterioration etc)
- ✓ Premiums

Internal communications

- ✓ Sales staff briefing
- ✓ Office staff briefing

Payments and money handling

- ✓ Bank charges
- ✓ Bad debt (cheques bouncing, invoices not met, etc)
- ✓ Delayed payments
- ✓ Collection costs
- ✓ Interest charges
- ✓ Credit card commission
- ✓ Cheque handling costs
- ✓ Instalment billing

Overheads

- ✓ Rent and uniform business charge

Overheads (ctd.)

☑ Staff

☑ Facilities

☑ Heat, light etc

Sales

☑ Initial sales

☑ Returns/uncompleted sales

☑ Reorder patterns

Financial calculations

☑ Response rate

Financial calculations (ctd.)

☑ Conversion rate (fulfilment to response ratio)

☑ Average order value

☑ Proportion acceptance

☑ Returns/cancellations ratio

☑ Proportion of returns refurbishable

☑ Bad debt ratio

☑ Method of payment analysis

TESTS AND ROLL-OUTS

You should have separate budgets for tests and roll-outs. Test budgets often show a loss, because the fixed costs of the campaign may not be depreciated over a large enough volume. The loss incurred by testing is called the cost of testing. If it is high, then you need to re-assess the benefits of testing. For example, if you ran a similar campaign in the same target market and got a response rate which would take the planned campaign well above break-even, then you might decide to run the full campaign without a test. Or you might decide to minimize risks by going for a larger test which, if the response rate is high enough, would cover costs. This shows that when it comes to testing, judgement still has an important role to play.

STANDARD FORMATS

Standard budgeting formats can be used where campaigns have common elements. The main types of direct marketing campaign have enough standard elements for standard formats to be used. Frequent direct marketing users are likely to have standard formats for the following types of campaign:

- A single offer mail order campaign.
- A catalogue.
- A mail campaign to generate leads for the sales force or dealers.
- An outbound telemarketing campaign to sell products directly.
- An outbound telemarketing campaign to generate leads.
- A media campaign to sell products.
- A media campaign to distribute catalogues.
- A media campaign to generate leads.

SPREADSHEETS

Computer spreadsheets are ideal for budgeting. Irrelevant sections can be deleted, so you only need one format for all kinds of campaigns. Rows can be deleted or inserted as necessary. Also, where many entries are constant, you can prepare a standard version with these entries held constant, eg postage rates on acknowledgement letters, assumed response rates. The same model can be used for showing both planned results and actual results, once the campaign is completed.

PLANNED VS ACTUAL RESULTS

In a budget, response and conversion rates would normally be based on test data. If a campaign involves media advertising, budgeted and out-turn figures might differ as it is not always possible to know what the costs will be for media advertising beforehand. For example, a media buying agency is normally instructed to buy a certain number of TVRs (television ratings), rather than to spend a certain budget.

SIMPLE BUDGETS

Many direct marketing campaigns don't require complex budgets. Suppose you are selling a book at £12, including post and packing. The cost of the book to you is £5.50. The cost of sending the book to the customer is 50p, leaving a gross margin per book of £6. The overheads carried by the promotion will be 10% of revenue, or £1.20 per book. To meet profit targets, you need a profit margin of 15%, or £1.80. This leaves £3 per book to cover mailing costs. The cost of each mailing will be 25p. To meet profit targets, one in 12 mailings (£3 divided by 25p) must yield a sale, or 8.3%. Suppose the highest response rate on any of your previous similar campaigns was 5%. This mailing looks unviable. So you might consider:

- Raising the price.
- Offering two books.
- Using the list of customers who actually bought in this campaign as a list for future campaigns, yielding higher response rates, thereby justifying the mailing on the basis of lifetime value.
- Improving the mailing piece to attract a higher response. This would increase the cost per mailing.
- Refining targeting, to get a higher response rate.

monitoring and control

Measurement **during** campaigns helps you check your strategy is working. Measurement **after** a campaign tells you what worked and what did not. In setting up your campaign, make sure the right information is reported at the right time to the right people (ie those who are in a position to do something about it). This means:

- Deciding what performance indicators are required. They must, of course, be measurable as well as useful.

- Making sure these indicators are actually measured. Ideally, they should not require special measuring techniques, but be picked up as a normal part of the campaign.
- Making sure that results are communicated to the right people.
- Ensuring that the actions indicated by these results are taken.

CONTROL INFORMATION

The control information you need during a campaign includes:

- Where your first communication is direct, the number of customers actually selected by the selection criteria (or the number of valid names on a list).
- Availability of stocks of initial mailing material, checking that numbers match selection/list numbers.
- Volumes actually dispatched, and timings of dispatch.
- Where your first communication is through broadcast or published media, that the advertisement/insert was according to schedule and that the right number of people actually received it.
- Numbers responding to your first communication and categories of response.
- Availability of response packs.
- Response pack mailings – timing and volumes (applying to every subsequent action step).
- Results of response pack mailings (category and timing) eg sales.

Flow rates of outbound and inbound communication are very important. They are the key to checking inventory of mailing material. Inbound rates are also critical in forecasting the final result, but obviously can only be understood if it is known when the relevant outbound step took place.

INFORMATION SOURCES

The above information comes from many sources. Where it comes from suppliers (eg media buying, mailing, response handling), your contract with them should specify provision of high quality, up-to-date statistics, as should the brief for each campaign. Many companies new to high volume direct marketing have had significant problems in this area. These can be avoided by attention to detail at an earlier stage. If you don't get these statistics from suppliers, you won't know the exact status of your campaign at a particular time.

WATCH OUT!

Most of the problems in this area are caused by clients failing to specify their requirements of suppliers in enough detail. Make sure you brief each supplier on:

○ *The data required.*

○ *The frequency of reporting.*

○ *Procedures for signalling problems.*

CONTINGENCIES

Contingency plans are required for all sorts of situation, for example, when:

● Responses are too low or high.
● Problems emerge with stocks of mailing or fulfilment material.
● Media schedules are altered for reasons beyond your control.

If response is too high, your fulfilment pack stocks may run out. Can you order extra stocks quickly (make sure you establish this in initial negotiations with your suppliers)? Can a later wave of outbound communication be deferred? Before taking a snap decision, however, the reason for the high volume needs to be established. Was the outbound mailing larger than expected? Was there a special reason why more people than usual might have seen the press advertisement? Has there been a high volume of responses from "friends and family" as well as from the target respondents?

If response is too low, check the achieved media schedule, your selection criteria or the list you used. Perhaps there were delays in the outbound communication. Were all the components of the pack included? Did the right response packs go to the right respondents?

SUPPLIER QUALITY AS REVEALED IN CONTROL STATISTICS

The statistics you receive are the key to quality. If you have used the right selection criteria, chosen the right lists or media, designed your offer and creative well, and so on, your control statistics tell you how well you have briefed your suppliers and how well they have observed the brief. Analyzing control statistics over several campaigns will tell you whether there is a fundamental problem in a particular area. For example, does a particular mailing house always mail out late, or does a fulfilment house always notify stock figures too late? Has your campaign manager's absence on business or holiday caused problems in the management of a campaign, suggesting that a sharing arrangement with colleagues would help?

*The problem with learning after the event is that by the time results are in, your next campaign may have started. Control statistics are forgotten. So keep them as a permanent record of your campaign's progress. For example, the rate at which responses arrive (**the response curve** – see Figure 21.2) for a particular type of product, target market and medium may help in interpreting early results next time a similar campaign is run.*

Fig 21.2

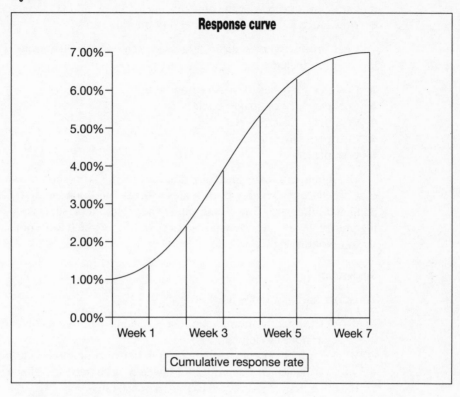

LEARNING FROM FINAL RESULTS

Monitoring and control during a campaign are closely related to final evaluation, except that while during a campaign basic flows and stocks (responses in and packs out) are evaluated, after a campaign, rates and ratios (eg profit per contact) are usually evaluated. There are many ways you can measure your campaign's effectiveness. Some are non-monetary (eg response rates). Some are cost ratios (eg cost per response, relative media cost productivities). In the end, the most important results are customer satisfaction and brand support, and how these are translated into financial measures, such as revenue and profit.

Intermediate criteria can be used to judge effectiveness. These are based on the **chain of productivity**, the ratios which determine the relationship between input and output. A simple example of such a chain is:

Profit = *Unit profit* x *Number of units sold*
Number of units sold = *Sales per response* x *Number of responses*
Number of responses = *Responses per customer reached* x *Number of customers reached*

Using intermediate measures, you could evaluate your campaign by, for example:

● The number of customers it reaches.
● How many responses it generates (of each type).

- Number of bookings made.
- Extra profit from the campaign.
- How much it increases customer lifetime value.

"Cost productivity" statistics are used to judge the effectiveness of different inputs. They include:

- Cost per 1000 mailed or per phone call.
- Cost per decision-maker contact.
- Cost per lead achieved.
- Cost per conversion.
- Cost per sale.

You should compare these for different media. You should also analyze the cost of different elements of the sales process (outbound contact, enquiry handling and fulfilment, concluding sale). These should be set against revenue and margins achieved (including any sales of products which were not the subject of the promotion).

Simple ratios

The most common ratios used here are:

CPM = Cost per thousand – the cost of making a thousand contacts, eg mailing a thousand letters.

OPM = Orders per thousand – the number of orders received per thousand contacts. Dividing this by 10 gives % order rate. In a single step contact strategy, this is equal to the response rate.

CPO = Cost per order – the cost of achieving an order.

The relationship between these is: $\text{CPO} = \dfrac{\text{CPM}}{\text{OPM}}$

That is, cost per order is equal to the cost of contact divided by the orders per contact. But such ratios don't tell you your return on promotional investment (ROP), which is the ratio or the difference between contribution achieved (back-end revenue less all direct costs including promotional costs) and up-front media or mailing/list costs. The latter is a the key measure because it is what you risk before you sell the first item.

Allowable cost per order

Even indicators with such distinguished mail order pedigrees as "allowable cost per order" should only be used in evaluating if you are sure that the situations being compared are comparable. For example, "allowable cost per order" helps in markets where all campaigns must follow a particular format because extensive testing and years of experience have shown that no other format works. There are many such situations in mail order. All such calculations start with the assumption of a pre-determined selling price, but price is determined, via the strength of demand, by your volume and profit targets.

EXAMPLE

Using cost ratios

The steps in using these ratios are:

1. Estimate your allowable CPO.

2. Estimate your media CPM.

3. Divide your CPM by your CPO to give your required OPM.

4. Divide OPM by 10 to give orders per hundred, ie your required response rate.

If you are using direct mail costing £500 per thousand to sell training manuals at, say, £50 and you can afford to spend £10 to acquire each order, you need an OPM of £500/£10 = 50 and a response rate of 50/10 = 5%. ○

Quality statistics

These include database quality statistics (eg gone-aways) and measures of the quality of the response handling process (eg average elapsed time before fulfilment pack sent out).

setting targets

As you use direct marketing more and more, you get a better idea about what is achievable. Examples include:

- The kinds of response rates that can be achieved in different markets for different types of offer and product.
- The cost levels that can be achieved for particular kinds of pack.
- Allowable cost per order.
- Conversion rates achievable on leads from particular kinds of campaign.
- Rate of growth of active customers (those having bought in a specified recent period) as a proportion of total customers on the database.

You can turn these figures into targets. Although your final campaign result is the most important figure, these other figures provide a check on the quality of different parts of campaign design. You can use these figures as benchmarks, to appraise management performance. Examples of the use of such benchmarks include:

- Response rates being used as a check on targeting.
- Pack cost figures being used as a check on design and print buying.
- Conversion rates being used as a check on sales force or telemarketing skills.
- Proportion of customers who are active being used as a check on quality of campaign planning.

For these reasons, the prime evaluation is whether the campaign achieves your business objectives. For example:

- To bring in an agreed profit.
- To contact a given number of neglected customers and motivate them to recontact you.
- To get a given number of users of a competitive product to try your product.

BUILDING YOUR DATABASE VALUE

Long-term performance across several or indeed all campaigns should also be evaluated. This evaluation helps answer questions such as:

- Should you recruit a particular customer type?
- How much should you pay to recruit new customers?
- Should a particular medium be used?
- How much credit should be extended?
- How frequently should campaigns be run?
- Is it worth reactivating lapsed customers?
- Which customers are profitable now and how profitable are they?

Much statistical experience is built into such models. The more experience you have with your database, the more easily you can develop such a model. Spreadsheets are often the best way of representing the model.

VALUING CUSTOMERS

Customers are expensive to acquire and not easy to keep. If you neglect acquisition and retention of customers, you will incur high marketing costs relative to any competitors that take more trouble. Your marketing information system must therefore give an accurate and up-to-date picture of acquisition and retention. The relevant management report is the **customer inventory**. This shows customer gains and losses, classified in various ways (eg by type of customer, type of product typically bought).

If acquiring customers is expensive, why do it? Over the period of a customer's relationship with you, the customer may buy many times, across all your product range, which is why we use lifetime value estimates.

To estimate the lifetime value of a group of customers, you need data on:

- All your marketing contacts with the customer.
- The responses and revenues that result from these contacts.
- The costs associated with each action and response.
- Change in status of customers, eg between being a customer and not being one, or from being an intense user to an infrequent user.

FREQUENCY AND RECENCY

The value of your customer base depends on how actively they buy.

Suppose all the customers on your database have bought large amounts of a wide range of products at good prices from you. However, if it is a long time since most of them bought (ie if recency is poor), then the value of your database is questionable. You should hesitate to value the database at all until customers' propensity to buy is tested by a new campaign. The same concerns apply to frequency, amount and category. Don't generalize from behaviour over the last few years if your customers are buying less often and smaller amounts from you each year.

GETTING THE CONCEPT OF LIFETIME VALUE ACCEPTED

The concept of customer lifetime value is well established in companies whose customers are all identifiable and with whom a succession of financial transactions is carried out. These include mail order and financial services companies. They routinely compare lifetime values of customers recruited from different media or lists and by different offers. Lifetime value is for them a key criterion in choice of list and medium. They also use statistical segmentation procedures to find what differentiates customers with different lifetime values. The variables that account for the difference are then used as criteria for targeting customers within lists or for searching for new lists.

EXAMPLE

A financial services company might discover that customers with a high lifetime value were married couples with three or more children, living in a particular housing type, both holding professional jobs and possessing certain store cards (as revealed by a questionnaire). Although this segment might not be large, its high value might warrant specific targeting, eg through advertisements in store card magazines, use of store mailing lists and use of media with higher than average proportions of such customers amongst their readers. ○

However, for many companies, lifetime value is a new concept, or one that is poorly understood. In some companies, the pressure to sell "new business" militates against using the concept. This can distort relationships with customers and even alienate customers with high lifetime values, as they may be neglected relative to their business potential. This problem can be resolved, although it may take time.

To get the concept of lifetime value accepted:

○ *First make sure that lifetime value statistics are available, at least on a sample, estimated basis.*

○ *Carry out tests to show the benefits of the concept, taking care to follow through and measure results.*

○ *Demonstrate the financial and customer-satisfaction benefits of the approach, being particularly careful to identify the cut-off points under different strategies.*

○ *Propose specific changes to policy in areas where using the concept is likely to pay off best.*

summary

This chapter has shown that the financial aspects of direct marketing are, in principle, simple. The key point to remember is that your aim is to find out what works in every element of your campaign and whom it works for, in the short and long-term. However, this is just the start. You must budget for your campaign to work, using the well-tried direct marketing formulae described in this chapter and provide contingencies for it if it doesn't. However, never forget that your budgets are based on assumptions and don't be surprised if your campaign doesn't go quite to plan or bring in the exact results you expected. The problem may be in your assumptions, not the market.

the integrated hit

- Classic marketing communications concepts – the proposition and the brand – are the key to integrating direct marketing with your overall marketing effort.

- Different media have different strengths in terms of their ability to convey a proposition or support branding.

what is "integrated communication"?

> **"Integrated communication"** is simply the deployment of all marketing communications media together in a consistent way. Your aim is to make each medium reinforce the other and avoid confusing customers. Productivity and quality are the outcome of integrated communication.

For example, if you are launching a new product, you may want to create national awareness for the product and then find customers for it. Television advertising followed by direct mail may be the best way. In consumer markets, the combination of television, mail, retail display and telephone can be particularly powerful. In industrial markets, exhibitions and seminars combined with mail and telephone can have similar power. However, for them to exercise this power, they must be planned and executed together. Because they are traditionally planned separately, special attention must be given to project-managing them together.

WATCH OUT! *As much direct marketing methodology derives from direct mail practice, the integration of telemarketing is often weak. So ensure that the telemarketing side of your campaigns is properly planned, briefed and managed.*

Integrated marketing communication merges the traditional concepts of different marketing disciplines. The **key thought** and **proposition** of your advertising campaign must transfer to your mail piece and telemarketing script for the three to work well together and for the right "take-out" (what customers will say about their contact with you) and consumer action (what customers do) to be achieved. The direct marketing concept of "managed dialogue", in which contacts with your customers occur in a structured way, must be applied to media advertising, which becomes the dialogue's "front end" – the incentive to your customer to start the dialogue.

FAST TRACK *As the dialogue continues, direct mail and telephone must be integrated with other actions, such as the sales call. Be careful to maintain the brand values you have so carefully and expensively established. This means adopting clear rules on copy and presentation in every medium.*

media integration

One of the key aims of your post-campaign analysis is to find out how different media work together best for your products in your target markets. There are few general rules on media integration – what works for you may not work for another company. What works in one target market may not work in another. Much depends upon your customers' media habits, in particular:

- What they view, read or listen to, whether they attend exhibitions and seminars etc.
- How they respond to different media (listen, give information, buy).

The quality of integration of direct with other marketing media has improved due to:

- The diffusion of knowledge about direct marketing techniques into the wider marketing community.
- The use of practical direct marketing techniques by other media – for example, use in leaflet distribution of print technologies pioneered in direct marketing.
- The use of database marketing to provide data needed for integrated marketing communications. This is because data is held on customers' responses to all media and can be analyzed not only in classic direct marketing ways (eg by type of response), but also using media-based approaches (eg by TV area).
- High costs in broadcast and published media, which force advertisers to examine ways of sharing tasks once undertaken by media advertising.
- Improved ability to handle multiple step contact strategies, involving a mix of media, due not only to better understanding of the roles played by different media, but also to increasing computerization of the process.
- Focus on accountability for marketing expenditure, producing a strong desire to find the most cost-effective media combination.

the meaning of integration

Even the best integrated campaign must deliver these:

- Your overall campaign must be as effective as possible, ie achieve results in terms of its objectives – awareness, trial, purchase etc, and as efficient as possible, ie achieve results economically.
- Your mandatories must be achieved, eg company or product branding is fully supported and enhanced, as few customers as possible are alienated and the foundation for future campaigns is laid and/or strengthened.

However, integration is not just about integrated campaigns. You might use each medium separately and still be considered good at integration. For example, a continuous backdrop of television and radio advertising might be used to maintain brand presence, with individual campaigns being carried out entirely by direct mail.

strengths and weaknesses of different media

A properly integrated marketing communications campaign uses the different media according to their strengths and weaknesses. A medium's suitability for a campaign depends on the nature of the campaign, ie objectives, products, offer, target market and so on.

To develop a good multiple-media campaign you need to know:

- Which media are acceptable and credible to different types of customer.
- Which media are right for different kinds of message.
- Which media are best for the different tasks involved in moving your customer towards the sale.
- Which media are the most cost-effective.
- Which media have the right volume capabilities (taking into account any time constraints).

Media choice depends on your campaign's nature, but each medium has general strengths and weaknesses.

DIRECT MAIL

Direct mail, like the telephone and other forms of directly addressable media, has all the advantages of personalization. Customers tend to pay more attention to communications that are addressed specifically to them. But name and address are not the only ways of personalizing. Any reference to facts and ideas that apply to individual customers or small groups of customers increases the "fit" between communication and customer. Finding generalized, but strong benefits that apply to large parts of the market is more difficult than finding benefits that apply to small groups, as the needs of customers in well-defined market segments can often be defined very tightly. The most perfect example of this is when the segmentation is purely by benefit.

FAST TRACK

Once the envelope is opened, direct mail has an additional advantage – its power. This is because – if only for a short time – your reader usually gives it full attention. This is an advantage it shares with the telephone. It makes direct mail a good carrier of strong, repeated propositions.

Direct mail can contain a lot of information – far more than an advertisement in broadcast or published media and far more than in a telephone call. This makes it ideal for the stage of a sales cycle when your customer is already interested and is preparing to make a choice about what to do. Also, if it is important for your customer to qualify themselves as candidates for your product or service, they may need a lot of information to do this. This information may be best delivered by direct mail.

IN THE REAL WORLD

Despite worries about "junk mail", most direct mail is generally liked and respected as a source of information. It is mail that is mistargeted, with offers that are inappropriate for the target market, that sullies the reputation of direct mail. Properly targeted mail is powerful mail.

The variety of print and design formats possible in a direct mail pack means that direct mail is good at carrying over other media's themes. You can reproduce ideas from your television or press advertising in the copy and illustrations. However, worries about your motives can cause customers to mistrust direct mail. So your mailing's tone must be carefully judged and consistent with your overall contact strategy tone to overcome possible mistrust.

A disadvantage of direct mail is reliance on list quality – whether the list is external or drawn from your own database. In an integrated campaign, nothing is as divisive as a high level of complaints from customers that they are receiving two or more copies of a mailing, or receiving mailings intended for other people. Somehow, this is different from customers watching a television advertisement that was not intended for them! The inevitable rivalries between advertising and direct marketing agencies, often played out in front of your senior management, are exacerbated in these circumstances. However, the higher quality your database and the more you update it through frequent promotions and data audits, the less frequently you'll encounter such problems.

WATCH OUT!

A disadvantage of direct mail, shared with all published and broadcast media but not with media involving face-to-face or voice to voice contact, is its inability to answer your individual customer's questions. This can be partly compensated for by explicit anticipation of their questions in the copy. The lack of limit to the length of copy in a letter allows you to do this.

Direct mail works best in an integrated campaign as a confirmer of branding (through its tone and perhaps through carrying themes over from other media) and through delivery of the volume of information needed to move customers through to the next stage in the sales cycle or qualify themselves.

INSERTS AND TIP-ONS

Inserts are more expensive than page advertising, but they have some of direct mail's advantages. Although not personalizable, they can carry the volumes of information and provide some of the variety of format. They are not as targetable as direct mail, but careful selection of media (and of editions within media) can improve your targeting. With modern inserting machinery, you can test different versions of an insert within the same publication, while using the same insert over different publications allows quick testing of media. You can also buy inserts regionally much later than off-the-page advertisements.

Despite their higher unit costs, inserts usually produce several times greater responses than page advertising. This is not just because they stand out more, but also because the response device is usually more substantial. Page advertising allows a coupon, with at most a section similar to a small order form. An insert can contain a complete order form. However, inserts usually produce lower response rates than direct mail. They may fall out of the enclosing medium, or be thrown away immediately, but with lower costs than direct mail, they play an important role. They often work in conjunction with direct mail campaigns as a trawl for new customers. Most of these points apply to tip-ons. Typically, they need to be smaller, but have the additional advantage of working together with page advertising.

PAGE ADVERTISING

Many of the advantages and disadvantages of page advertising are implicit in the above. Cheaper than inserts or direct mail, page advertising is excellent for raising awareness or triggering a first response based on limited information. It is a powerful deliverer of branding, although combining delivery of branding with response generation can be difficult. This is because it is hard to produce copy designed to generate a response (focusing the customer on the coupon or the Freephone number) which also develops or reinforces branding.

Where prospects already have much of the information they need, page advertising may be the best way for you to reach new customers in a broadly defined market. Technical magazines are a good example of this, eg computer magazines, usually dominated by page after page of software and hardware listings.

FAST TRACK

If you acquire customers through page advertising, find ways to reinforce your relationship with them by direct mail and telephone.

While direct mail depends on list quality, page advertising depends upon accuracy of circulation figures (achieved as opposed to target) and the position of advertising in the publication and on the page. However, low cost advertising (in poor page and publication positions) can work wonders, particularly if readers are likely to look for the advertisement (eg in a special advertising section which self-qualified readers tend to look at). For example, readers about to make a holiday decision tend to examine pages of holiday advertisements.

IN THE REAL WORLD

In buying page advertising, you may need to negotiate with publishers' sales offices. So your advertising effectiveness depends on media buying quality. This in turn depends on good briefing of media buyers.

CATALOGUES

If you are selling a wide range of products to customers who are likely to want more than one item, a catalogue may be right for you. But high catalogue production costs mean you need to qualify customers before giving them the catalogue. Sometimes you'll need to distribute the catalogue as the first contact, as part of a test. Of course, for catalogue retailers, wide distribution of the catalogue is the prime mode of generating traffic.

Catalogues can contain vast amounts of information – about your company, your products and the uses to which they can be put. This information is usually viewed as highly credible by readers. The style of a catalogue – repeated statements of product specifications and prices – creates this credibility. However, it also creates a weakness – inability to focus on specific products or types of customer, given the volume of information. So catalogues are often the basis for subsequent mail and telemarketing campaigns. These stimulate customers to consult their catalogues. Catalogue price promotions are powerful, as they are based on reductions from a published former price. To verify this, your customer has only to consult your catalogue.

IN THE REAL WORLD

Properly targeted customers keep their catalogues and therefore its cost can be depreciated over many contacts. However, this brings the accompanying risk of dating – hence the need for merchandising to be carefully controlled in line with catalogue publishing cycles.

THE TELEPHONE

The telephone is one of the most flexible media. It can be used either as the core medium or as support to almost any other medium, whether in its inbound form, for customers seeking to progress the sale or have queries resolved, or in its outbound form, to identify and qualify customers and to take orders.

The telephone is a powerful medium. It demands attention (once the connection is made), but intrusiveness can destroy the call. The very power of the telephone means that you can use it to get a high level of commitment from your customers. For new customers, whose relationship with your company has just started, commitment may need to be backed up **quickly** by written confirmation. Absence of visual contact and immediate written confirmation can weaken commitment, so follow-up must be delivered by other media, such as direct mail or a sales force call. Slow follow-up reduces commitment.

If the first connection is not with the right person, the telephone allows you to find the right person quickly, while a letter may just be returned with no further information. So for customers who have high sales potential but who are hard to track down, the telephone is a good medium. This **interactivity** means that the telephone is excellent for answering questions, handling objections and resolving queries. It works well as a follow-up to direct mail, which may have delivered the information the customer needs to stimulate the questions.

IN THE REAL WORLD

The telephone is most acceptable as a marketing medium when used within an existing relationship. Here, quality of commitment is less suspect.

With modern systems and approaches (eg computerized scripting and operator training), telephone is as measurable and testable as mail. It has the added advantage that testing can be carried out in small volumes, only limited by the statistical validity of the sample size. For example, set-up costs for a variation in script are usually less than for a mail pack. Telemarketing is also flexible, so if your customer does not want the product or service promoted by the campaign, an immediate needs-analysis allows your operator to up-sell or cross-sell.

High cost per contact is offset by depth and effectiveness of telephone contact. Also, as the telephone is often an excellent substitute for a field sales call costing 10 times as much, high cost is usually not a barrier to its use.

TELEVISION AND RADIO

These are the least targetable media, but the most powerful at developing branding and generating awareness. They are therefore typically used at the initial stages of an integrated campaign, to be followed up by telephone or mail, and thereafter to keep your brand image strong, reinforcing your customers' propensity to respond. The value of television as a response generator has been proved through off-peak, low cost and long response advertisements, and on occasional peak-time national campaigns (eg for utility privatization, when the campaigns were linked to Freepost and Freephone numbers).

Teletext has a combination of the advantages and disadvantages of press and television. Its restricted coverage means that it is most often used as a supplement to other media, for covering known teletext users. It can give excellent results combined with inbound telemarketing, as the telephone number can be advertised prominently and the consumer can hold the page while writing it down. In the UK this segment is up-market, so the additional coverage is worth considering.

The disadvantages of teletext – limited audience and creative limitation – should of course be taken into account, but because the medium is so highly testable, these can be overcome.

THE SALES FORCE

The sales force is usually used for in-depth diagnostic work, query resolution and closing the sale, particularly for complex products (eg financial services, technical products and services). But sales staff are expensive, so it is important that every customer they visit is a good quality prospect. Your sales force must structure visits to customers as effectively as possible. Visits should only take place when face-to-face presence is needed to initiate contact or move your customer through the sales cycle.

IN THE REAL WORLD

You can deploy your sales force in tight combination with other direct marketing approaches. Direct marketing approaches can help sales staff to call on more prospects who really do want to place large orders and less prospects who are just "testing the water". Time spent looking for new business or servicing marginal accounts can be saved. Information on existing accounts and on new customers can be provided from your customer database. Telemarketers can work closely with field sales staff to deliver more business.

Using your database to support your sales force and its management

Your customer database can be used to support sales force management, by:

- Providing key sales productivity ratios, such as sales per call and calls per day, and data on productivity of individual sales staff.
- Aiding sales call and journey planning.
- Monitoring customer behaviour, such as buying cycles and order values, so sales staff can establish when customers are ready to buy, how often and what sort of purchase levels they may reach.

Your database marketing system can achieve the above by:

- Gathering and processing leads, whether via direct mail, trade or national press advertising, telephone marketing, TV and radio, inserted or delivered leaflet, catalogues or exhibitions. These leads are delivered, prioritized, to sales staff, with the assurance that the customer was targeted as a good prospect, has responded to a campaign, and has already received information on the product or service.
- Rationalizing prospecting, enabling your sales staff to spend more time converting prospects and developing more business with existing customers. The database marketing approach makes it easier for you to identify and reach opportunity markets and segments, ensuring that your sales staff are used for the task for which they are most needed – making the most profitable sales.
- Gathering prospect data, enabling your sales staff to plan their own sales efforts and prepare more thoroughly for their approach to the customer. The breadth and depth of customer information gives sales staff a deeper understanding of the customer and his needs, enabling them to tailor their proposals more effectively and to determine sales strategy more precisely – from which customer staff will be called on, to what needs to be discussed when they are seen.
- Getting information to your customers, helping them to move faster towards purchase, ensuring that sales staff are not just information providers.
- Identifying which prospects are "hottest" and when they are likely to buy. This helps you schedule visits. It also means that customers who want to buy will be dealt with quickly. Your system should ensure that sales staff know when the customer receives the information, preventing waste of time before the call.
- Enabling further communications or actions to be triggered automatically (eg follow-up sales or service activities), as part of the contact strategy.

- Sustaining customer loyalty, reducing the required frequency of "mainten-ance" visits, and allowing sales staff to concentrate on moving forward sales cycles or resolving serious problems. Provided the communication is relevant, and not for its own sake, many customers prefer maintenance activity to be by mail or telephone. Campaign co-ordination ensures that your customers receive a structured, non-overlapping flow of communication about products and services which meet their needs.

In many campaigns, sales staff form the last link in the chain – the final element of the contact strategy which delivers the business. This does not mean that they have to follow up every lead that arrives. Some leads will be low priority. Others may arrive at a difficult time, when existing customers are crying out for attention. So you should devise a scoring system for prioritizing leads, eg according to likely size of order, whether other suppliers have been asked to tender, urgency of requirement. When a high priority lead arrives, it means that a customer has expressed a need and is expecting to hear from the salesperson.

WATCH OUT!

No salesperson should be a market researcher, but the system should provide a streamlined framework to encourage sales staff to help maintain database quality by maintaining data on customer profiles and needs. However, if this is a problem area for you, then experience shows that outbound telemarketing is more effective than field sales when it comes to gathering customer data during the sales process.

The sales office and the database

Many sales forces are supported by a sales office, which may also act as a telesales centre and perhaps also take on service functions. Staff are normally carrying out one or two basic direct marketing tasks, such as response handling – dealing with inbound enquiries, or fulfilment – ensuring your customers get what they want (eg a product brochure, confirmation of order entry, delivery or installation). Many such staff feel their work is cut out just dealing with the existing volume of enquiries coming in. However, a customer database can help them.

How a customer database can help sales office staff

- Providing improved marketing databases for identifying the best prospects for particular services and products. This means that the leads coming to your offices will be higher quality and that better prospects will be identified for telemarketing campaigns.
- Getting leads to your offices quickly, ensuring that they are fresh. This means that the customer is more likely to commit to the next stage of the sales cycle and less likely to have pursued enquiries with competitive suppliers.
- Prioritizing leads. This ensures that sales staff know which leads to give atten-tion to first.
- Making sure, through careful targeting of campaigns and copy design, that leads are high quality.

- Providing a mechanism for actioning and following up leads derived from tele-marketing campaigns more quickly and effectively.
- In some cases, automatically sending customers the information they need. This enables your sales office staff to concentrate on scheduling sales appointments with the right customers and on closing orders. It also enables your telemarketing staff to concentrate on moving the customer to the next stage in the sales cycle rather than providing information.
- Ensuring that the leads received contain more relevant information than before, giving staff a flying start in moving to the next stage in the sales cycle.
- Improving the basis for monitoring the sales cycle by providing better reports on open orders, etc.
- Facilitating co-ordination of local sales office efforts with those of your other marketing functions – sales staff, other channels, telemarketing, etc as part of a coherent contact strategy.

In a business where coverage of many small to medium size customers (business or consumer) is important, where potential sales do not justify a calling sales force, but do justify a more proactive marketing stance than setting up a retail outlet and relying on customers to call, using direct marketing enables the sales office to serve as a remote account management office, deploying a combination of mail and telephone. The most important asset which enables this approach to be taken is information on the database which indicates customer potential in terms of what, how much, how frequently and when they buy, and details of how to contact them.

OTHER MEDIA

You can use many other media in an integrated campaign, eg to generate leads and reinforce your branding. A steady background of relevant and favourable media comment, generated by a good PR campaign, should be used as cost-effective support to a multi-media campaign. If your industry is one in which exhibitions are used, some visits to exhibitions will be towards the end of the contact strategy, to be followed by a sales force close on the stand or shortly after, while others will be at the very beginning, when the customer is in the search phase of the buying cycle. Poster campaigns, particularly in well-targeted sites, have frequently been used to reinforce multi-media campaigns. Cross-tracks campaigns aimed at commuters at railway stations are frequently used to reinforce business to business campaigns. Sales promotions are often used to add value to the use of other media (particularly print media) and to add strength to the customer's motivation to move to the next stage in the sale. Finally, new electronic media have a whole host of applications, but depend very much on the individual's response to the medium (or even ability to use it).

how integration is achieved

Here's what you need to do to make integration work.

TIME

Make enough time to develop your campaign. You will need more documentation for an integrated campaign. Your brief must contain everything that agencies responsible for advertising, direct marketing, sales promotion, exhibitions and sales force motivation need. Your campaign must march according to the communications discipline with the longest lead time. In some cases this may be the exhibition discipline, in other cases direct marketing. If you want to test a new television advertising approach, this discipline may have the longest lead time, particularly if longer-term factors such as wear-out need to be tested.

Integrated campaigns usually require long overall campaign times. For example, the brand awareness component may need to be strongly established before your customer receives a direct communication. So the overall time from campaign conception to completion may be much longer.

COMMUNICATION AND INVOLVEMENT

You will need to involve more agencies and more of your own staff than in a normal single-medium campaign. So make sure that communication between them is high quality. All parties should be involved in the development of the campaign right from the beginning. This helps you avoid ideas which work well in one medium but cause immense problems in another.

VARIETY OF RESULTS

Integrated campaigns yield a variety of results and should be designed to do so. Awareness, positiveness of attitude, customer satisfaction with treatment by the company, agreement to a sales visit, receipt of information, agreement to visit an exhibition and – of course – a purchase, are all results which might come out of a campaign. These results must be measured in your sales results and through research.

This variety of results must be planned for and the value of each result understood.

FAST TRACK

CAREFUL BUDGETING

- Your integrated campaigns should cost less for a given task, because each medium is used for the purpose most suited to it. You won't be using direct mail to raise awareness, nor television to generate response. However, using several media together tends to increase the minimum effective size of the integrated campaign. Also, some media have a minimum effective volume of usage.

Integrated campaigns tend to be larger, and therefore require more careful budgeting.

WATCH OUT!

PLANNING AND CONTROL

As your campaign progresses, you need tight planning and control. You need to co-ordinate the timing of different media and control media buying and mailing times tightly. Tight budget control is also essential. You can easily lose financial control in the plethora of activities of a major multi-media campaign. You may find gaps at the last minute (eg a piece of print missing) and be tempted to throw money at the problem, rather than try to solve it cost-effectively.

THE INTEGRATING MANAGER

You need integrating managers for integrated campaigns – managers who understand the essentials of all marketing communication, not necessarily all the details. They must have a clear idea of what each medium can do and how it needs to be managed to deliver what it promises.

RESULTS EVALUATION

You need to analyze the results of all the media you used in a campaign, to see how well they worked in combination. Too much evaluation is "stand-alone", using different methods for each medium.

FAST TRACK

You must develop a common language for measuring and assessing different kinds of performance.

Performance measures that apply to every medium

- What customers each medium reached.
- What immediate effect each medium had.
- Whether the customer responded, and how.
- What the final outcome was, in terms of sales (or other fundamental objectives).

the concepts of integration

BRANDING

The concept which unites all marketing communications and makes your relationship with customers more coherent is *branding*.

> Your "**brand**" is the complete set of values which your customers derive from your company's offering. These values are created by your marketing mix (of which communication is one part) on customer perceptions.

It is not just your **current** marketing mix that matters. Customers have memories. Successful deployment of the marketing mix over a period of years leads to very strong and positive branding. Your brand remains valuable even after your investment in creating it is reduced. A strong brand can survive weak marketing for a period. However, like any asset, your brand can depreciate, particularly if it is poorly maintained. Investing in a brand usually requires maintaining the value added by the product range and continually reinforcing it with positive messages through promotion and/or customer service. However, the more focused your marketing, the easier and cheaper it is to develop branding. In very large markets, finding the branding which stands out and making it stick in customers minds, is an expensive business. This because it is not cheap to create a product or service which appeals strongly to a large number of people and then promote it extensively.

IN THE REAL WORLD

Creating a brand is considered one of the best and most long-term routes to survival and growth. However, creating a brand is not easy. It takes years of hard work. Once established, your brand is one of the best barriers to entry by competitors. It is a psychological barrier in your customers' minds that makes them less willing to try other experiences. It also makes them more willing to pay higher prices.

Successful branding also depends on your taking some hard decisions. Perhaps the most important is what kind of brand you want to create.

Types of brand you can create

- **Classic stand-alone** – Persil, Oxo.
- **Corporate** – Heinz, Volkswagen, BA, BT.
- **Classic range** – Sunsilk, Jaeger Men.
- **Corporate range** – Heinz Weightwatchers.
- **Sub-brands** – Persil Washing-up Liquid, BA Executive Club.

- **International** – IBM, Kodak.
- **Regional** – Watney Coombe Reid.
- **Manufacturer's** – Crosse & Blackwell.
- **Retail** – Sainsbury's Home base, BhS, Marks & Spencer.
- **Wholesale** – Nurdin & Peacock.

You need to distinguish between **company brands** and **product brands**. Company branding is for an entire company and product branding for an individual product. Company branding is important where your customers make separate decisions on which supplier to buy from and which product to buy. For example, a package tour operator might want to create a branding associated with high quality of all of its packages, and separate branding for its tours to particular areas or at different times of the year.

The key here is to be realistic about what you can achieve with your branding and in particular whether you want to combine any of the above. Financial services companies tend to combine several of the above in their product brands, often falling between (at least) two stools by combining the (often long) company name with a product description and a hint at the target market.

BRAND VALUES

Branding your product is not just a question of a particular set of product features. Nor is it created by a single communication campaign. It is something that exists in customers' minds. The aim of branding is to get **brand values** associated with your **brand name**. This means that whenever the consumer sees your brand name, your brand values are recalled. When your brand name is well established, you can get your promotional messages over much more easily, because when customers hear or see your brand name, recognise it and (ideally) recall its values, they are more receptive to further messages. Direct marketing thrives in a strongly branded environment. Your customers are more willing to listen to your telephone message, to open your envelope and to accept a visit from your sales person.

BRAND PROPOSITION

You use customer benefits and brand values in the form of your brand's proposition.

> **Brand propositions** are the **words** that express the values and benefits of your brands most succinctly, as the idea which you want to occur in people's minds when they see, hear of or buy your brands.

In an integrated campaign, you must present this proposition across the different media, if each medium is to reinforce the others. How you do this depends on how your **creative execution of the proposition differs across different media**.

> **Creative execution** refers simply to the graphical and verbal ideas used to express your proposition, ie what your customer sees in your communication. Put more simply, these are the "words and pictures".

At one extreme, your creative execution can be fully integrated. You use the same pictures and words in different media. The TV sound track may be modified for use on the radio. The words from the sound track may be incorporated in the mailing copy. The images from the TV advertisement may appear in the brochure or as a backdrop to the exhibition stand. At the other extreme, the brand proposition may be the same, but the creative execution very different. However, irrespective of the degree of creative integration, your proposition should always be the same in every medium within a campaign.

TONE OF VOICE

Marketing communication speaks to customers – whether through the voice, copy, or pictures. The tone of that speech is critical. **Tone of voice** must be consistent with your branding. Cheap and cheerful brands can be communicated in light-hearted tones. Serious brands need to be communicated in serious tones. The tone must be consistent with the **brand personality**.

Brand personality refers to the embodiment of your brand's values in personal attributes (eg serious, expert, cheerful, professional, helpful, trustworthy). It gives agencies a lot of help in determining how the product is to be presented.

BRAND SUPPORT

This refers to how your brand is supported by:

- The features of your product or service.
- How it is promoted.

As was stressed above, your brand must be supported by both..

summary

This chapter may seem a little theoretical in its concepts. However, even a cursory examination of the most successful multiple-media campaign will reveal the importance of sticking to the above principles. Conversely, campaigns which fail in this respect clearly often do so because of failure to observe these rules.

In this chapter, we stressed that managing multiple-media integrated campaigns depends critically on good management of every element of the campaign. This begs the question of who is going to do the managing – the subject of our next and final chapter.

23

organizing for the hit

- You need many skills for quality direct marketing – for example, general management, analysis, project management, IT expertise and statistics.

- You're unlikely to find all these skills in one person, which is just one reason why direct marketing requires teams.

- Deploying external suppliers to meet the needs of your internal customers is an essential requirement for direct marketing success – but unfortunately one which is often lacking.

introduction

Despite direct marketing's reliance on technique and technology, only people do direct marketing. So in this chapter, we examine the jobs direct marketers do and how they can best be organised.

who works in direct marketing?

There is of course no ideal direct marketing organization. However, certain kinds of post occur in most direct marketing organizations.

THE DIRECT MARKETING MANAGER

This person is the leader of the direct marketing organization, often reporting either to a more general senior marketing manager (sometimes head of the marketing communications or marketing services organization) or, more rarely, to a non-marketing person. In some companies, there is no direct marketing manager and direct marketing specialists are quite junior, reporting in to marketing middle management. The highest level of seniority of specialist direct marketers is achieved in the largest companies and/or those with the most commitment to the discipline. The lowest level is achieved in smaller companies and/or those with least commitment.

THE DIRECT MARKETING SPECIALIST

This is the most commonly encountered direct marketing type. Often recruited from an agency or another user, the specialist usually carries the burden of developing campaigns and making them work.

THE SYSTEMS SPECIALIST

In smaller companies, much of the systems work is contracted to external suppliers. Here, there are unlikely to be any systems specialists dedicated to direct marketing. In larger companies which have their own customer database, there may be many in-house systems specialists involved in direct marketing. They are usually assigned to support marketing systems by the IT manager. Some will be only temporarily involved, but in large companies, a permanent team is needed to support marketing systems and develop them further.

Systems specialists often help integrate direct marketers' work with mainstream marketing, perhaps by drawing customer data from more general marketing systems and feeding back data gathered from direct marketing campaigns into marketing systems. Or they develop decision support systems which can be used in all marketing contexts (eg management reporting systems). IT specialists also play a key role in liaising with external suppliers such as computer bureaux and data suppliers.

THE STATISTICIAN

If you are in the early stages of using direct marketing, your statistical expertise is likely to be supplied as part of a package deal with your direct marketing agency, which will undertake to carry out (or use specialist suppliers to carry out) any statistical analyses needed. These analyses are likely to be quite simple, eg comparing results of different tests, different selections within a campaign, and so on. As you get more sophisticated in your use of data – particularly if you develop your own database, you may need to use advanced statistical techniques to analyze customers and group them into categories likely to be more responsive to different offers. At this stage, the strategic advantage gained from this may make this a highly sensitive competitive issue. You may be worried about using external suppliers. Also, the depth of the analysis required means that there are real gains in having internal experts. They know your company, your customers, your strategies and your data.

IN THE REAL WORLD

Good business statisticians are rare birds. They don't require great skills in statistical manipulation, which is the job of sophisticated computer packages – which even tell them what is worth analyzing. Good direct marketing statisticians must have insight and creativity. They are not statistical purists. They must be prepared to live by the central rule of direct marketing – what works, works. Most direct marketing statistics are "dirty statistics", which don't observe nice theoretical, pure statistical rules, designed to provide scientific degrees of certainty in making predictions, rather than find patterns which can be shown to continue (or not!) by testing.

direct marketing users in the marketing organization

The wider team involved in direct marketing may also include the following.

USERS

Users are responsible for putting together campaigns. They may be specialists (direct marketers) or generalists (marketers with other accountabilities, but who do some direct marketing themselves).

INTERNAL CUSTOMERS

Internal customers ask/brief specialists to produce campaigns to meet their needs, eg brand managers.

MARKET RESEARCH

Market research staff may use data generated by or recruited for direct marketing to reach research conclusions for use in the wider marketing organization.

SUPPORT

These provide various support functions needed by your users. They include specialists in print, data analysis systems support (who help marketing staff operate database and campaign management systems) and database management (who ensure that your customer database is the quality and size required to meet your needs).

SENIOR MARKETING MANAGEMENT

Those who secure funding, create direction and manage resources.

who's responsible for the workload?

You can allocate workload between specialists and users in many ways. At one extreme, users may do most of the work and specialists may provide infrastructure (eg the customer database, the agency roster, campaign scheduling approaches). In this case, users become "doers". At the other, users may brief specialists, who act on their behalf with all suppliers. In this case, they are "internal customers". In a large organization, there are also "influencers" of direct marketing – who can make things easy or hard for direct marketers and users. Senior marketing management usually control the financial resources which allow direct marketers to recruit staff, invest in systems and pay agencies.

staff capabilities

Although the broad management skills requirements are common across most industries, different types or sizes of companies need different capabilities. The major differences are likely to be as follows.

SMALLER COMPANIES

If your company is small, you probably won't be able to afford many or even any dedicated direct marketing staff. You may even have no marketing staff. So your manager responsible for direct marketing will usually be co-ordinating external suppliers (often small themselves) to achieve effective low-cost campaigns. For this, you'll need a hard working marketing all-rounder who is good at liaising with a wide range of people.

LARGER COMPANIES

If your company is large, you probably can afford specialists – and you'll need them. Their tasks are likely to be precisely allocated as part of an overall plan. As specialists, they will be "pitting their wits" against their opposite numbers in competitive companies, to gain an advantage over them. They will probably be working as members of a large in-house team which works as much by consensus as by instruction. The team needs to be communicated with, listened to and influenced, rather than told what to do.

CONSUMER MARKETERS

If you are marketing mainly to consumers, you may be an intense user of "mass-market" media – mail, inbound telemarketing, published and broadcast media. You may also be using consumer data from third parties and need to be familiar with the kinds of analysis carried out on such data to segment the market.

Business to business companies

If you are selling to businesses, you'll still need experience in mass marketing if these businesses are small (whether as final or trade customers). However, if your market is mainly larger organizations, your staff will need strengths in telemarketing (especially telephone account management) and using direct marketing in support of sales staff or large agents. In the latter case, your staff need to be strong in communicating, influencing, negotiation and functioning as part of a team. Sales forces are rightfully suspicious of new approaches to marketing which involve addressing people they see as "their" customers.

LONG-TERM RELATIONSHIP MARKETERS

If you aim to develop long-term customer relationships (or have potential for so doing) eg if your customers buy often, or if you have other products and services to sell after the "main sale", you'll need database marketing expertise, as you'll probably find an in-house customer database cost-effective.

OPERATIONS-INTENSE COMPANIES

WATCH OUT!

Companies with "real" operations facilities (whether service or "hard" product eg manufacturing, transport, product retailing) have more constraints on their flexibility to customer needs (eg inventory, capacity) than companies without such facilities (eg personal or financial services).

If you have "real" operations, you should aim to plan further ahead and remain closely in touch with the inventory or capacity situation. If you haven't such operations, you may even be able to create products specifically for direct marketing campaigns.

THE EFFECT OF YOUR COMPANY'S HERITAGE

This is best demonstrated by example. If you have a strong engineering heritage, your direct marketers need to work closely with engineering management. They need to show them how to market benefits rather than sell features and to design products to fit markets rather than find markets for pre-designed products.

A sales force-driven company needs to think of direct marketing as more than just a lead-generating device, rather a way of managing markets.

recruiting direct marketing staff

Too much direct marketing recruitment focuses only on technical direct marketing skills to the exclusion of management skills and personality requirements. Too many direct marketers become real experts at targeting, media selection and judging creative, but are hopeless at managing a complex network of relationships or project-managing a large campaign. Your recruitment should include all marketers. It is easier to make a good direct marketer out of a good marketer or manager than the other way round. Training in direct marketing is easier to achieve than creating the right personality. Experience can usually be created quickly by a period of secondment to the agency, or by taking a junior role on a number of campaigns.

EXAMPLE

In a multinational computer company, a programme of telemarketing off a computer supplies catalogue was being extended from the UK to the rest of Europe. The best implementation was in Germany, where the manager was an engineer by training. After he was given proper direct marketing training, his thoroughness ensured that the catalogue was properly produced, suppliers were briefed well and systems worked. ○

after the investment?

If you've spent good money on recruitment and training, work hard to keep your staff:

● Reward them for achievement. Build evaluation of their campaigns into their appraisal, and reward success by increased remuneration and promotion.

- Allow them to work towards success steadily, by giving staff small campaigns to work on initially, then build them to being able to handle large campaigns.
- Manage their workload. Direct marketing succeeds through management of detail. Do not expect staff to succeed with massive workload fluctuations. Give good notice of campaigns.
- Let them contribute expertise to strategy development. Accept and develop their ideas. Give credit for them.
- Let them express how they feel about how they're managed and what they're learning, in work and training.

supplier management

You're likely to use many suppliers in each campaign, such as:

- Direct marketing agencies.
- List suppliers and brokers.
- Media buyers.
- Computer bureaux.
- Letter shops/mailing houses.
- Fulfilment houses.
- Print creative providers.
- Paper and envelope providers.
- Premium providers.
- Data providers.
- Telemarketing agencies.
- Print production.

If you have integrated campaigns, the wider circle of suppliers may also include:

- Advertising and PR agencies.
- Market research agencies.

So many suppliers are available that you can achieve excellent direct marketing without a single in-house specialist. You can contract everything out – from campaign strategy and implementation to data management. To control this network of suppliers, you might ask most of them to sub-contract through your direct marketing agency. At the other extreme, you might handle as much as possible in-house, including traditional agency functions such as copywriting and lay-out design, as many mail order companies do. The general rule is that the greater the strategic importance of direct marketing to you and the greater the integration required between direct marketing and the rest of the marketing mix, the more is carried out in-house.

SHOULD YOU CONTRACT OUT?

Advantages

- Lower overheads – your suppliers are hired on a job basis. For best results, a strategic agreement may be required, with longer-term fee commitments. This is likely for conventional agency functions (see below) and database management functions, which both require longer-term relationships. Telemarketing agencies and fulfilment houses also benefit from stable relationships, so consider longer-term contracts here too.

- Lower prices – suppliers constantly compete for work. However, costs of competition may lead to higher fees (hidden pitching costs), and constant evaluation of pitches and quotes is time-consuming for you too.
- Variety – new experience is constantly fed into your company, supplementing your own.
- Customer-orientation – in-house staff tend to be less customer-oriented than (some!) agencies, who know that if their performance falters, they may lose the contract.

Disadvantages

- Management control and communication problems – suppliers take time to learn to work with you and each other. Frequent changing of suppliers can cause communications problems and loss of job control.
- Strategic control – if your database is kept outside, there may be security risks. If too much policy is generated outside, key skills may not be available in future. Agencies may learn from you, not vice versa.

THE KEY NEED – CLOSE CO-OPERATION AND STRATEGIC UNDERSTANDING

Many models of client-supplier relationship work – there is no ideal. The issue is not how much you contract out, but how you handle contracting. Try to remain flexible about this issue and decide on the basis of strategic need and costs. Always aim to manage the relationship professionally, over the long term.

Hiring and firing suppliers from campaign to campaign certainly never works.

WATCH OUT!

Because suppliers need to work with each other over many campaigns, teamwork needs to be created between suppliers themselves and between the suppliers and the various internal departments involved. On each campaign, the team should be brought together as early as possible, in order to agree the work programme and sort out any potential problems. Many inter-supplier problems are caused by centralization of communication. In practice, it is best if suppliers work closely with each other according to a tight brief from the client. This is much better than their having to rely on the client being at the centre of a network of communication.

supplier selection

Selection of suppliers is an important first step and the following criteria should be applied:

- Creativity – do they provide that extra spark, but one which is consistent with the brief? For agencies, this may depend on the quality of the creative brief as well as on the quality of creative staff.
- Quality – is their work of a consistently high standard and is this high standard a result of good management rather than chance?
- Reliability – can they be relied upon to perform well every time?
- Ability to observe deadlines – do they meet all their deadlines? If there are problems, do they inform the client quickly enough, or try to hide the problems?
- Ability to understand client needs.
- Openness – are they honest with clients?
- Ability to take criticism and bounce back with better solutions.
- Price – do they give good value for money? This does not mean being cheap. Can they account properly for the money that clients pay them?
- Ability to work with others (the client and other suppliers). Do they enter into the team spirit, and not try to look good at others' expense? Do they accept problems as team problems?
- Ability to add value – do they execute the brief blindly, or do they help achieve more by identifying weaknesses in the brief and remedying them?

Don't hesitate to emphasize **management quality** rather than creativity. Direct marketing relies greatly for its effectiveness on "managerial" factors. It is good management that translates the strategy of the campaign – targeting, timing, offer, creative and media – into action. In selecting a supplier, it is worth paying close attention to managerial factors such as:

- Their management processes.
- The management experience of staff.
- Budgetary and costing processes.
- Their client's experiences (eg do they deliver on time, of the right quality, within budget).

is one-stop shopping an advantage?

Some agencies will offer you a very full range of services. The main advantage of this is that inter-supplier communication and control problems are minimized (if **their** internal communications are good!). This can reduce the time to produce campaigns and improve quality, as long as the agency's internal procedures are quality-oriented

One-stop shopping can be just a ploy to make it easier for the agency to sell. So if you are considering using a one-stop agency, ask for evidence of the agency's internal campaign management procedures, in particular those concerning briefing, campaign project management, and financial control. Such an agency should also be asked for reference clients, who can testify that one-stop means more than one juicy contract for the agency!

rules of good supplier management

DON'T FORGET!

○ *Always brief suppliers clearly at the beginning of each campaign and communicate with them clearly during development and implementation. Give clear instructions and cover what is to be achieved, by when, by whom and at what cost. Response to instructions should as far as possible be put in writing by suppliers, eg through contact reports, which should summarize their understanding of your instructions. Without these reports, it can be very difficult to establish who said what or agreed to do what.*

○ *Develop and explain the criteria by which you'll be judging the supplier's performance.*

○ *Give clear feedback on performance, based on the agreed criteria. Set and stick to high standards.*

○ *Recognize good performance, by stability of future contract and public recognition.*

○ *Punish bad performance, by querying or refusing invoices, or negotiating down fees. Eventually, a repitch should be asked for. Working closely with suppliers during a campaign should not prevent you being tough if things go wrong. This is the essence of any commercial relationship. Management by fear is not the right approach. Give early warning of potential problems, so the supplier has time to correct them. Both you and suppliers benefit from this. However, poor performance which is the result of an agreed experiment should **never** be punished. This is a good way to destroy all creativity.*

Once your supplier is on board and working with you on campaigns, apply these "good management" rules.

controlling supplier costs

It should not be too difficult for you to control supplier costs. For each activity, obtain a proper quote from each supplier. For a competitive tender, compare quotes and select the best value for money, not the cheapest. If you use a small number of agencies, perhaps on a retainer basis, retain the right to examine their cost structures and compare them with other agencies. For work agencies buy in, set clear cost targets. In all circumstances, use professional negotiating skills – for new contracts, retainer fees and problem resolution.

COST OVERRUNS

There are several reasons why cost overruns occur, often occurring simultaneously. They are listed below, along with possible solutions.

Last-minute copy changes and missed approval deadlines

These changes may be caused by changes in your requirements, or be stimulated by inspection of final copy. To avoid this, always take copy seriously well before the final version. Where "final-copy-stimulated" revisions are a severe problem, then they can be removed by using desktop publishing techniques as an intermediate production stage. Producing something looking very like the final copy helps focus attention.

If you detect slackness in this area, it may be because your staff are not budget-accountable. If they are not, then make them so. Otherwise, occasionally exercise the ultimate sanction of withdrawing a promotion if the costs over-run too much. If your staff are budget-accountable, they may just be unaware of the costs of late changes. So make them aware of the costs of late changes early enough for them to avoid them.

Lack of criteria for judging supplier costs

In media buying and TV advertising production there are now established benchmarks for costs. Such benchmarks are less well established for direct marketing. But when you've run several campaigns, you will have enough data on media, print and telemarketing costs to establish your own benchmarks. If you're new to direct marketing, ask agencies for client references and benchmark quotes against what other clients pay.

Lack of negotiation with suppliers

Remember you're a negotiator, not just a budget estimator and user. Never make an estimate on the basis of a single quote. You may do this under time pressure, because you have no time for competitive quotes. Train all your buyers in negotiation. Develop a negotiating strategy with each supplier. This includes situations of cost over-run, where additional billing should never be accepted without query and negotiation. Finally, prepare briefs as early as possible to give yourself time to negotiate.

Lack of feeling of cost-accountability

None of the above will work unless your staff feel cost-accountable. Take a leadership position on this. Devise a system for cost-reporting to indicate where or with whom problems lie. Success must be rewarded in appraisal, visibility and promotion. Ability to manage costs should be seen as an entry-gate to more senior management positions and a natural development of professionalism.

Lack of supplier cost-control

Many suppliers lack cost-control systems which account properly for your money. If their systems don't do this, then ask them to install a system or risk deletion from your list of approved suppliers.

Your lack of cost-control system

If you have no proper cost control system, you will find it hard to control supplier costs.

What you need in a cost control system

- Proper procedures for recording costs against cost centres.
- Reporting procedures, including include simple reports on performance relative to budget and benchmark, and reports on who is over- and under-running on budgets, with exception reports for severe cases.
- Budgetary rules. For example, no work without job number and budget cleared, no agreement without negotiation and reference to benchmarks, no change to specifications without cost implications being negotiated and agreed.
- Benchmark processes. For example, a database of costs, time-estimates and charges from different suppliers for different kinds of task.
- Management processes. For example, clear and fast processes for determining and modifying budgets, so that suppliers are not encouraged to work ahead of budget because budget agreement is not finalized.
- Management review. Budgetary performance should become an important item in your management meetings and in your suppliers' review. Issues to be reviewed in this way include whether suppliers, in response to your brief, offer alternatives with significantly different costs and benefits; whether suppliers stick to budgets; whether proper communications budgeting is practised and whether staff have the right resources and skills.

managing the strategic relationship with suppliers

You might consider an arrangement with your suppliers in which they receive an annually negotiated fee for their consultancy, account management, planning and creative work. All other items are charged at cost, with no mark-up and only when agreed. In this situation, achieving cost-effectiveness depends heavily on fee/mark-up negotiations and on close vetting of **content** of work, as you are not using competitive tendering. If you use this approach, include in your contracts the installation by suppliers of quality and cost-control procedures (including progress reporting). The estimated and out-turn costs of every campaign should be published as part of the cost control process, using standard formats (as used in the request for tender). Target cost levels should be developed from these, and budget-setting should be based upon analysis of these costs.

finalizing contracts

The aim of the contract is to:

- Ensure detailed specification of the supplier's deliverable.
- Embody it in a form which is an agreed management and legal basis for monitoring delivery, paying and resolving problems.

Your contract with your supplier should flow naturally out of the summarized conclusion to the negotiation. However, the problem with many negotiations is that, accidentally or deliberately, they fail to cover every aspect of the subsequent relationship. This may be discovered when the formal contract is being drawn up and may result in a return to negotiation. There is only one answer to this – a persistent, almost dogmatic attention to detail, an insistence that the agreement be fully documented and that it be used as the basis for a contract.

A good contract must be:

- Based on a clear understanding by both sides of the requirements of the situation, the resources required to deal with it, the resources actually available, likely problems and so on.
- Clearly committed to by both sides.
- Properly documented, with deliverables, timing and resources clearly specified, in a form accessible to and agreed by both sides.
- Followed through professionally, so whenever there is a risk of outcomes not meeting requirements, early warning signs stimulate corrective action.
- Reviewed afterwards, with any learning points identified and used to improve the relationship.
- Correctly positioned in relationship to other agreements (concurrent, past or future).

Obviously, the level of detail agreed and contracted to varies with the type of project and the closeness of the relationship. A close working relationship does mean that certain things can be assumed. There may also be a framework agreement against which individual agreements are made.

A good contract specifies:

- What is delivered – at the level of detail needed to ensure that it can be managed and quality-controlled on both sides, including progress checks. This should cover commitments of both sides – not just the supplier's.
- By whom it is delivered (individuals and teams, including contact names and when and how to access them).
- By when – overall and for particular stages.
- At what cost – overall and for individual elements of work (again, the level of detail depending on the type of work and the relationship).
- How delivery is to be measured, including types of review, milestones etc.
- Whether payment is to be by inputs (time/resources) or outputs (results).
- Prices (of delivered units), fees (where an overall package has been agreed), or rates (where resources are being paid for on a unit basis).
- Terms of payment (invoicing, payment period, late payment, interest charges).

- Problem-handling (what to do if something goes wrong).
- How learning will be incorporated into the management of the relationship.
- Escape clauses – how contract terms might be changed and why.

summary

In this chapter we have explored some of the main issues involved in managing the direct marketing organization – your own and suppliers'. It should be clear from this that direct marketing is more likely to deliver results when a longer-term approach is used – in developing your own direct marketing organization and in managing relationships with suppliers.

Indeed, this applies to most of what we have covered in this book, whether it be to the use of media, to establishing a database, or to planning and implementing campaigns

We hope that this book gives you the feeling that direct marketing is a professional discipline, which can be learnt. It is not a witch's cookbook, but a series of simple – but not short – recipes. Like all recipes, the more you use it, the better you will get, and the more the result will suit your tastes (objectives). Used once in a while, as a tactical fill in, your chances of success are not so high. We hope we have encouraged you to take the route to becoming a cordon bleu direct marketer.

index